For Orley Ashenfelter,

with warm Regards,

Ukandi G. Damachi

DEVELOPMENT PATHS IN AFRICA AND CHINA

*Other publications of the International
Institute for Labour Studies*

*

EMPLOYMENT PROBLEMS OF AUTOMATION
AND ADVANCED TECHNOLOGY
edited by Jack Stieber

COLLECTIVE BARGAINING IN AFRICAN COUNTRIES
*by B. C. Roberts and
L. Greyfié de Bellecombe*

AUTOMATION ON SHIPBOARD
edited by G. J. Bonwick

INDUSTRIAL RELATIONS AND ECONOMIC DEVELOPMENT
edited by Arthur Ross

THE LABOUR MARKET AND INFLATION
edited by Anthony D. Smith

WAGE POLICY ISSUES IN ECONOMIC DEVELOPMENT
edited by Anthony D. Smith

TRANSNATIONAL INDUSTRIAL RELATIONS
edited by Hans Günter

TRADE UNION FOREIGN POLICY
by Jeffrey Harrod

RURAL PROTEST: PEASANT MOVEMENTS
AND SOCIAL CHANGE
edited by Henry A. Landsberger

*Publication of the International Industrial
Relations Association*

*

INDUSTRIAL RELATIONS: CONTEMPORARY ISSUES
edited by B. C. Roberts

DEVELOPMENT PATHS IN AFRICA AND CHINA

Edited by

UKANDI G. DAMACHI
International Institute for Labour Studies, Geneva

GUY ROUTH
University of Sussex

ABDEL-RAHMAN E. ALI TAHA
University of Khartoum

First published 1976 by
THE MACMILLAN PRESS LTD
London and Basingstoke
Associated companies in New York
Dublin Melbourne Johannesburg and Madras

SBN 333 18987 6

Photoset, printed and bound
in Great Britain by
REDWOOD BURN LIMITED
Trowbridge & Esher

Contents

List of Tables and a Graph

Foreword

At no time have development strategies been subjected to more constant and critical scrutiny, nor goals and objectives, plans and priorities so thoroughly questioned, appraised and re-examined as they are today. Each country selects its own road to economic salvation in keeping with national requirements, resources, ideologies, and the genius and tradition of its people.

It has been the concern of the International Institute for Labour Studies to make such contribution as it can to ensure that in charting the course of economic development the essential social and human goals of all development are not forgotten, that overall economic progress is not accompanied by a deepening of social inequalities and injustices, that the benefits of development are equitably distributed and that in the pursuit of economic growth, basic human rights, needs and aspirations are not ignored. Within this framework, the IILS undertakes and encourages the study of the development experience of various countries.

This volume represents one such effort. It brings together the results of separate and independent studies carried out by various collaborators of the IILS. The fact that some of these parallel studies came to fruition at the same time has led to the fortuitous but happy juxtaposition of analyses of development efforts in a certain number of young and newly independent countries of Africa with a review of the experience of the ancient and vast developing nation that is China. It is hoped that the lively contrasts in the nature, magnitude, gravity or urgency of development problems and of the options adopted in seeking their solution will make both stimulating and instructive reading. This volume is presented to our readers not as a compendium of ready-made solutions but rather as a stimulant to continued searching analysis of development options and decisions.

ALBERT TÉVOÉDJRÈ
Director, International Institute for Labour Studies

Preface

Studies of development and under-development have been produced in large numbers since the countries of Africa and Asia achieved independence: papers in learned journals, textbooks, monographs, anthologies and symposia have multiplied and specialist journals have been established. 'Of making many books there is no end.' Then why make another? The reader must, of course, judge from the contents of this one whether it would have been more seemly for its authors to remain silent. It may help him to his judgement if we begin by saying how the book came to be conceived and what the common influences were to which the authors have been exposed.

Five of the studies that follow are derived from talks and discussions at the Internship Course held at the International Institute for Labour Studies in Geneva from April to June 1973. The theme of the course was 'Active Labour Policy Development'. There were thirty-six participants from thirty-two countries, some in Eastern or Western Europe, but most in the Caribbean, Africa, Asia or Oceania. The purposes of the course were, amongst others, to focus attention on the broader issues of labour and social policy that are relevant to economic and social changes in the developing countries of the world; to contribute to the further development of a carefully selected group of younger national leaders from trade union organisations, employers' associations and governments; to stimulate the exchange of experiences among developing and developed countries relating to problems of formulating, implementing and evaluating labour and social policy as part of the process of development; and to encourage learning across frontiers as a means of widening the perspective of participants.

Guy Routh directed the course, Abdel-Rahman Ali Taha and Ukandi Damachi were Teaching Fellows; Norman Scott came from the nearby Graduate Institute for International Studies. A significant part of whatever merit is contained in their contributions to the present volume is attributable to their exposure to so many critical minds from so many countries.

Views of problems and of how or how not to solve them tend to get fixed in national cultures; yet the identification of serious problems and the discovery of their solution often requires a changed perspective. Not infrequently, indeed, problems linger on, unsolved and often unspecified, until the occurrence of a crisis in which, suddenly, the unthinkable becomes the obvious. It is one of the characteristics of international study sessions such as those held at the IILS that different perspectives are revealed, with a potential for insight and understanding, without the intervention of crises; these perspectives may emerge from the consideration of countries with striking similarities and differences, such as those African countries studied here, and *a fortiori* from a consideration of China. Indeed, one of the factors that encouraged us to prepare this volume was the intellectual excitement engendered by such a juxtaposition.

These Internship Courses are the more lively because they are 'free from the need of making recommendations or of taking policy decisions'. Thus the views of the authors of the papers now presented are their own, though those who participated may sometimes discern the influence of K. F. Walker, Hans Günter or Robert S. Ray, or one or other of the many specialists of the International Labour Office by whose contributions the proceedings were enlivened.

The intellectual soil has been further enriched by the influence of the Institute of Development Studies at the University of Sussex. From that Institute came leaders of the ILO Employment Missions to Colombia, Sri Lanka and Kenya whose reports have done so much to add operational power to development thinking. It was by this link that Frances Stewart and Charles Harvey were drawn into the enterprise.

It has become a stereotype to say in introductions that, despite the acknowledgements, the responsibility for what follows belongs to the authors alone. It means something more in this case, for each contributor has been positively encouraged to develop his or her personal views in the hope that, by exciting agreement or disagreement, they will help to generate the hard thought required for the solution of development problems.

UKANDI DAMACHI
GUY ROUTH
ABDEL-RAHMAN E. ALI TAHA

Acknowledgements

For a book of this magnitude to be written, there must be many helping hands. We first of all want to thank the former Director of the International Institute for Labour Studies, Professor Kenneth Walker, for his foresight and wisdom in sponsoring this work which in our opinion will provide fresh thinking in development studies.

The support from the Institute staff not only facilitated our work, but also helped us to make a rather ambitious deadline. The encouragement and co-operation from Mr Oscar Ribeiro, the Director's deputy, and Mr Oldrich Cerny, the Chief Administrator, coupled with the administrative expertise of Mr Jean Favre as well as the typing speed and accuracy of the Institute secretaries, contributed greatly to the successful completion of this work.

To Dorothy Hagy, Mary Vick Wilson, Lawrence Leüba, M. G. Samaki, Yolande Diallo, Ode Okore and Edwin Edoboh, Dr Damachi extends his thanks for their helping him in one way or another when this book was being written.

Also thanks and appreciation from Dr Ali Taha to his wife, Amal, whose understanding and co-operation proved very useful during the course of this work.

The editors and publishers wish to thank the following who have kindly given permission for the use of copyright material: George Allen & Unwin Ltd, for tables from *The Economies of Africa*, edited by P. Robson and D. A. Lury, and from *A Study of Contemporary Ghana*, vol. I: *The Economy of Ghana*, edited by W. Birmingham et al.; Federal Ministry of Information, Lagos, for tables from the *Nigeria Handbook 1973* and *Economic and Statistical Review 1970*; International Labour Office, Geneva, for tables from ILO publications; Manpower Planning, Training and Zambianisation, Zambia, for a table from *Copperbelt of Zambia Mining Industry Yearbook 1966*; Ministry of Information and Broadcasting, Nairobi, for tables from *Economic Survey 1969*;

Ministry of Labour, Social Welfare and Co-operatives, Accra, for a table on Statistics of Unemployment; National Planning Commission, Department of Statistics, Khartoum, for tables from *The National Income Accounts and Supporting Tables, 1969;* Praeger Publishers, Inc., for a table from *China Trade Prospects and United States Policy,* edited by Alexander Eckstein.

The publishers have made every effort to trace the copyright-holders, but if they have inadvertently overlooked any they will be pleased to make the necessary arrangement at the first opportunity.

Biographical Notes on the Contributors

UKANDI G. DAMACHI is a Staff Associate at the International Institute for Labour Studies, Geneva. He was Hicks Fellow in Industrial Relations at Princeton University, 1970–3; a research associate at the Russell Sage Foundation, 1969–70; and an English-speaking Union Scholar to the European Economic Community, 1967. Dr Damachi has taught at the New School for Social Research and at Lincoln University, Pennsylvania, and has done fieldwork in Ghana. Damachi received his Ph. D. and an M.A. from Princeton University, an M.A. from the University of Illinois and his B.A., with honours, from the National University of Ireland.

He is the author of *Nigerian Modernization: The Colonial Legacy, From Black Africa, The Role of Trade Unions in the Development Process: a Case-Study of Ghana,* and co-editor (with Hans Dieter Seibel) of *Social Change and Economic Development in Nigeria.* His forthcoming books are: *African Management Practices* and *Leadership Ideology in Africa: African Leaders' Attitudes toward Socioeconomic Development.* He has also published a number of articles.

GUY ROUTH is Reader in Economics in the School of African and Asian Studies at the University of Sussex and Associate Fellow of the Institute of Development Studies, also at Sussex. He has previously been Senior Research Officer at the National Institute of Economic and Social Research, London, and has taught at the University of Dar es Salaam. He was General Secretary of the Industrial Council for Clothing Industry (Transvaal) until he was banned by the South African government in 1954.

He is the author of *Occupation and Pay in Great Britain, 1906–1960, The Origin of Economic Ideas,* and joint editor with E. I. Livingstone et al. of *The Teaching of Economics in Africa.*

ABDEL-RAHMAN E. ALI TAHA is Lecturer in Business Administration at the University of Khartoum. He was previously a

Teaching and Research Fellow at the International Institute for Labour Studies, Geneva, and is currently a member of the Board of Directors, Sudan Airways. He has also participated in various arbitration boards, wage tribunals and other government commissions in the Sudan.

Dr Ali Taha received his Ph.D. from the University of California (Los Angeles); an M.A. and B.S. from the University of California (Berkeley). He has published numerous articles in the field of labour and industrial relations.

CHARLES HARVEY, who has a degree in History, worked for four years at the Bank of England. He was a graduate student and taught at the University of York; he then taught for four years at the University of Zambia, worked for the Study Project on External Investment in South Africa and Namibia, and is currently a Fellow of the Institute of Development Studies at the University of Sussex.

He is co-author of a book on United Kingdom exports, co-editor (and part-author) of a book on economic independence and the takeover of the copper mines in Zambia, and the author of numerous articles on credit, banking, taxation, inflation, mining in Zambia and foreign investment in South Africa. He is currently writing a textbook on macro-economics for Zambian students.

NORMAN B. SCOTT is Visiting Professor in Comparative Economic Systems at the Graduate Institute of International Studies, Geneva, and a member of the Scientific Council of the Asian Research and Documentation Centre. He was born in Scotland, and studied economics, philosophy and politics at the Universities of Glasgow and Belgrade. He was a Research Fellow and Assistant Lecturer in Political Economy at the University of Glasgow, 1956–9. Since 1960 he has been a member of the secretariat of the United Nations Economic Commission for Europe and of the three general conferences of the United Nations Conference on Trade and Development. He has spent one month on a study tour in China.

Professor Scott has published research monographs and articles in scientific journals on cost-benefit analysis, labour migration, the politics of economic planning, technological policy, and the trade of socialist and developing countries; these include 'East-West Enterprise-to-Enterprise Co-operation', in H. Günter (ed.), *Transnational Industrial Relations* and 'Trade', in R. Symonds (ed.), *International Targets for Development*.

The text of Chapter 8 has been written by the author in his personal capacity and in no way engages the responsibility of the secretariat with which he is associated.

FRANCES STEWART is Senior Research Officer at the Institute of Commonwealth Studies, Oxford. She worked for some years as an economist in the Civil Service before going to Nairobi (1967–9) as lecturer in the Department of Economics. She was a member of the 1972 ILO Employment Mission to Kenya and has been a consultant to the Ford Foundation and UNCTAD. She is currently working on problems of technology and employment in developing countries and has published a number of papers on that subject.

1 Introduction

UKANDI G. DAMACHI, GUY ROUTH AND
ABDEL-RAHMAN E. ALI TAHA

'The progressive state', said Adam Smith, 'is in reality the cheerful and the hearty state to all the different orders of society. The stationary is dull; the declining melancholy.'[1] But how was this most favourable state to be achieved? Here, his prescription was somewhat obscure, even self-contradictory. In part, it was a matter of leaving it to the 'invisible hand' – that is, to every man to mind his own business. Authority to control such affairs could not safely be entrusted to any government, and 'would nowhere be so dangerous as in the hands of a man who had folly and presumption enough to fancy himself fit to excercise it.'[2] Smith cited China as an example of a country that had achieved the stationary state and acquired the full complement of riches consistent with the nature of its laws and institutions, where 'the oppression of the poor must establish the monopoly of the rich, who, by engrossing the whole trade to themselves, will be able to make very large profits.' But in the ultimate stage of opulence, from which a country could advance no further, both the wages of labour and the profits of stock would probably be very low.[3]

Economic doctrine was purified as time went by, so that by the end of the nineteenth century a state of *perfect competition* was postulated where, by everyone seeking his own interest, resources would be allocated and income distributed so as to maximise the sum total of utility. Later, the doctrine was amended by the Keynesian rules: governments might and should intervene when entrepreneurs were unwilling to invest all that people wanted to save and where, as a result, idle capacity co-existed with unemployment.

There the account stood until the vast political changes of the second half of our own century. Myrdal notes three changes, closely interrelated: 'first, the rapid liquidation of the colonial power structure; second, the emergence of a craving for development in the underdeveloped countries themselves, or rather among those who think, speak, and act on their behalf; and, third, the international tensions, culminating in the cold war, that have made the fate of the underdeveloped countries a matter of foreign policy concern in the developed countries.'[4]

Not unnaturally, it was to economists that the colonial governments turned in the 1950s, as did the newly-independent governments in the 1960s, when it was desired to move previously stable or stagnant economies on to the development path. But here was a paradox: while economists had brought to the highest point of perfection their demonstration of the self-operating power of private enterprise and the evils of state intervention, they were now being invited to design the very operation against which they had warned. There was certain preliminary work for which they were well equipped: the collection and arrangement of statistics, a stock-taking of natural, human and industrial resources, the construction of a system of national accounts. Then in their tool-box there were a few models that, with a little adaptation, might be suitable for the new task. There was the long-established theory of comparative advantage that told a country that even though there was no product in which it had an *absolute* advantage, it could still benefit through international trade by exporting to another country that product in which it had the least disadvantage, while the theory of course applied *mutatis mutandis* to the other country. But no industrialised country seemed willing to accept goods on this basis. Trade continued to be in those tropical agricultural products or in minerals in which the poor countries' advantage was absolute. When, as in textiles, they demonstrated their ability to compete, markets were closed by tariffs, quotas or embargoes.

There were, however, also certain growth models – von Neumann (1938); Harrod (1939); Rosenstein-Rodan (1943); Nurkse (1953); Lewis (1955); Hirschman (1958).[5] If one knew what made an economy grow, one would surely know how to make it grow faster? An immediate difficulty was that the models were schematic of competitive economies that were already going concerns, and did not purport to explain the process of transformation from a subsistence to a capitalist society.

Further, they were explorations in how a model with a small number of variables might conceivably operate: a system with two inputs, labour and capital, from which were generated income divided between consumption and savings. Growth of output would be determined by growth of population, the consumption function relating consumption (and hence savings) to income, the propensity to invest and the capital-output ratio. There were no governments nor international trade, for the one would make the system indeterminate and the other inconveniently complicated.

These models clearly generated (and still generate) much intellectual excitement amongst those who were engaged in creating, developing or teaching them, but those who mastered them remained ill equipped to deal with the problems of the real world. This difficulty was heightened for economists who applied themselves to the problems of the newly-independent countries because even the terminology of industrialised countries did not apply. In Myrdal's words,

> Our main point is that while in the Western world an analysis in 'economic' terms – markets and prices, employment and unemployment, consumption and savings, investment and output – that abstracts from modes and levels of living and from attitudes, institutions, and culture may make sense and lead to valid inferences, an analogous procedure plainly does not in underdeveloped countries. There one cannot make such abstractions; a realistic analysis must deal with the problems in terms that are attitudinal and institutional and take into account the very low levels of living and culture.[6]

It is not surprising, then, that the first-generation plans formulated in Asia, Africa and Latin America should resemble works of abstract art, their shape unconstrained by considerations of reality. In this, governments and planners conspired together in a game of make-believe while decisions were made piecemeal to meet the exigencies of the moment; '. . . the next generation of policy-makers will look back at the almost complete domination of development thinking by economics in the 1950s as a (bizarre) transient historical phenomenon . . .'[7]

These early plans were combinations of what it was hoped to

do in the public sector, together with guesses of what would happen in the private sector. They were frequently overtaken by unpredictable changes in commodity prices or in foreign aid tied to ventures not foreseen in the plan. Sometimes the expenditure of available funds was delayed by technical or administrative obstacles; sometimes projects ran out of funds before completion; predicted levels of private saving and investment were rarely achieved.

This is not to assert that the face of the continents was not being changed: schools, hospitals, roads, railways, airports, telephones, radio and television stations have appeared; towns have grown into cities, old cities been transformed into new; new élites in business, administration and the professions have joined the traditional élites or replaced them. Growth in real GDP has been somewhat erratic but has compared not unfavourably with that in many industrialised countries, though on a *per capita* basis the comparison has of course been much less favourable. The Pearson Commission arrived at an average annual rise for the period 1960–7 of 1·6 per cent *per capita* for Africa and 1·7 per cent for South Asia.[8]

Is an increase of 1·6 per cent per head per year enough to qualify for Adam Smith's progressive state – cheerful and hearty? One must not underrate people's desire for stability; modest aims minimise disappointment, and peasants who have not been bitten by the bug of rising expectations are content if this year is no worse than last. But having made all such allowances, a rise of $1·60 from a base of perhaps $100 per year hardly qualifies for the epithets cheerful or hearty. And, at that rate, it would take forty-four years to reach the modest level of $200 per year.

There are other considerations, however, that lead to the conclusion that this rate of increase from this initial level is dangerously low. First of all, the *distribution* of income in the poor countries is possibly even more skew than in the rich. A sizeable number of the gainfully employed receive incomes in excess of $5000 a year and a sizeable number of probably less than $50. Secondly, a very high proportion are engaged in agriculture and at the mercy of fluctuations both in the yields of their products, due to uncertain climates, and in their prices, due to uncertain world markets. Thirdly, the poorest countries whose people are most at risk and least able to accumulate savings cannot afford the expense of systems of social security. These are the elements of the syndrome of poverty which, when they come together, can lead to the horrors that we have witnessed in recent years in Bangladesh and across a broad band of Africa.

An adjunct of the domination of development thinking by economics was its interpretation in terms of growth of GNP. But at the same time that the wealthy countries, with their insatiable appetites for more, began to be criticised for their raids on the mineral resources of the poor countries, so doubts began to be expressed as to the legitimacy of growth in GNP as an index of progress. Instead, emphasis began to be laid on the broader concept of 'modernisation'; less on the quantity of material production and more on efforts to improve the quality of life.[9] One conflict in particular had become conspicuous: that between the productivity of labour and employment opportunities. If an industry were to survive in the modern world, it had to be able to meet international standards of price and quality, which required a search for labour-saving innovations. Thus we had the spectacle of production rising, sometimes with impressive rapidity, while employment remained static or even declined. Modernisation, it seemed, had introduced a virtuous circle that had somehow turned vicious.

The first segments of the circle precluded argument: one, the introduction of modern medicine and hygiene that radically reduced morbidity and mortality; two, the extension of education that radically reduced illiteracy; three, the introduction of mechanisation and mass production that replaced imports and produced potential exports. The first, for which the WHO has done so much, turned stable populations into rapidly expanding ones; the second, the special concern of UNESCO, greatly increased the supply of educated workers; the third, with the aid of various international and national agencies, greatly raised production without substantially raising jobs.

Rising generations, driven by land shortage and rising expectations, converged on the towns in search of jobs and a new life and met, in large part, frustration; so the focus was now on the provision of jobs as an end in itself. In the country, of course, there was always something to do and various edifying forms of recreation; town life, by contrast, with landless families crowded into single rooms, resulted in social deprivation and, if employment were irregular, physical deprivation as well. As a contribution towards the alleviation of this problem, the ILO World Employment Programme was adopted by the International Labour Conference in 1969.[10]

Dudley Seers, who headed the first employment mission (to Colombia) in terms of this programme, afterwards wrote:

> Perhaps the hardest step for those who have worked for many years in the development field is to realise the limited relevance in itself of the rate of economic growth. Even those who accept employment as a specific objective often fall back on the argument that the way to achieve the necessary increase in employment is to accelerate the rate of economic growth. Yet it is clear, by now, that fast economic growth is not sufficient to raise employment at a fast pace; moreover, one common result is that part of the population is left behind and inequalities become even greater. In fact, if growth is concentrated in a few capital-intensive industries, as it tends to be when it is really fast, the effect may be to raise productivity rather than employment, and also to lift wages to levels higher than other industries can pay, especially agriculture, thus *reducing* the employment they provide. This is a particular danger in countries where the dynamic sector is petroleum, mining or tourism.
>
> Those who draw up targets for income rather than employment are in effect saying that to raise the income of the unemployed is no more important than to raise the income of the rest of the community. This does not seem to us morally (or politically) defensible. What a development plan needs to concentrate on is first an employment target and then – to achieve the target – not so much the *pace* as the *process* of growth, i.e. the changing balance between sectors (and within them) and between town and country.[11]

It is fascinating to watch the development of this line of thought through the reports on Ceylon[12] and Kenya.[13] Fascinating, too, to see that economists have relinquished their monopoly and drawn in political scientists, sociologists, geographers, anthropologists, educationists, agriculturalists, natural scientists and engineers.[14] Frances Stewart, who was a member of the Kenya mission, comments in her contribution to the present volume, 'Economists tend to regard policy as the autonomous factor to be manipulated by eager, rational decision makers in the pursuit of declared objectives. Policies too are part of the fabric of social struggle, and are the outcome as well as, in turn, a cause of historical developments.'[15]

So we see, in what follows, the representation of the stories of seven countries, six of them African, the other China. Within the statistics, narrative and analysis of each chapter, the human drama is portrayed: man's age-old dream of mastery of the forces of nature, near in principle but still elusive, that is mixed inextricably with his need to master himself. The same characters appear and reappear: the peasants whose patience seems without limit; the politicians with their grand designs; the sharp-operators pursuing, and sometimes realising, their dreams of avarice; the élite torn between idealism and a comfortable feeling that their personal dreams have already come true; the military, watchful from the wings and occasionally taking the stage.

Of course, there is no one formula or model that applies to all these countries or, for that matter, to any one of them. While they share certain characteristics, there are striking contrasts between them in natural endowment, social and economic structure, systems of behaviour and belief and in the policies and personalities of their rulers. Kenya, Tanzania and Zambia have enjoyed political stability, with the same heads of state from independence to the present day; Ghana, Nigeria and the Sudan have seen the violent overthrow of governments and the application of different political philosophies. Nigeria has suffered an enervating civil war.

Each of the African countries has certain unique features that give it special interest for the student of development. Tanzania has a sparse population and abundant land but few natural resources. It is the most socialist of the six African countries, with some features that invite comparison with China – most strikingly, its *ujamaa* village movement. Is it because of its lack of natural resources that the government has been able to maintain good relations with both east and west?

Ghana and the Sudan were the first of this group of countries to achieve independence: the one in 1957, the other in 1956. Each has had four styles of government since that time, and each is heavily dependent on a single crop. In Ghana, cocoa accounts for 10 per cent of GDP and a third of government revenue. The Sudan is even more dependent on cotton and cottonseed, which account for a fifth of GDP and two-thirds of exports.

Sudan is the largest country in Africa, with an area of nearly a million square miles, but Nigeria is the most populous. Its political history, since independence in 1960, has been even more stormy. 'The key factors in the apparent ease with which the national economy had absorbed the strains and stresses of the civil war were the rapid rise in the production of petroleum and the continued high performance of the agricultural sector. Following closely behind these two key factors was the increasing volume of investment.'[16]

In contrast to the other countries, Kenya had a substantial population of white settlers who were engaged not only in government and trade but in farming the splendid Kenyan highlands. Some of this ethnic hierarchy remains today, though the process of Kenyanisation has proceeded apace. Kenya and Tanzania are neighbours and members of the East African Community, but there are striking differences between them. Kenya, with its capitalist orientation, is industrially dominant and has proved attractive to foreign capital. One complication, as Frances Stewart shows, is that dividend outflow is treading hard on the heels of capital inflow.[17]

Like Kenya and Tanzania, Zambia has enjoyed stable government. Its economy is even more monocultural than those of Ghana and Sudan, with copper providing 90 per cent of export proceeds, 40–50 per cent of GDP and 60 per cent of government revenue.[18] Charles Harvey writes, 'The most fundamental points are that Zambia has become even more heavily urbanised than in 1964, and that the urban sector and thus the economy is more than ever dependent on copper.' But alternative exports must be developed, for the copper will not last forever, and living with its price fluctuations is difficult, not to say nerve-wracking.[19]

There are great poverty, immense problems and underlying conflicts daunting to the human intellect and will. And yet

China, itself one-third the size of Africa and with nearly three times its population, seems to be tackling problems no less daunting with immense audacity and verve. These great experiments excite the curiosity of the rest of the world, who have resigned themselves to co-exist with problems, many of them seemingly inherent in human nature, which the Chinese have set themselves to solve. From that country come tales as startling, in their way, as those brought back by Marco Polo six centuries ago. Do their methods work in their own country? Is there something that can be learnt from them and applied to improve the way of life of people in Africa?

We present what follows in the hope that the consideration of each country will aid the understanding of all countries, and that, through such studies, the development path of each may be made easier and more direct.

2 Development Paths in Tanzania

GUY ROUTH

For socialism the basic purpose is the well being of the people, and the basic assumption is an acceptance of human equality. For socialism there must be a belief that every individual man and woman, whatever colour, shape, race, creed, religion, or sex, is an equal member of society with equal rights in the society and equal duties to it. Julius K. Nyerere[1]

There was a time, not so long ago, when it was thought that all that was needed was the removal of the imperial yoke, and then all good things would follow. This was a plausible view, for Hobson and, following him, Lenin, had taught us that the imperial powers were drawing great wealth from their colonial empires.[2] Once this process were ended, this wealth would surely be freed for the betterment of those from whose land and labour it was drawn?

Further support came from the knowledge that traditional societies were in some important respects superior to the western capitalist societies by which they were ruled. Instead of the self-seeking of the Western way, in terms of which it was a virtue and duty for man to prey upon man, there was an ethic that came much nearer to the Christian doctrine. Neighbour and stranger were treated with consideration, there was an instant and unquestioning willingness to share. Disputes were settled by discussion, verdicts implemented by force of public opinion and without the intervention of police.[3] The principal disturbing factor was the tribal migration in process of which Africa was gradually peopled; but there was, at the same time, a balance between man and nature and a maintenance of social order by systems characterised by a remarkable economy of effort.[4] Of course I am not pretending that they lived an idyllic existence – all I am saying is that in some important respects

10

they were superior to the Europeans who were applying their technological advances to the extermination of each other and to the subjection of the peoples of Asia, Africa and America.

Arabs, Portuguese and Indians participated in the trade in ivory, spices and slaves, but it was not until the 1880s that Tanzania was brought within the formal imperial system, first by the German East African Company and then by the German government. The First World War was extended to East Africa and after the war, Tanganyika (as it had been named) was mandated to the British. In 1953, the Tanganyika African National Union was established (taking over the Tanganyika African Association that had been set up in the 1920s) with Julius Nyerere as its leader. Seven years later, it became the government of the country, and in December 1961, Tanganyika won its independence.[5]

The literature on development devotes much space to 'the colonial heritage'. One school maintains that the association with the metropolitan country, both during the colonial era and in the neo-colonial era that follows, actively generates underdevelopment.[6] Ann Seidman describes, with reference to East and West Africa, the emergence of the dual economy, with export enclave and traditional agrarian hinterland. 'This concept rejects the notion that increased global production, perhaps benefiting a limited *elite*, constitutes "development" in any meaningful sense . . .'[7]

But any balance sheet purporting to set the debits against the credits of the colonial era must have in it many subjective evaluations. We begin in a period without national identity, with a multitude of tribes at various levels of independence, some engaged in slave-trade at the expense of others. The Germans seize a great portion of East Africa, forcibly putting down resistance. Their coercive policies provoke the Maji Maji rebellion in which, from 1905 to 1907, many tribes united against them. The rebellion and the famine that followed are thought to have cost 75,000 African lives.[8] But the Germans actively developed the country with the idea of colonising it in the style of South Africa, Rhodesia or Kenya. They built railways and introduced plantation agriculture. British policy, by contrast, actively sought to re-establish traditional tribal society, with indirect rule administered by chiefs. If chiefs did not exist, they proceeded to create them. The extension of education and health services went on at a leisurely pace. In 1926, a Legislative Council was established dominated by senior government officials, but with five European and two Asian appointed members. It was not until 1945 that two African chiefs were included.[9] By 1959, 375,000 children were receiving primary and 47,000 post-primary education, about one in four of children aged between six and sixteen. By 1948 the largest town, Dar es Salaam, had a population of 69,000. Tanga, the centre for the sisal industry, was one-third as big, and Tabora, the next largest, was half the size of Tanga. In 1958, there were about 500 medical practitioners for a population of nearly 9 million – about 1 to 18,000.

The population census of 1957 showed 56 per cent of African males and 59 per cent of African females to be over 14 – about five million, then, of working age. But in 1961, the last year before Independence, fewer than 400,000 of these were working as wage- or salary-earners in the modern sector and, of these, only about 20,000 were employed in factories. About half of the wage- and salary-earners were engaged as agricultural workers on plantations or estates.

Thus, by the time the British handed over power, more than 90 per cent of the population were country-dwellers making their living as subsistence farmers, very much as they had been fifty years before. Public expenditure was covered by public revenue except for a development grant varying between £1m. and £2m. a year, which disposes of the idea that the attitude of the mother country was especially maternal.

What were the advantages derived by the British from the association? The 1957 census shows that there were 7516 British European males in the country, and 6661 British European females. 10,442 were gainfully employed, 3000 in the public service, 159 in banking and insurance, 707 in trade.[10] British banks had a comfortable little business in Tanganyika – Barclays D.C. & O. with twenty-six branches in 1965, the Standard with nineteen and National and Grindlays with nine. Loans and advances of all commercial banks totalled £15m. at the end of 1960, so that they might have earned somewhere near £1m. in interest. One might have thought that the imperial connection would have given Britain a near monopoly of trade, but in 1960 only a little over a third of imports came from the United Kingdom: £10m. worth. Did the United Kingdom have a monopsony of Tanganyikan exports? No, for again it took about a third. Fortunes were being made from sisal production, exports of which were valued at £15m. in 1960, but there were probably as many Greek and Asian owners as British.

The upshot, I suggest, is that there were a few vested interests that would become clamorous if their interests were threatened – colonial civil servants, banks, traders, plantation owners. But the political psychology of imperialism is such that large amounts of public money are at times spent to protect much smaller amounts of private money. One lesson of the past ten years is how little, in fact, business connections depend on governmental and administrative ties and how much on customary, cultural and even sentimental relationships.

There is, however, another aspect of the colonial heritage that deserves consideration, and that is a psychological one. The representatives of the imperial power were superbly confident of their own superiority. They were, and their belief was implicit, superior in intelligence, culture, morals and beauty, and they worked very hard, albeit without conscious design, at implanting these illusions in the minds of those they ruled. Friedland quotes a story of Tom Mboya's:[11]

> One day in 1951, when one of my European colleagues was away on leave . . . I was busy in the laboratory with some tests when a European woman came in with a sample bottle of milk. She looked around for a few moments and did not say anything. 'Good morning, madam,' I said. When I spoke she turned around and asked, 'Is there anybody here?'

So non-whites were also in some curious sense non-people. If they knew what was good for them, they had to accept the role in which their rulers cast them and act the part of good-humoured morons eager to obey. Of course not all Europeans were like that, and many of the exceptions amongst the officials and businessmen stayed on after Independence to see the new country on its way. But the exclusiveness and privilege of the European enclaves was very compelling and it required great perception and goodwill to resist it.

The psychological heritage has taken contrasting forms:

some people have been, as it were, innoculated against racial-
ism by seeing it at work; others have yielded to it and turned it
against the whites; others have zestfully embraced the privileges that were once the prerogative of a white skin, so that class
relationships are revealed without the mask of colour.

The Tanganyika African National Union was the only party to
win seats in parliament, so that Tanganyika was *de facto* a one-
party state. It became one *de jure* by the new constitution of
1962.[12] This was a considerable advantage to a country setting
out on the path of independent development and was itself occasioned by three circumstances: since the mass of the people
were subsistence farmers, the interests vested in property (the
class of landlords and capitalists) carried little weight at the
polls; the tribal structure of the country, constituted of a multitude of small tribes, was not such as to allow tribal dominance
nor to encourage tribal rivalry, phenomena that have plagued
other African countries;[13] the country had Swahili as a common language.

I visited Tanganyika four months after Independence so was
able to witness at first hand and share in the excitement sur-
rounding the birth of a nation. Dar es Salaam was full of visitors
coming to tender homage or advice. Capitalist and Communist, World Bank and multinational corporation, British
and American, ICFTU and WFTU, Arab and Israeli – they
were all there, hopefully pressing their suits. Julius Nyerere had
just retired from the prime ministership so as to devote himself
to the building up of TANU, though before very long he was to
be brought back to government as President under the new constitution. I was taken to see him at his Oyster Bay house, where
he received us without appointment or other formality. Later,
at a reception at the Israeli Embassy, cabinet ministers could
be approached as easily. Wherever one went, in hotels or tea-
rooms, groups would be discussing aspects of policy.

But how to meet the challenge that confronted the new
government? With the imperial yoke removed, surely a surge of
progress should follow? But progress did not come of itself, it
required a multitude of decisions by a multitude of people who
both wanted to progress and knew how to. The will was there –

but the knowledge? The ministers did not yet know how to run their own departments and were in awe of the ex-colonial service departmental heads whose thought still dominated the day-to-day running of the government. Results would have been more spectacular if oppression had been more marked, but as it was there were no landlords from whose rents the peasants could be freed, no princely estates to give to the land-hungry, no corrupt officials from which to rid the public. Just a very poor, very beautiful country whose somewhat sparse population of subsistence farmers had somehow to be shown the road to progress and persuaded to follow it.

There were a few ideas that were widely accepted: a plan must be formulated and economists found to formulate it; manufacturing industry must be built up and foreign corporations attracted to do so; aid must be sought from abroad; large-scale farms must replace peasant holdings. So a plan was formulated to take cognisance of these things – but meanwhile a crisis had arisen with regard to the trade unions.

INDUSTRIAL RELATIONS AND INCOMES POLICY

The colonial government had enacted the Regulation of Wages and Terms of Employment Ordinance in 1953, in terms of which statutory (that is, legally enforceable) minimum wages could be fixed.[14] Then, on the eve of Independence, a Territorial Minimum Wages Board was established, to lay down minimum rates for employees in different areas of the country.[15]

Its report, presented in March 1962, demonstrated the inadequacy of current rates of pay, even though they had increased substantially over the previous five years. Data collected by the Labour Division, covering between 350,000 and 400,000 African employees, showed an increase in pay of 68 per cent between 1956 and 1961, when retail prices had risen by only 10 per cent. Real wages had, by this reckoning, risen by 53 per cent. Even so, they remained low: average monthly earnings in July 1961 were Shs. 117 in manufacturing and Shs. 115 in construction, while the Board calculated the cost of basic needs for an adult male working in Dar es Salaam at Shs. 104 per month.[16] But would not the payment of adequate wages cause a drastic fall in employment? Donald Chesworth later summarised policy on this point:[17]

At an early stage in its work this board had been clearly informed by the Minister of Labour that the Government appreciated that any immediate rise in wages would lead to redundancy. This was acceptable to the Government as being in accordance with its policy that there should be a smaller number of workers in paid employment earning a comparatively higher wage, rather than a greater number employed at a lower wage. In its report the board described this statement of government policy as having been an important contributory factor in its unanimous decision to recommend that minimum wages should be introduced at a level substantially higher than the then general level of wages, and in its agreement that a 'bachelor' wage was socially and economically undesirable. Its position was summarised in the statement that 'in the conditions of Tanganyika higher minimum wages will lead to redundancy, but that the smaller labour force will be much more settled and efficient, and that families of urban wage earners will be able much more easily to live together as family units.'

On the Board's recommendations, the following monthly rates were laid down for adult workers:

Dar es Salaam and Tanga urban areas	Shs. 150
Eighteen main townships	Shs. 125
All other areas	Shs. 100

Non-plantation agricultural workers and workers on tea plantations were excluded from the operation of the order.

The order came in the middle of a period of rapid wage increases which had amounted to 29 per cent in the average from 1961 to 1962, followed by 33 per cent (incorporating the effects of the wage order) between June 1962 and June 1963. Then came a modest rise of 7 per cent between 1963 and 1964. Thus between 1956 and 1964, money earnings had more than trebled. In the ensuing four years, to mid-1968, there was a further rise of just over 40 per cent.[18] *A priori,* this might be expected to have a devastating effect on wage and salary employment, but the statistics reveal no functional relationship between the two. A major reduction did take place on sisal plantations, but this was due to the ending of migrant labour and the system of employing wives and children, and to an agreement to increase output for men.

During the colonial period, relations between the Tanganyika Federation of Labour and the Tanganyika African National Union had been close. M.A. Bienefeld records:

> 1961, the year that culminated in the achievement of independence, had seen a sharp reduction in the wave of strikes that had accompanied the last years of the struggle for Uhuru. From 197 and 195 in the two preceding years the number of strikes recorded had fallen to 108. But now in 1962, the first year of independence, strikes proliferated once again with 148 recorded disputes entailing a loss of 417,474 man-days.[19]

This sort of thing presents the governments of newly-independent countries with an awkward dilemma. Colonial governments have been attacked for their proscription of trade union rights; should national parties, now in power, practise what they have condemned? The answer seems to be that independent trade unions will be tolerated only to the extent that their pursuit of sectional interests does not clash with the government's conception of the general good. So strikes were outlawed by the Trade Disputes (Settlement) Act no. 41 of 1962 which substituted conciliation, negotiation and, in the last resort, arbitration.

The minimum wage provisions had, of course, been prescribed by the government rather than won by the trade unions, and the government now proceeded to ease the wage-earner's lot by three further bits of legislation. The Severance Allowance Act no. 57 of 1962 prescribed fifteen days' pay for each year of service on termination of employment (excluding those summarily dismissed for any good legal cause). The Security of Employment Act no. 62 of 1964 curtailed the right of employers to dismiss their workers. An elaborate Disciplinary Code is included in the Regulations to the Act (Government Notice no. 98/1965). It lays down in great detail the breaches of discipline that workers are liable to commit, and the remedies open to the employer. A provision of great importance is for the establishment of a workers' committee in every concern employing ten or more union members whose pay does not exceed £420 per annum. Employers must consult these committees on the application of the Disciplinary Code as well as on the promotion of efficiency, safety, welfare, redundancy and on industrial relations in general.

Thirdly, the National Provident Act, no. 36 of 1964 established a fund to which employers were required to contribute on behalf of each worker an amount equal to 5 per cent of his wage, while deducting and contributing from his wage a like amount. This gives the worker a useful source of funds when he retires or loses his job, as well as being a source of capital for government expenditure.

In January 1964, differences between government and unions were brought to a head by an army mutiny, in which it was alleged that some union leaders were involved. By the National Union of Tanganyika Workers (Establishment) Act no. 18/1964, the Tanganyika Federation of Labour and its constituent unions were absorbed into a single National Union of Tanganyika Workers (henceforth known as NUTA, to complement the political party TANU). The emphasis in the constitution laid down in the Act is on the national responsibility of the union. Its activities must further a national wages policy. It must affiliate to TANU, shall do everything in its power to promote the policies of TANU and encourage its members to join. The President of the Republic appoints the general secretary and deputy general secretary of the Union and may dissolve it and replace it by another if he is satisfied that it has failed adequately to carry out its objects.

Section 6 makes provision for the enforcement of the 'union shop' when half or more of the employees of an establishment are union members. In such a case the Minister of Labour may direct the employer to require his employees to join the union within two months, and to deduct union dues from wages and transmit them to the union.

Workers continued to obtain substantial increases in wages after 1964, but at a declining rate: 15 per cent between 1964 and 1965, and 6 per cent between 1965 and 1966. But there were many complaints about the inadequacy of the new union, and in May 1966 the President established a commission to inquire into its affairs. Many complaints were unearthed, from the neglect of individual grievances to the soliciting of gifts from employers, but it is not really possible from the commission's report to gauge the extent to which the complaints were justified.[20]

The Union is undoubtedly in a difficult position. It is given a monopoly of trade union organisation, so that there is nothing against which its performance may be measured;[21] the union shop and the check-off system remove some of the voluntary quality of membership and make it less necessary for officials to persuade workers to join and maintain their membership. At the same time, incomes policy severely restricts its ability to win for its members what they most want from their union – increases in pay.

For the sake of exposition, I take you now to the subject of planning, and shall return later to that of incomes policy and the problems that this occasions for industrial relations.

PLANNING

Every government has, of course, to plan how to raise money and what to spend it on. But government is a going concern, the broad lines of the budget defined by custom and practice. So the colonial government had its plans for education, health, justice, communication, while in the East African Common Services Organization it provided the foundation for what was to become the East African Community. But serious planning, designed to change the face of the country, did not begin until 1963. For the First Five-Year Plan the government assembled a team drawn from a number of capitalist countries and headed by a Frenchman on loan from the Bureau de Plan.

As with many of the newly-independent countries, this exercise had in it a large element of planning-for-planning's-sake. A plan is an exercise in public relations, an advertisement of the good intentions of the government. It may also enable the toiling masses to suffer the hardships of the present in silence and enjoy the foretaste of the better things to come.

The First Five-Year Plan was not meant to be of this nature, but in the event the outcome did not bear much resemblance to the plan. Perhaps the best one can say for it is that it provided a very useful, perhaps indispensable, rehearsal for the Second

Five-Year Development Plan. The technicians who drafted the first plan laboured under difficulties that were really insuperable. Firstly, the philosophy of the government was still somewhat amorphous. It was still believed that it was desirable and possible to leave a great deal of industrial development to investment by foreign corporations. It was also hoped that 78 per cent of the finance of the public sector plan would be provided from abroad. In the event, foreign corporations proved very timid of investing in the country, thereby possibly contributing to the left-turn that the government took in 1967. Public finance from abroad, too, disappointed, amounting to only about half the planned level.[22] The fall in the price of sisal was another disappointment. A fall had been anticipated, but not from the Shs. 2167 per ton of 1964 to the Shs. 1394 of 1965 or Shs. 1018 of 1967.[23] Sisal contributed nearly one-third of export earnings in 1964 and less than one-eighth in 1967.   But as serious in their own way were the difficulties of administration with which the formulation and the implementation of the plan were hindered. Prime responsibility for the plan was given to a new Ministry of Economic Affairs and Development Planning between whom and the Treasury there was a built-in struggle for power.[24] Each government department was supposed to complete a questionnaire in which they elaborated their own part of the plan but most of them lacked the information and the expertise to do this. In the end, the planning team had to do most of this work themselves with no guarantee that the ministries concerned would be willing or able to carry out the intentions attributed to them.

The result was that by 1969 not much more than three-quarters of the planned expenditure had been spent. Ministries, particularly in the first three years of the plan, had had difficulty in spending even those funds that were allocated to them. In part, this is a matter of organisation: departments are needed to plan, assess, cost and implement, with all the necessary arrangements for communication, supervision and authority. In part, it is a matter of men, from planning to implementation, with the requisite training and experience.

But apart from all these considerations, there came, in the very middle of the plan period, a radical switch in direction signalled by the Arusha Declaration.[25] The Declaration begins with a declaration of human rights – including freedom of expression, movement, religious belief and association. In Part Two it goes on to enunciate a policy of socialism; in Part Three, of self-reliance. There was to be a new emphasis on agriculture, for the previous emphasis on manufacturing had been mistaken.

With more material impact, TANU and government leaders were directed to divest themselves of shares and directorships in privately-owned enterprises, of houses for rent to others and of additional salaries. This applied equally to husbands and wives.[26]

Within two weeks, a massive programme of nationalisation had been implemented: banks had been taken over by the National Bank of Commerce, insurance companies by the National Insurance Corporation, importers, exporters and wholesalers by the State Trading Corporation. Food-processing firms had also been taken over, while partnership agreements giving the government a majority share were proposed for breweries, the British American Tobacco, Bata, Metal Box, the Tanganyika Extract Company and Tanganyika Portland Cement.

In Latin America, such announcements are followed by political and military crises; in Tanzania, the scheme went through with hardly an angry word. Bata refused on principle to enter into a partnership agreement and its factories were taken over and renamed 'Bora'. Metal Box refused to enter an agreement that gave them a minority shareholding, so that each side now has a 50 per cent holding in the company. Barclays D.C. & O. and the Standard Banks decided at first on non-co-operation and removed their British staff. The Goan sub-managers,[27] with a university economist, and staff hastily recruited in the Netherlands, had to fill their places and Tanzanians were hastily trained to take on new responsibilities. A crisis was averted and, in its first five months of existence, the National Bank of Commerce made a profit of Shs. 6m. Before long, Barclays and the Standard cut their losses by entering into new business arrangements with the NBC, to the profit and satisfaction of all.

The Second Five-Year Plan was conceptually very different from the first. The country was now set firmly on the socialist path. The President, presenting the plan to Parliament, gave the first priority as the provision of an adequate diet for all, the second, the provision of good and, if possible, attractive clothing; the third, decent housing; the fourth, education.[28]

The basic plan committed the government only to those projects that it expected to carry out in the first two years, and other than that presented only a framework within which annual plans were to be defined. Instead of the plans for the transformation of agriculture by the establishment of large-scale, mechanised state farms, the Government, since October 1967, had been elaborating plans for *ujamaa* (socialist) villages[29] and for the introduction of the ox rather than the tractor. Food production could be improved on the principle of self-reliance. 'Our present attitude to food is the result of ignorance, indifference and indolence. Many of our people do not realise what they can do, or why it is important that they should; and they find it easier to carry on in the old fashion than to make the effort to change the condition of their life . . . '[30]

The First Plan had achieved a growth rate of 5 per cent compared with the aim of 6·7 per cent and the Second Plan aimed at a rate of 6·5 per cent. Even so, the chances of a child going to school, 46 per cent in 1964, had risen only to 47 per cent in 1969, partly because population growth, at 2·7 per cent per year, was higher than had been thought. Even at the end of the Second Plan, there would be primary school places for only 52 per cent of those eligible, while universal primary education would not be achieved until 1989.

Notwithstanding the lessons that had been learnt, clarification of policy, greater abundance of trained manpower and control of the so-called commanding heights of the economy, the report on the Annual Plan for 1972–3 reveals a considerable difference between plan and achievement.[31] Real growth in 1971–2 was estimated at 4·5 per cent. There had been a large increase in wage employment, but the origins of growth had differed from those expected. Agricultural output had declined because of poor weather and severe organisational difficulties, manufacture had grown less than had been planned, and the real growth had come from a constructional boom and in education, health, water, power and administration.

The Arusha Declaration came in the middle of the First

Plan; another important change in strategy has come in the middle of the Second Plan – that is a switch, in the middle of 1972, to regional planning.

The most important change in the planning structure in 1972 is the decentralization of many government functions to the Regions. Last year's Annual Plan pointed out the problems raised by the highly centralized structure of government existing at the time: 'Regional and District heads tend to work vertically to their ministries rather than horizontally as members of Regional/District teams. Decisions are still largely made in Dar es Salaam, with insufficient reference to, or consultation with either Regional Officers or the Regional Development Planning Committees. High-level manpower and decision-making power are concentrated at the centre, and the regions have little scope for initiating or influencing projects. This has led to urban bias in project preparation and implementation, poor co-ordination at the project level, and an undesirable separation of the planning process from the people for whom the plans are made'.

Decentralization of responsibility for development planning and plan implementation was the answer to this. A new type of Regional and District administration is being created in which the civil servants in the Region or District will work together as a team to draw up their development plans and will have the responsibility for implementing these plans. Thus, for example, the Regional Medical Officer will no longer be responsible to the Ministry of Health in Dar es Salaam. He will instead be directly responsible to the Regional Administration, although he will continue to receive advice and certain technical services from the ministry.[32]

Regional Development Committees had, in fact, been set up some years ago, but with indifferent results. One reason for the non-implementation of some really quite good plans seems to have been that mentioned above: the lack of administrative machinery for the co-ordination at local level of the activities of administrators from different departments. Thus local initiative would lose itself in the sands because someone in some department at headquarters in Dar es Salaam had not been sold the idea. Sometimes the plans were too complex and wide ranging to be capable of implementation; sometimes the implementing agencies lacked funds and manpower to act on them; sometimes the plans simply did not get to those whose co-operation was required.[33]

UJAMAA

I have mentioned that more than 90 per cent of the Tanzanian population are subsistence farmers. At the end of 1967, I conducted a survey of 156 peasant households: 960 people including 149 husbands and 192 wives. Their plots of land averaged 5.8 acres. Only eighteen households said that they did not always get enough to eat and more than half said they had sufficient variety in their diet. It is one of the benefits of farming in the tropics that plants grow quickly and luxuriantly. So bananas, potatoes, cassava, groundnuts, yams, green or dried beans, maize were frequently mentioned. Housing was to a great extent at the discretion of the household, for typically it consisted of a frame of unplaned timber plastered with mud, and a thatched roof. So a striking feature revealed by the inquiry was not the poverty but rather the austerity of peasant life – the almost total absence of superfluities. An inventory of 120 households of 749 people showed that they had between them 187 beds, 405 chairs, 123 tables, 13 bicycles, 12 radios, 57 goats, 45 sheep, 195 cattle, 589 fowls and 55 pigs. Cash income per household averaged Shs. 1349 per year, but with a wide dispersion, a wide range between regions and within regions and a mean deviation of Shs. 1063.[34]

A question asked, 'What are the chief hardships, difficulties or worries from which you suffer?' Of course, there was no shortage of troubles: difficulties of marketing produce, lack of money, ill-health, childrens' education, falling coffee prices. The next question asked the extent to which these things had been alleviated in recent years. Ten considered that things had got worse and the rest were almost equally divided between those who saw no improvement and those who thought there had been some.

They were then asked what improvements they anticipated in the next five years; 92 anticipated some, 43 that things would stay the same and only one that they would actually get worse.

Of the improvements, three-fifths were the sort of things they would have to do for themselves, the rest things that would have to be done by or with government agencies.

And on the comparative advantages of town and country: country people were independent with regard to food, while in towns even wild spinach had to be bought. On the other hand, towns had social amenities, good roads, easier work, more abundant money. 'Townspeople are richer with many modern things such as electricity. The town is good for making money through business. The townspeople are the ones who control the government and hence favour themselves.' But with all this, the concensus was that life in the country was better, both for the parents and for their children, except for the boys and then only if they could get good jobs. 'The weather in the town is very uncomfortable. Townspeople live amidst all evils. No good children can be reared in the town.'

From these interviews there emerges a picture of the non-acquisitive society, where most of the needs of life are filled without the intercession of money, where the aim is to sustain life no better and no worse than last year or the year before. He who expects little, one might say, wants little and needs little. So the sleep of the peasant is undisturbed by dreams of avarice. As much of the day as needs be is devoted to meeting his simple needs and the rest to the pleasures of idleness, drinking and talk. And by and large, his lot is not so unenviable. He is king of his little family circle, a man of importance with immense authority over his wife and children. Far from being hostages to fortune, they are his capital and investment, the children his security against the frailties of old age.

But of course, Western medicine and hygiene have upset the balance that nature ruthlessly maintained, and now each year 350,000 more people are being born in Tanzania than die. The more favourable agricultural areas are already over-populated so that less favourable areas have to be brought into cultivation. The other great agency of change is education, for to teach a person to read and write is, in a way, like teaching a blind man to see: it gives him a new perceptive faculty, and the lust for education is everywhere in evidence in Africa.

Given these factors, the complexities of the situation mount. Liberation from the parasitic and other diseases that flourish in

the tropics leads to the necessity for birth control, which in turn
requires education and the liberation of women if it is to be effective. And all require the creation of more resources, which
can only be created if the peasant is disturbed from the austere
balance of his life. Somehow in him there must be aroused the
drive of rising expectations, a dynamic envy of those who are
richer than he, or, in a West African phrase, he must be given
the wants.[35] But why, you may ask, can his wants not be limited
to literacy and health, with the way of life otherwise
unchanged? It is true that the peasant family must find school
fees for primary (though not for secondary) education and
hospital fees for the mission (though not for the public) hospitals. But it seems to me that the population and education
explosions are not susceptible to being contained in that way.
Birth control, education, liberation of women, capital creation
for expanded output and employment – these seem to be part of
the same socio-political package.

If that is accepted the question becomes, how to achieve rural
development? The crucial choice is between the path of the
kulaks or the path of *ujamaa*. And, as variables, state farms or
privately-owned plantations: There has already been a considerable advance by the kulaks. In the inquiry referred to
above, the families with comparatively high income were those
who had diversified their activities by running a butchery,
shop, mill or motor-lorry. The tobacco farmers of Iringa are
already earning incomes of £1000 or £2000 a year. John Iliffe
records:

> By 1959, some 270 Africans in the Northern Province were
> farming more than 50 acres each. At the old Groundnut
> Scheme area at Urambo, a group of smallholders was estab-
> lished by the East African Tobacco Company to grow to-
> bacco under close supervision and with the use of hired
> labour. By 1965 their average holding under mechanical cul-
> tivation was 21 acres at any time, and established farmers
> earned an average of Shs. 12,790 a year (less the costs of culti-
> vation), perhaps ten times as much as the average cotton
> grower in Sukumaland. Plots of 25 acres were noted in the
> densely-populated lake plains of Rungwe in the mid-1950s,
> where the average holding was 1½-2 acres per family. 'It must

be understood', the rules of the Nguu Coffee Growers Society stated bluntly, 'that the aim of this Society is to enable members to own farms without working on them themselves.'. . .

It was estimated in 1949 that 10 per cent of Iraqw households owned 75 per cent of the tribe's cattle. A study of a small area of Bulambia in Rungwe district in the late 1960s showed that 10 per cent of the households owned 45 per cent of the most desirable riverine land, and 34 per cent of the households owned none, while the wealthiest 20 per cent of peasant families held 67 per cent of the government and party offices in the area.[36]

In rejecting this move to capitalist agriculture, Julius Nyerere argues as follows:

Certainly at the moment everyone has a choice between working for others or farming on his own. In Tanzania's circumstances it may therefore seem unnecessary to be worrying about the implications of agricultural capitalist development – implications which will not reveal themselves in their full force until a shortage of land becomes a problem for our nation. But there are already local shortages of land in popular, fertile and well-watered areas. And in any case, if we allow this pattern of agriculture to grow, we shall continue to move further and further away from our goal of human equality. The small-scale capitalist agriculture we now have is not really a danger; but our feet are on the wrong path, and if we continue to encourage or even help the development of agricultural capitalism we shall never become a socialist state. On the contrary, we shall be continuing the break-up of the traditional concepts of human equality based on sharing all the necessities of life and on a universal obligation to work.[37]

So the Tanzanian answer was to group people together in *ujamaa* villages. 'They would live together in a village; they would farm together; market together; and undertake the provision of local services and small local requirements as a community.'[38]

By 1972, there were about 4400 *ujamaa* villages, in which lived 11 per cent of the population of the Tanzanian mainland,

and the movement was being promoted region by region. In July 1972, 'Operation Kigoma' was to begin, in terms of which 8000 families were to be settled in 23 *ujamaa* villages. Ten dispensaries and some primary schools were to be provided and 24,000 acres to be ploughed. Phase Two of 'Operation Dodoma' would involve the settlement of an additional 56,000 families.[39]

As one might expect, reports from the villages tell widely divergent stories. Some have been highly successful, with outstanding and dedicated men using their gifts to inspire their fellows. But sometimes the spirit of *ujamaa* has been doused by the over-enthusiasm of a Regional Commissioner. I.K.S. Musoke tells the story of the establishment of Rugazi Ujamaa Village.[40] The Regional Commissioner called a meeting on 16 April 1968.

> The session was opened by the Regional Commissioner with the statement that he had 'started war' in the region and that anybody opposing it would find himself in a precarious position . . . Only three people were allowed to air their views, and this not without the Regional Commissioner's interruptions, especially when they seemed to go off the track that he wanted them to follow.[41]

One objector was the local Member of Parliament, who reminded the Commissioner that the last two world wars had been started by Germany which, on both occasions, had come to a sticky end.[42]

Out of forty-two settlers interviewed at Rugazi, thirty-six said they had been compelled to go to the village. There were complaints that leaders were consolidating and expanding their own private landholdings and operating them along capitalistic lines. 'People began to complain about this and argued that if the projects which the leaders were urging them to undertake were good, why were the leaders themselves practising the opposite.'

But in other areas, Musoke found little evidence of intimidation. 'The reasons are that these areas are the least fertile in Bukoba and have produced only small quantities of coffee and food crops. So when the chance of moving in the Ujamaa villages came to the people and they were promised some aid, they would not let this golden chance slip through their fingers.'[43]

All the time, of course, experience is accumulating and the President himself sets an example by joining a village to which he frequently repairs to help with the manual labour. It is this political element – the wholehearted participation of local and national leaders – that will decide the winner of the race between kulak agriculture and *ujamaa*.

INCOMES POLICY

'Looking at the productive achievements in Tanzania since Independence, *it is clear that the economy has been carried forward materially on the backs of the rural producers, and not so much from the so-called modern sectors that have absorbed so much investment.*'[44] This was the theme, too, of the report presented by Professor H. A. Turner in 1967: 'There seems no doubt that there is a very large discrepancy between the living standards of the *average* wage earner and the *average* smallholder, and that this discrepancy has substantially increased in recent years.'[45]

Accordingly, Turner offered a formula for the setting of the minimum wage:

A minimum wage which gives unskilled and inexperienced workers the same living standard as the small farmer (taking into account the different amounts of work which a regular employee on the one hand, and a small holder and his family on the other, may be required to perform) is therefore fair as between the smallholders and the employed workers. It is also sound in an economic sense, in that it represents the wage which will normally be required to persuade a potential farmer to consider becoming a wage-earner instead.

Unfortunately, the simplicity of these ideas becomes lost in socio-economic complexity as soon as the process of quantification is begun. The trouble is that no one knows what the living standards of the average smallholder are nor how they have moved over time. The estimates for subsistence production in the National Accounts are based on a survey of 161 households in the Morogoro and Bagamoyo regions in 1961 and 1962, amended from year to year by estimates of crop yields. The results of the Central Statistical Bureau's large-scale household budgetary survey of 1969 are still not available, and until they are the national income estimates on this score will remain bits of creative statistical artistry of the most impressionistic kind.

Cash crop production has increased very considerably over the last ten years, doubling or trebling in most cases. Sisal has been the conspicuous exception, but it was grown on estates, not on smallholdings. It is true that there have been marked inefficiencies in marketing, but since the government has begun staffing farmers' co-operatives the position has improved.

The inquiry, described above, into peasant households, was followed by one into urban households, where respondents were asked to compare life in the country (from which most of them had come) with life in the town. I give some extracts from the replies:

> When he got employed he sent for his family to join him. Since then he has made a lot of debt mainly for food and medical care. Today he earns Shs. 205 [per month], and pays Shs. 40 for lodging [one room], and Shs. 100 to 150 for food. He remains with very little for other basic expenditure. Financially, he says he would prefer to go back to the rural area but he says he can't go back in the Shamba after having been used to town life. Working for someone as he is doing today is better, he says, as one expects to get a reward at each end of month, while shamba work is full of uncertainty.

> Work in the Shamba is difficult and needs patience. One has to work very hard during the rainy season. As the rains ease, work is continuously reduced to the minimum till harvest. At least, there is time to rest between harvest and the coming rains of the next year. Conversely, today she has to be on duty no matter whether it is Sunday or whether it is during the dry season.

> Her husband is messenger with BAT. She says the country is better only at the harvesting season when one gets plenty of food and money to spend, otherwise the town is better when your husband has employment. At home there is plenty of work while here she feels she is idle. In the country, although the work is arduous, there is something to keep one busy. Here, she feels she is depending too much on her husband. At

home she did play a part in feeding the family, but she has not got that role here.

He finds the country very peaceful while in the town, there are many thefts, robberies and killings. Life in the country is cheaper. The snag is that there are not opportunities for employment and the means of securing a regular income are quite a problem. The work in the country needs plenty of energy but there is no supervision. Here you are under the constant watch of the boss and always one lives in constant fear of losing employment. This makes life uncertain. The wife finds her work here boring because it is always domestic work. [But despite all this] they think they are better off in the town than in the country.

Thus from a flat earth with two dimensions – effort and income – we are taken to a world of many qualities whose net balance is not easily assessed. The economist's lack of understanding of the urban-rural relationship is matched by his misplaced sympathy for the 'underemployment' of the peasant, when it is precisely the aim of the peasant to be as underemployed as is consistent with achieving his austere objectives.

The government did succeed in severely limiting the rise in wages and salaries after 1967. Following Turner's suggestion, the Permanent Labour Tribunal was established at the end of 1967.[46] Collective agreements could not be implemented without the Tribunal's consent and would be limited to 5 per cent a year. Strikes and lock-outs are prohibited (except in certain unlikely circumstances) under penalty of fine and/or imprisonment.[47]

Apart from any rural/urban differential, real or imagined, the Government has applied itself to narrowing the difference between those at the minimum and those at the top of the pay scale. We have noted how politicians, senior civil servants and officials in the public corporations (or parastatals as they are called) were required to divest themselves of shares, houses to let and salaries in excess of one. At the end of 1966, on the President's initiative, top salaries in the public service were cut by 20 per cent.[48] While they have been held at this level, the minimum wage has been substantially increased, from Shs. 180 per month for Dar es Salaam at the time of the Turner Report, to

Shs. 240 in June 1972.

A weakness of incomes policy that I observed at the time was that it gave no organic role to the trade union. This had already become partially bureaucratised by the Act of 1964. Interviews with 241 workers in Dar es Salaam in September and October 1967 showed that 210 were members of NUTA. Of these, 130 considered that they had had no help from the union in the past; 148 that they were receiving no services from the union in the present; 125 expected to get no services in the future. As for ways in which services could be improved, 64 respondents had no suggestions to make. Heading the list of suggestions made by the others were higher pay and a reduction of inequalities; next, social services – clinics, housing, schooling, etc.; better treatment of workers by their employers; more member participation in the management of the union; a higher quality of union official; regulation of hours of work; elected leaders, independent of party or government.[49]

In a paper prepared at the International Institute for Labour Studies in 1969 I wrote, 'National incomes policies are at their least satisfactory in the role they ascribe to trade unions, and this, it seems to me, is because their designers overlook the most important feature of trade unions – that they institutionalize needs and tendencies that are present in the workers in the first place. Collect a group of workers anywhere, to do anything, and before long they will have produced a crop of common hopes and common grievances.'

Since then we have seen that even in South Africa, where penalties against illegal strikes are even more severe than in Tanzania, the authorities have been powerless to suppress manifestations of discontent. In South Africa, they are now being compelled, by force of circumstances, to change the law, if only to enable leaders to emerge, without fear of arrest, with whom settlements can be negotiated.

It is significant that between August 1971 and March 1972 more than 45,000 man-days of work were lost through strikes,[50] inspired, it seems, by Clause 15 of TANU Guidelines, 1971.[51] This clause maintained, *inter alia*, that 'The Tanzanian leader has to be a person who respects people, scorns ostentation and who is not a tyrant.' On a subsequent strike by bus drivers the Dar es Salaam government-owned daily commented: 'It is sad that the Workers' Committees should have been so out of touch with the run of feelings among the workers. It is sad that NUTA regional or national headquarters should have been ignorant of the rise of tempers and demands. And it is sad that Government should have been caught unawares about the state of industrial relations . . .[52]

In fine, the question is not if workers shall be allowed to have grievances, nor whether in the estimation of Western-trained economists they *ought* to have grievances, but whether in fact they *do* have grievances. The first thing is to find out, and this can be done only by trade unions that they feel to be their own, with officials whom they feel they can trust. And, having found out, the next thing is to resolve them, and this, too, can only be done on the same conditions.

EMPLOYMENT CREATION

The ILO World Employment Programme, adopted in 1969, marked a change in viewpoint on the problems of development. In the early days of Independence, wage- and salary- (or *employee-*) employment had been regarded as a means to increased production; now the focus was on unemployment as a social evil, and the provision of productive employment as an end in itself. It is strange to remember, by contrast, that in the early years of Tanzanian Independence, the aim of policy was actually the *reduction* of wage employment.

The rationale of such a policy was concerned with the nature of wage employment in colonial Africa: migratory contract male labourers recruited for mines and estates for periods short enough to enable them to return to wives and families who would themselves remain in occupation of their tribal land, the whole process urged on by taxation and contained by master and servant laws. The beauty of this system, in the eyes of the employers, was that it was not necessary to pay a living wage, but only one calculated to provide the surplus necessary for the family to meet its cash requirements.[53]

Reaction against this policy gathered strength as Independence approached. The average earnings of adult male employees (as shown in the annual census of the Central Statistical Bureau) rose by 43 per cent between June 1956 and June 1961. But at the latter date the average was still only Shs. 126 a month and a major part of the policy of the TANU government was to bring about a substantial increase in wages so as to replace migrant labour with its 'bachelor wage' by a permanent and concomitantly more efficient labour force with united families. This round of increases was, in fact, ushered in by the collective agreement arrived at on the Central Joint Council for the Sisal Industry in 1960, in terms of which basic wages were to be doubled, output per man increased by 30 per cent and the labour of wives and children to be withdrawn. In the event, between mid-1962 and mid-1963, employment on sisal estates fell by 20 per cent, earnings rose by 50 per cent and output remained constant.

The government proceeded to implement its policy by the appointment of the Territorial Minimum Wages Board in 1961, believing that a smaller number of workers at a higher wage was preferable to a larger number at a lower wage. The Board agreed that a bachelor wage was socially and economically undesirable. ' . . . in the conditions of Tanganyika higher minimum wages will lead to redundancy, but . . . the smaller labour force will be much more settled and efficient, and . . . families of urban wage earners will be able much more easily to live together as family units.'[54]

Earnings rose by 22 per cent between June 1961 and June 1962; by 29 per cent in the ensuing twelve months and by between 11 and 13 per cent in each of the following two years. The cumulative result was a rise in average monthly earnings from Shs. 88 in 1956 to Shs. 285 in 1967. On the other hand, employment, that had risen slightly between 1956 and 1957, fell by nearly 21 per cent in the ensuing eight years. A careless reading of the statistics has led some economists to proclaim a functional relationship between employment and pay and to argue that it was the rise in the one that caused the fall in the other. This leads them to a simplistic solution of the problem: pushing employment up is a matter of keeping pay down.

The most drastic fall in employment did, indeed, occur between 1962 and 1963, when earnings rose 29 per cent, but a substantial amount of each was engineered by the union and employers in the sisal industry which accounted for over 40 per cent of the total fall in employment. There was also a reduction of one-third in employment in building, but this was due to uncertainty associated with Independence rather than the rise in pay. The following year, building activity recovered and employment rose by 19 per cent.

Between 1962 and 1967, the Central Statistical Bureau recorded a fall in employment of 50,630, but this is compounded of a fall of nearly 80,000 in agriculture and 2300 in mining, with a rise of 25,000 in the remaining industries. The falls after 1963 were occasioned mainly by the catastrophic fall in sisal prices and the exhaustion of mineral deposits.

The fact is that economic generalisations, in this context, are devoid of operational significance. Capital/output, capital/employment, pay/employment ratios vary widely from project to project and, over time, within a project. In factory production, one knows that between $2500 and $5000 in capital is required for each worker employed, but whether the job will survive depends, of course, on the survival of the factory which depends, again, on the cost and quality of its products and whether people can be persuaded to buy them. Every project has to be examined in all its complexity of detail and, once established, so managed as to survive amidst all the hazards of the business world.

The employment objectives of the Second Five-Year Plan are in fact quite modest: a growth in jobs outside agriculture of about 7 per cent a year, the same as the anticipated growth in urban population. By 1974, there would be 348,000 jobs in the modern sector outside agriculture, of which 57,000 would be in manufacturing. This includes, at higher levels of training an intake of:

3850 university graduates
12,330 secondary school graduates with 1–3 years' additional training
13,100 with direct entry from secondary school[55]

Mention should be made, too, of the National Small Industries Corporation which offers a link between the modern and the informal sector (to use the terminology of the Kenya report). The Corporation specialises in providing workshops for handicraftsmen. These are equipped with machinery for common use and allow the craftsmen to enjoy the advantage of power tools. In addition, the Corporation gives practical and financial help for the promotion of arts and crafts.

There are two reasons for the modesty of these programmes: one is the emphasis, already mentioned, on the decentralisation of planning that constitutes an important part of regional development in the Second Plan; the other, still more important – indeed, the element that differentiates Tanzania from most other UDCs – is the conversion of agriculture to *ujamaa*.

It is pre-eminently the existence of the *ujamaa* villages and the need and facilities for establishing new ones that, in a very basic way, solves the unemployment problem for Tanzania. Like the Chinese, the Tanzanians are trying to diversify village life by encouraging the development of crafts so that there is place in them for shoemakers, woodworkers, potters, blacksmiths and tailors as well as farmers.

Of course, this is not an easy solution for all the problems of unemployment. It is not easy for those who have grown used to town life to reconcile themselves to life in the country, and no doubt, some people will be temperamentally incapable of making the adjustment. The preference for white-collar jobs is often written down to the colonial heritage, but it is in fact a worldwide phenomenon, a desire to escape the physical strain and dirt associated with manual toil for the greater ease and status of mental effort. Tanzania is no exception in this respect, as Walter Fischer noted in July 1967:

> At present the majority of job-seekers registered at L.E.O.s (Local Employment Offices) consists of unskilled *young men* (most of them primary school leavers but also boys from the villages). Some attended typing courses but their skill is usually quite poor. Generally they are not prepared to accept work on the estates but prefer town life and are looking for the so called 'white collar jobs'. Therefore placement is rather difficult.[56]

Is the campaign for *ujamaa* villages strong enough to turn back the flood of young people to the towns? It is certainly being conducted with considerable political drive, with MPs and other leaders being expected to include membership of a village in their activities and the President himself setting an example in this respect. Whether the campaign can be sustained will depend of course on how far the villages can deliver the goods and how far, particularly, they can offer scope for the development of the talents and personality of the young. They have, somehow, to successfully rival the towns in this respect – a problem that the Chinese, too, are vigorously confronting.

THE TANZANIAN PATH

Tanzania has chosen a socialist path that is in many ways unique for Africa. The bold programme of public ownership initiated at Arusha in 1967 seems to have been eminently successful, but in the words of the Annual Plan for 1972–73, 'the best way to increase output and export growth is to get better results from investments that have already been made and institutions already created. This will come, in effect, from thousands of individual decisions to help improve the efficiency and management and parastatal projects.'[57]

The government has staked heavily on the success of the *ujamaa village* experiment. If it succeeds they will, *ipso facto*, solve a number of other problems – more especially that of employment creation. With a population density of less than 40 per square mile, there will be room for the creation of new villages on virgin land for some time to come. The villagers, together with the workers of the towns, may, too, give Tanzanian socialism an organised class base that it has so far been without.

Thus far, the moral force of socialism has enabled those who are socialists for moral reasons to take the same path as nationalists seeking national identity and self-seekers after the jobs and businesses of Asians or white expatriates. But soon there will be not much more to be had from these sources, and then it will be a matter of reconciling the élite and the farming entrepreneurs with the aims of socialism. As Richard Jolly, Dudley Seers and Hans Singer put it, 'But we now see more clearly that the heart of employment strategy lies not in making economic projections, or finding ways of removing biases towards capital intensity, but in the balance of political forces, and the capacity of political leadership in government and outside to mobilise support in ways which will make changes successful.[58]

Running a country is an appallingly complex and exacting business and nothing would be more out of place, in this context, than complacency. We are asking people to leave one system that was essentially conservative, bounded by the possible and the available, and which by almost a process of race memory they knew to work, and offering another way of life with different values, risks and rewards. Between the known of the old system and the Promised Land of socialism lies a wilderness whose navigation requires leadership of Mosaic quality. I give the last word to Mr G. K. Mubiru of Sumbawanga. His letter appeared on 18 January 1973, in the correspondence columns of the *Daily News* which, like those of the *Standard* before it, so often give testimony of the independent spirit that is a feature of so many Tanzanians: 'We have few dedicated people, we all seem to be paying lip service to socialism, we think we can live in two worlds, no you cannot eat the cake and have it, not in Tanzania at least.'

3 The Development Path in Ghana

UKANDI G. DAMACHI

The Ghanaian development path is strewn with a variety of experiences. To gain a bird's-eye view of this path, we shall analyse it from a five-point perspective, (1) socio-economic and politico-administrative, (2) social relations, (3) employment, (4) incomes policy, and (5) the impact of government strategies.

SOCIO-ECONOMIC AND POLITICO-ADMINISTRATIVE ASPECTS

Ghana, formerly the Gold Coast, achieved independence from Britain on 6 March 1957. Today it is a republican state.

The population was estimated at 6.7 million in 1960; but the 1970 census put the total population at 8.5 million. This represented an annual growth rate of 2.4 per cent between 1960 and 1970.[1]

The economy, which is basically agricultural, engages about two-thirds of the labour force; the other one-third is evenly divided between services and production in manufacturing and crafts.

Cocoa is the main crop and leading export. In 1960, cocoa export revenue accounted for 18 per cent of government income; in 1969 this went up to 25 per cent and in 1970 it was estimated at approximately a third of the total revenue.[2] Other major exports are lumber, gold, manganese and diamonds, while important imports include machinery, iron and other metals, foods and textiles.[3] *Per capita* income – about US $150 per year in 1963 – is higher than in most other African countries.

With regard to the level and structure of economic activity in Ghana, the period 1955–62, for example, witnessed a high growth of the Gross Domestic Product estimated at a total of 40 per cent. This amounted to an average compound annual growth rate of 4.8 per cent. In real terms (that is, in constant prices) and taking the Gross Domestic Product of 1955 at 1960 prices (£G 355 m.)[4] as 100, the performance of the economy during the seven years was as follows:[5]

$$
\begin{aligned}
1956 &= 106 \\
1957 &= 109 \\
1958 &= 108 \\
1959 &= 122 \\
1960 &= 132 \\
1961 &= 134 \\
1962 &= 139
\end{aligned}
$$

During this period, between 1955 and 1960, the population of Ghana was estimated to have grown at the rate of 2.5 per cent per annum and at 2.6 per cent thereafter, which when compared with the annual growth in GDP, still showed a substantial increase in the average levels of over 2 per cent per annum.

However, the economic growth of the country failed to keep abreast with the increase in population throughout most of the 1960s. Nevertheless, at the same period, the GDP grew at an average annual rate of about 2.5 per cent which indeed was less than the estimated rate of population growth of some 2.6–3 per cent. Consequently, although the GDP (in real terms) per head rose by 15 per cent, *per capita* incomes showed a decline in real terms during the 1960s. The last two years, 1961 and 1962, however, showed a more satisfactory growth in the economy because of a determined effort to increase the rate of investment and job opportunities. (We shall analyse this point in more detail later on.) Table 3.1 illustrates the growth trend in the economy during the 1960s.

As demonstrated in Table 3.1, the gross national product in constant prices grew by about 4 per cent per annum between 1968 and 1970. There was almost no growth between 1965 and 1966 because of certain factors which resulted from the then government economic policy. (These factors will be discussed later in the chapter.)

Estimates of the industrial origin of the gross domestic product of Ghana for the same period are summed up in Tables 3.2 and 3.3 respectively. Differences in the base year for market prices make the separation of the tables necessary. Table 3.2

TABLE 3.1 Expenditure on gross national product, 1960–70, at constant 1960 prices (Nc million)

	1960	1965	1966	1967	1968	1969	1970*
1 Private consumption expenditure	694	722	689	724	757	797	825
2 General government consumption	96	165	172	193	213	226	254
3 Gross domestic fixed capital formation	194	250	207	154	142	155	160
4 Changes in stocks	+22	−9	+16	+7		+11	+14
5 Domestic expenditure	1006	1128	1084	1078	1112	1189	1264
6 Exports of goods and non-factor services	246	334	306	288	288	277	289
7 Imports of goods and non-factor services	−206	−350	−277	−233	−251	−268	−305
8 Expenditure on gross domestic products	956	1122	1113	1113	1149	1198	1248
9 Net factor income from abroad	−10	−19	−14	−17	−29	−32	−35
10 Expenditure on gross national product	946	1093	1099	1116	1120	1166	1213
11 *Per capita* gross national product (Nc)	141	142	138	137	134	136	138
12 Rate of growth in gross national product	2.9 †		0.5	1.5	0.4	4.1	4.0

* Provisional.

† For Period 1960–5.

Note: Ghana went over to a decimal currency in July 1965. The monetary unit became the cedi; divided into 100 pesewas. Nc1 = US $1·40. But on 8 July 1967, the par value of the new cedi was reduced, representing a devaluation of 30 per cent. Currently the new cedi is equivalent to US $1·0.

Source: Ghana Ministry of Finance, Budget Estimate for 1971–2.

summarises the data for the two terminal years of the period, and averages for two sub-periods: 1955–7 and 1959–61.

Moreover, Table 3.2 gives a picture of the sectoral structure of the Ghanaian economy. Agriculture (i.e. items 1 to 3) appears to be the largest single element for it accounts for slightly over 50 per cent of the total GDP. The production and distribution of agricultural products (that is item 2) relate almost entirely to local foodstuffs. It is this latter which includes the subsistence element of production. But it should be noted, of course, that a true subsistence sector in the sense of a large area, or areas, having little or no contact with the market economy does not exist in Ghana. Notwithstanding the importance of subsistence production, there is no part of the country which does not produce a surplus and market that surplus. It is, therefore, more appropriate to speak of the traditional and modern elements of the economy rather than the popularly preferred dichotomy of subsistence and market economy. The basic distinction between modern and traditional sectors is in the techniques of production. In the modern sector relatively advanced technology is used for production while the traditional sector still relies on the 'knife-and-hoe' means of production.

Item 6 (in Table 3.2) which covers a variety of recorded private activities in construction, transport and various services, constitutes another important sector of the economy. An estimate based on an input-output table of the economy for 1960 indicates that 37 per cent of gross value added was contributed by private service activities, with distribution services especially large.[6] On the other hand, manufacturing accounted for only 1.1–2 per cent while mining declined from 4.9 to 4.5 per cent. After 1961 and especially in the late 1960s (see Table 3.3) the share of manufacturing went up – jumping from 2 to 7.6 per cent in 1968 and 7.9 per cent in 1969. Construction's contribution also showed a slight increase from 3.6 per cent in 1968 to 4 per cent in 1969. Mining, however, continued to decline in its share of the total GDP.

The contribution of cocoa to the GDP is stagnant. This was due to a steady decline of the price of cocoa in the world market. Between 1958 and 1961, for example, the price of cocoa fell from $985.6 per ton to $504 per ton. In

TABLE 3.2 Gross domestic product by industry of origin at 1960 market prices

Sector	1955 Ncm.	1955 %	1961 Ncm.	1961 %	1955–7 %	1959–61 %
1 Cocoa	88	12·2	142	14·5	12·9	14·9
2 Agricultural production and distribution (including agricultural exports)	238	32·9	296	30·3	32·5	30·7
3 Forestry and sawmilling	32	4·4	50	5·1	4·8	5·5
4 Mining	32	4·4	40	4·1	4·8	4·4
5 Manufacturing	6	0·8	22	2·3	1·1	2·0
6 Other recorded private industries	116	16·0	158	16·2	16·1	16·2
7 Net rent, personal and other household services	64	8·8	92	9·4	9·1	9·3
8 Government enterprises and public corporations	10	1·4	20	2·0	1·5	1·9
9 General government	36	5·0	52	5·3	5·0	5·1
10 Residual items	102	14·1	104	10·7	12·2	9·9
GDP at constant 1960 market prices	724	100·0	976	100·0	100·0	100·0

Note: Item 6 covers recorded construction, transport and various recorded services. The residual item represents the difference between the total of items 1 to 9 and the expenditure of the GDP. This residual incorporates errors and omissions on handicrafts, petty trade (apart from food distribution) and other unrecorded activities.

Source: P. Robson and D. A. Lury, *The Economies of Africa* (London: Allen and Unwin, 1969) p. 83.

TABLE 3.3 Estimated composition of gross domestic product, 1968 and 1969, at 1968 prices (million)

Sector	1968		1969	
	Value	%	Value	%
Agriculture	528·0	25·4	544·0	24·4
Forestry	79·9	3·8	81·2	3·6
Cocoa	177·3	8·6	228·5	10·2
Fishing	15·4	0·7	17·5	0·8
Mining	45·9	2·4	47·3	2·1
Construction	74·2	3·6	80·9	4·0
Manufacturing	157·4	7·6	176·0	7·9
Fuel and electricity	47·3	2·3	50·0	2·2
Transport and services	948·6	45·6	998·0	44·8
Total GDP	2074	100·0	2223·4	100·0

Source: Ghana Ministry of Finance and Economic Affairs, *Guideline for a Five-Year Rolling Plan* (Accra: Government Printer, Sep 1969).

1962, it fell still lower to $476 per ton. Over this same period, Ghana increased her production. In 1958, Ghana produced 255,000 tons of cocoa. In 1961 this had been increased to 432,000 tons. But as a result of the dramatic fall in cocoa prices over the same period, Ghana was receiving as much foreign exchange for 432,000 tons in 1961 as she did for 255,000 tons in 1958.[7] But by the end of 1973, the price had recovered to over $1000 a ton.

Despite the unstable price of cocoa, it provided (and still provides) the main source of foreign exchange earnings. In 1962, the proportion was 60 per cent and in 1963 almost 64 per cent.[8] Consequently, cocoa was (and is) the main source of government revenue. But the considerable increase in the weight of manufacturing and government enterprises and corporations in the domestic product (See Tables 3.2 and 3.3) is a clear indication of modernisation.

With regard to sectoral inter-dependence, Ghana conforms to the structure of most developing economies in having a rather low degree of integration between the sectors of the economy. Agriculture, cocoa and forestry are almost totally independent of locally produced inputs. However, significant levels of dependence are found in construction, public utilities and electricity, and especially manufacturing. In manufacturing, purchases from other sectors account for 42 per cent of the value of output at producer prices. On the whole, only 8 per cent of the output of the sectors of the economy consisted of intermediate goods used in the production system.[9] In this respect also, Ghana is at present in a transitional stage. The rapid expansion of the industrial sector in the 1960s created a greater amount of inter-independence in the economy and this change in the productive structure is likely to continue in the future even if at a slower pace.

Now let us consider the politico-administrative aspects of Ghana. Up to the present, Ghana has experienced five types of political leadership, namely (1) the British Colonial Rule which lasted till 1957[10] when the country became independent; (2) the Nkrumah years, 1957–66; (3) the National Liberation Council (NLC) Phase, 1966–9; (4) the Busia Era, 1970–2; and (5) the National Redemption Council phase, 1972 to the present.[11]

In each of these phases, the government had its own peculiar set of objectives and problems. Also, the development policies of the political leaders were based on their respective political ideologies and ambitions. Accordingly, the colonial administrators were primarily interested in preserving the interests of the colonial masters, so any form of development was to bolster the colonial power. However, faced with manpower problems, especially shortage of skilled labour, and lack of a committed labour force, the British colonial government adopted a labour policy of encouraging guidance-type trade unionism which accorded legal recognition to house unions that were extremely weak and decentralised. To implement this policy, the first Labour Department of the colonial government was set up in 1938 to encourage, and to assist in, the formation of responsible trade unions and industrial negotiating machinery. The impact of this British labour policy on industrial relations, employment and incomes will be discussed later on.

With Independence in 1957, Nkrumah became the first Prime Minister of Ghana and continued in that capacity until 1960 when he declared Ghana a republic and himself its first president. With the transition to a republican state, Ghana, almost simultaneously, passed from a parliamentary form of government to a one-party state. Nkrumah's government considered as necessary a process of exerting control over the agents of development if the multi-faceted problem of socio-economic development was to be tackled successfully.

What were some of these problems? First, at Independence, many Ghanaians were living at extreme poverty level. Education, health service, housing and social security were all at very rudimentary stages; and illiteracy was prevalent. The government, therefore, had the responsibility of raising the living standards of Ghanaians by promoting social and economic development.

Secondly, the economic development which had taken place during the colonial era was one-sidedly directed toward the production of primary commodities for export to non-African countries. There had been little industrialisation and little had been done to develop domestic markets for Ghana's own products. The structure of the economy at Independence still reflected the colonial pattern which existed in the early 1900s.

As demonstrated in Tables 3.2 and 3.3, cocoa lopsidedly accounted for the national income.

As a result, the economy of Ghana was (and still is) predominantly agricultural. But the structure of agricultural production in Ghana revealed a number of significant features which were also problematic. Shifting cultivation was widespread. In 1963, for example, the government estimated that about 40 per cent of the total cultivated land was under shifting cultivation. Farming was carried on in small-holdings – the average size of a holding being estimated to be about 6.2 acres. Moreover, a large proportion of the total number of fields was (and still is) devoted to the cultivation of cocoa.

Too many people were therefore locked up in agriculture to permit adequate attention to other sectors. Ghana's rate of employment in the agricultural sector was 62 per cent of its working population in 1960, compared with the United States 12 per cent, United Kingdom 5 per cent, West Germany 15 per cent, Denmark 23 per cent and Japan 39 per cent.[12] Furthermore, despite the high percentage of employment in agriculture, productivity was low; holdings were uneconomic, and production methods were largely rudimentary.

Agricultural characteristics of this sort constituted another source of problem for the government. Firstly, Ghanaian agricultural production was not enough to make Ghana self-sufficient in food. As a result, Ghana relied, and still relies, on food importation. In 1963 imports of food, drink and tobacco comprised 10.3 per cent of Ghana's total import bill.[13]

Secondly, since Ghana was primarily an agricultural country, she had to rely on importation for almost all her needs of manufactured goods. These consisted of goods needed for both current consumption and for productive processes such as capital-intensive equipment. For instance, in 1963 imports of textiles and clothing accounted for 13.2 per cent of Ghana's total import bill and imports of other non-durable consumer goods for 9.1 per cent. Imports of capital equipment accounted for 24.7 per cent.

Thirdly, in order to pay for these imported goods, Ghana had to earn enough foreign exchange in currencies such as sterling, dollar and deutschmark.

But Ghana relied on cocoa for most of her revenue. Accordingly, the world market price of this essential product became very important to the government. Nkrumah's government ran into economic difficulties because of the steady drop in the price of cocoa in the world market. As I have indicated earlier, between 1958 and 1961 the price of cocoa fell from $985.6 per ton to $504 per ton. Thus, as mentioned above, in 1961, although Ghana had increased production to a record level of 432,000 tons she was receiving only as much foreign exchange as she did for 255,000 tons in 1958.[14]

While Ghana's export earnings were falling as a result of the catastrophic decline in the world cocoa price, government expenditure was rising. Moreover, consumer demand for imported goods was generally high throughout the period. All this was reflected in the import figures. Imports increased from $218.4 m. in 1958 to $383.6 m. in 1961. The balance of payments, which had shown a surplus of $33.6 m. in 1958, registered a deficit of $145.6 m. in 1961! Such deterioration in the balance of payments was due mainly to the high rate of government expenditure for capital equipment (some of it unproductive) and for development projects and current consumption. Consequently, the nation's reserves of foreign exchanges which had been drawn steadily since 1959 were at last exhausted, and it faced a severe foreign exchange crisis. Worse still, it had acquired a heavy burden of foreign debt, largely in suppliers' credits and was in arrears of its current payments. Thus, the economy had reached a point where the traditional basic structure had become incapable of coping with its growing needs.

Confronted with these basic economic and social problems, the Nkrumah government adopted a policy of economic diversification. It became necessary for the government to effect an agricultural revolution which involved diversification of cash crops for exports and for local consumption. This entailed more extensive use of machinery and technology as well as scientific methods and research in order to increase agricultural productivity. The establishment of manufacturing and processing industries to provide employment for the people was also considered an aspect of economic diversification.

The Nkrumah government attempted to achieve these goals through development planning based on Nkrumah's concept of

African socialism.[15] Economic planning of a sort had existed in Ghana since April 1951, during the colonial period, when the First Five-Year Plan was launched. This plan was extended to include a Consolidation Plan which ended in 1959. It was followed by the Second Development Plan which extended to 1964. These plans were mainly public investment programmes which involved the spending by government of some $381 m. The emphasis on these plans was on infrastructural development and the provision of a variety of social services and amenities as necessary prerequisites to a meaningful economic and industrial development. Thus $288 m. of the total $381 m. disbursed (i.e., 76 per cent of the total) was spent on infrastructural development. Substantial sums were also spent on education, housing, medical facilities, and urban and rural water supplies.

The Seven-Year Development Plan which was inaugurated in 1964 and was expected to run to 1970, was different from the previous ones[16] in that it was comprehensive in scope and production-oriented. It attempted to define the government's socialist policies in terms of economic development. The plan envisaged a rate of growth of 5.5 per cent per annum for the Ghana economy over the plan period. It aimed at a total expenditure of some $1333 m. on development projects in the public sector over the period, with a forecast for some $1512 in the private sector. Within the overall framework of changing the structure of the economy from a heavy dependence on primary products to medium and heavy manufacturing based on modern technology, the plan aimed at making Ghana a net exporter of foodstuffs and a producer of basic lines of manufactured consumer goods.

The actual performance of the plan was disappointing for the following reasons. First, the government could not raise the estimated capital to implement the plan; and secondly, the few items of heavy equipment and machinery acquired by the government were not operated at full capacity because of lack of markets and low national demand. Another reason was that the country lacked the skilled personnel to operate such equipment and machinery. The average annual growth rate *per capita* (GNP) as estimated by the World Bank was only .04 per cent[17] instead of the 5.5 per cent envisaged in the plan. Besides, between 1960 and 1965, Ghana had incurred a heavy burden of foreign debt that was to weigh upon its balance of payments and to restrict its choice in economic policy for some years to come.

Estimates of the magnitude of the foreign debt have varied widely. In mid-1966 a comprehensive estimate of the country's foreign obligations as of February 1966 amounted to the equivalent of US \$448.6 m. in medium-term debt, scheduled to mature within five years at 6 per cent interest, and about US \$71.1 m. in long-term debt, with average maturity of nineteen years at 5 per cent interest.[18]

With this problem unresolved, the National Liberation Council which came into power in February 1966, after a successful coup against the Nkrumah government, inherited a legacy of high inflation, a heavy burden of foreign debts and a highly centralised bureaucratic structure.

The country, however, emerged from the Nkrumah years with some important physical assets – most notably the impressive Akosombo Dam on the Volta River, which cost the equivalent of about US \$414 m. and which is capable of meeting the country's foreseeable needs for hydroelectric power. But the economic outlook was bleak. Foreign exchange resources had been reduced to the vanishing point by 1965 and since then have been negative, with debt repayment and servicing obligations outweighing net foreign exchange earnings. As a result, the assets created during the regime of the National Liberation Council were not adequate to make up for the liabilities incurred.

Also, the military government had difficulty in gearing up the existing 'socialist' administrative apparatus to carry out the new shift in policy which was to place greater emphasis on assistance to private enterprises. With heavy debt obligations and very limited funds, the NLC government (1966–9) inherited an entire range of state enterprises and projects that must either be rendered productive – usually under mixed private and state ownership – or gradually phased out.

On the whole, as summarised by E. N. Omaboe, then Chairman of the Economic Committee of the National Liberation Council, the economic problems facing the country at the time were:[19]

1 the correction of the imbalance in the country's foreign payments position;
2 the arrest of the inflationary pressures to which the economy had been subjected during the Nkrumah regime;
3 the provision of more job openings for the rising population of the country; and
4 the restoration of balance of the government's budget.

Faced with these problems, the NLC government introduced a stabilisation programme designed to curb demand pressure on the balance of payments by restraining domestic credit expansion and curtailing spending as well as by an initial strict control on imports. At the same time, it accepted responsibility for the debts incurred under the previous government, although a few of the more obviously uneconomic contracts were subsequently cancelled. The effect of these government policies remained limited in 1966. In that year, there was a severe drop in the cocoa price coinciding with a reduction in the volume of cocoa exports because of heavy rains and floods. Imports were cut back, but there was none the less a payment deficit on current account to the amount of US $125 m. It was offset by an increase in foreign investment, by new official loans, and by sizeable drawings on the IMF accounts. Some current payments were in arrears and there were very substantial arrears in transfers of profits and dividends of foreign-owned firms as well as on debt payments. To redress some of the imbalance in external payments, the government devalued the cedi in 1967.

After the period of retrenchment from 1966 to 1969, the civilian government under Busia resolved to return to a policy of expansion. The balance of payments position remained a serious restraint on development expenditure and growth, however, and along with external debt service charges, unemployment and inflation, remained one of the principal problems confronting the government. About 220,631 persons were reported unemployed – a total of about 25 per cent of the wage and salary labour force in the modern sector.[20]

With the problems of inflation and unemployment unresolved, the Busia government (1970–2) proposed to redouble its efforts to correct some of the structural problems in the economy. Accordingly, the government relied on private foreign investment both for reviving flagging industries and for creating new ones. The investors also provided much needed business expertise. Since the implementation of Busia's proposals, Ghana had remained a predominantly private enterprise economy. Business management by politicians, begun under the Nkrumah regime, had not achieved the anticipated results. The Busia government, of a somewhat more conservative complexion, was more tilted to favour private enterprise, often in joint participation with the government. As a result, foreign investors were invited to participate with the government in a joint operation and management of the former state enterprises while foreign investments were also encouraged in new projects or enterprises.

However, the government was firmly resolved that such foreign participation should be to the benefit of Ghana. Already saddled with a number of unproductive or shoddy projects which were carried into the Nkrumah regime and the NLC regime by British and other European contractors, the Busia government resolved that the new foreign investment approved should be able in time to be self-supportive. Besides, the government was to participate in most projects on equal basis with the foreign investors to safeguard the national interest. There was accordingly a provision in most of the investment agreements which ensured that Ghanaian personnel were employed in both labour and managerial positions wherever available.

All these government measures failed to improve the balance of payments and to solve the unemployment problem. As a last effort to arrest the chaotic economic condition of the country, the Busia government devalued the Ghana cedi by 48.3 per cent. The devaluation only helped to worsen the already pathetic situation. For example, it increased the cost of imports from the United States by 80 per cent. Imports from countries whose currencies were tied up with the dollar went up in cost by 93 per cent following the devaluation of the dollar. Besides, since most of the industries in Ghana depend on raw materials imported from abroad, domestic selling prices according to an estimate by the Ghana Manufacturers' Association, went up by between 50 and 70 per cent.[21]

The benefits expected from devaluation, an increase in export earnings, for instance – were not realised since Ghana's main exports, cocoa, timber and minerals, are all exported in an unprocessed form and sold at prices dictated from abroad. This meant that devaluation failed to cause their appreciation in terms of the cedi; rather, the foreign exchange earnings from these exports remained at the level decided by overseas purchasers.

With these daunting economic and social problems plaguing the country, the military under the leadership of Colonel Acheanpong took over power from the Busia government in a bloodless coup on the morning of 13 January 1972. Colonel Acheanpong quickly set up the new government of the National Redemption Council (1972 to the present) with himself as its chairman. The NRC government revalued the cedi by 42 per cent, that is, it was now worth US $0.78 instead of US $0.55. The expensive 180-day credit system, which had inflated the cost of imports of consumer goods and industrial raw materials, was abolished.

More significant, the government rejected all the debt settlements concluded either multilaterally or bilaterally with creditor countries since 24 February 1966, the day of the first coup. (The debts that were the subject of these settlements had been contracted under the Nkrumah regime in respect of contractor-financed projects which were generally believed to have been inflated in cost through corrupt deals between the contractors and the politicians to whom they sold the ideas for the projects.)[22] The debt settlements which were concluded in 1966, 1968 and 1970 had merely served to push up the size of the debts because of a staggering moratorium interest (40 per cent of the original sum) that was charged each time short-term relief was offered by the creditor countries.

The government therefore decided to cancel the debts (about US $34.7 m.) owed to British companies, the Parkinson Howard Group of Companies, Seawork Limited, Newport Shipbuilding and Engineering Company, and Swan Hunter and Richardson, for reasons that the contracts were 'tainted and illicited by corruption and other illegality'.[23] On the other hand, the remaining medium-term debts worth US $294 m. were to be paid only if the following conditions were satisfied:[24]

1 All those creditors who maintained that Ghana was indebted to them must establish before the National Redemption Council the validity of the contracts under which those debt obligations were incurred.

2 No arrangement for the servicing of debt obligations which would result in 'economic suicide' for Ghana would be accepted. Therefore, even where any debt was established as valid, it would only be repaid on terms currently applicable to credits granted by the International Development Association (IDA). In other words, such debts would be paid over a fifty-year period, including ten years of grace. Since all the previous debt settlements had been rejected, the capital amounts that would be considered for repayment would be exclusive of all accumulated moratorium interest.

3 Debts arising out of suppliers' credits contracted after 24 February 1966, and short-term debts arising from arrears on import credits, 180-day credits and liabilities of service payments, as well as long-term loans granted by the World Bank, the IDA, the government of the United States of America and the governments of other donor countries would, however, be fully repaid.

The National Redemption Council's rather unprecedented action on the debts was received with joy throughout the country. This was due to the fact that throughout the late sixties, debt servicing obligations had been corroding Ghana's foreign exchange earnings and thus preventing the importation of the machinery and equipment needed for the country's industrialisation programme. Moreover, many of the debts had in fact been paid off, though compound interest and other forms of usurious practices had kept them at a perpetually high level.

To control the unnecessary high cost of imported goods, the government centralised the importation of all essential consumer goods and industrial raw materials. An 'Essential Commodities Committee' was set up, charged with the following duties:[25]

1 to establish both national and regional consumption requirements;
2 to obtain the necessary tenders and quotations from local and overseas suppliers;
3 to arrange the placement of orders; and
4 to take delivery of stocks and ensure their fair and equitable distribution throughout the country.

With the formation of this committee, small importers and retail traders resorted to 'hoarding' of goods in order to cause temporary shortages out of which they could recoup the profits now lost to them through direct importation by the committee. The NRC government has yet to devise means of coping with the hoarders. Meanwhile it has advised Ghanaian consumers to rely more on local food and less on imports during the period of temporary shortages as a way of putting the hoarders out of business. Such a solution, however, merely begs the problem, for the Ghanaian consumer, like other consumers in most developing countries, believes that any imported product is automatically superior to a local brand. Besides, like consumers everywhere, he shops to meet his personal needs and not to fulfil a political objective of the government.

From this discussion of the problems that confronted the various governments in Ghana, we realise that since the inception of Ghana's independence in 1957, her problems have been basically the same. What has changed over the years has been the approach used by the different governments to solve them. These problems have been how to modernise the economy, and how to create jobs for the ever-increasing population and thereby maintain an equitable society with equal justice for all Ghanaians.

In trying to find an answer to these problems, the Nkrumah government adopted the ideology of African Socialism. The government felt the quickest way out was rapid industrialisation based on a socialist model. The cost of such a model was so heavy that it ran the economy into great debts and chronic deficit in the balance of payments. Consequently, a country which started as a promising developing nation suddenly found itself barely able to exist.

Not surprisingly, Nkrumah's economic failure was blamed on his socialist policies. Accordingly, the subsequent governments decided to try other models of development. The NLC government reverted to the attempt to combine a little bit of socialism with the capitalist model. Such a mixed model did little to alleviate Ghana's economic and social problems. It was then not unexpected that the Busia government went all out for the capitalist model, hoping that it was the panacea to the socio-economic ills of Ghana. His government relied on developing both the agricultural sector and the modern or industrial sector simultaneously. While the intention was good, the finances were limited – hence the eventual failure.

The NRC government that succeeded the Busia regime felt that the main reason why the previous regimes had failed was due to the fact that they were relying on foreign ideologies and models. Consequently, they were trying to industrialise the country on a porous base since there was no indigenous ideology which stressed the need to feed oneself before thinking of a modern industrial society. The government therefore launched 'Operation Feed Yourself' as an indigenous ideology which would motivate the people to increase local food and thereby set the stage for rapid industrialisation. Such a policy seems to answer what one Ghanaian newspaper had suggested to be Ghana's number one political problem, and that is 'the problem with the Ghanaians and their milk'. If the Ghanaians were provided with milk (i.e., food) the political system would then run smoothly, uninterrupted by military coups or mass protest.

So we can see that Ghana has gone first from colonialism through African Socialism, a mixed system of socialism-capitalism, to undiluted capitalism and to what is now known as 'Operation Feed Yourself' which is a policy of self-reliance. In going through these various ideologies, the population was mobilised by each government for the sake of implementing the respective government development policies.

SOCIAL RELATIONS

In this section, we shall attempt to depict how the various governments attempted to harness the co-operation of organised groups (e.g., the trade unions and employers' associations) and non-organised groups (e.g., the masses) to foster the development process.

With regard to the trade unions, the governments expected them to play a dual role; first, defending or protecting the interests of wage-earners, and secondly, participating in a national effort to conquer political and economic dependence. To help the extremely weak and loosely structured trade union organisation (a colonial legacy) play this dualistic role, the Nkrumah government passed the Industrial Relations Act, 1958, introducing a 'new structure' which sought to avert the problems that confronted the unions during the colonial rule.[26]

The Industrial Relations Act, 1958 (IRA, 1953), later amended by the Industrial Relations Amendment Acts of 1959 and 1965 respectively, had four principal parts. One of the two most important of these was the creation of 'A strong centralized trade union organization, whose central body is recognized by the Government and is given certain powers and duties, and over which the Government would be able to exercise some supervision to ensure that the powers were not abused.'[27]

In essence the IRA, 1958 and its amendments centralised the unions into a 'root and branch' trade unionism and gave it legal recognition.

The other part of the Act restructured the methods of collective bargaining and negotiation and stipulated the circumstance in which a strike (or lock-out) could legally take place. Accordingly, the Act established the Ghana Trade Union Congress (TUC) as a corporate body to act as the spokesman and representative of all the trade unions in Ghana. Similarly, trade unions were not only legally recognised by both the government and all managements, but were also the legally accredited bodies to undertake the task of collective bargaining and negotiation in establishments for and on behalf of all workers. In short, the Act made collective bargaining compulsory. Refusal on the part of the management to bargain with a union could result in the imposition of a fine.

The new system certainly resulted in a very close relationship between the trade union movement and the Nkrumah government. The IRA, 1958 gave the minister responsible for labour power to effectively dissolve unions by withholding or withdrawing their certification for collective bargaining with employers, denying them the advantage of the check-off system, or the right to strike. Similarly, the President of the Republic could freeze the funds of the TUC in the event of any action considered not to be conducive to the public good. It could thus be said that the trade union movement was legally subordinated to the government. The unions did not seem to resent this. On the contrary, some of the trade union leaders were keen on mobilising the trade union movement behind the government. Also, the unions were attracted by the prospects of achieving a functional arrangement with the government.

As a matter of fact, the desire for co-operation between the trade union movement and the government occasioned the IRA, 1958. Politically, the trade union movement was subordinate to Nkrumah's Convention People's Party (CPP) which was in power. Consequently, any cabinet decision taken had to be supported by the TUC and its affiliates. Thus, such union subordination did not prevent the unions from participating actively in the government and party activities. In fact, the Secretary General of the TUC was at the time a cabinet minister. Nevertheless, the TUC's strength within the political machinery was dependent on its ability to mobilise the unions in support of the government's programmes.

To make the civil service more responsive to national priorities, the Nkrumah government passed the Civil Service Act, 1960. In accordance with this Act, all civil servants were now members of trade unions. This afforded the TUC complete membership of the work force and thus the opportunity to channel its activities toward productivity and toward achieving industrial peace which was almost nil during the twilight of colonialism. With the passage of the Act, therefore, the government consolidated the position of the TUC as an organ of the CPP.

With the new pattern of industrial relations, where collective bargaining was made compulsory, the government encouraged the employers to form an association to facilitate the industry-wide bargaining stipulated by the IRA, 1958. Immediately, the Ghana Employers' Association was formed, and by 1959 it was extended from the industrial to the national level.

The Association represents most of the employers in Ghana. It consults with employers for advice and guidance on economic, social and technical issues. Like the TUC, the GEA is actively involved in collective bargaining and negotiations. It is the accredited representative of and spokesman, at the national level, for employers' organisations.

Since the TUC was now well organised and administered, the government used it as a socialising agent. To propagate the government socialist policies, and to mobilise and socialise the masses for the national goals, the TUC executives organised adult education programmes in rural areas. This aspect of organised labour as a socialising agent becomes all the more important if we note that in spite of the fact that tribal differences and jealousies existed among the workers and the masses, attempts were being made to unite all of them behind the party to promote national development.

Also, to foster national development, the Nkrumah government mobilised the youth into the 'Ghana Youth Brigade', the women (married or single) into the 'Ghana Women's Association', and centralised the students into a national union – the 'National Union of Ghana Students' (NUGS). To encourage the farmers to produce more, marketing boards were set up to buy their produce. With such a broad mobilisation scheme, the country was put, according to the government, 'at war with economic backwardness and neo-colonialism'.

The NLC government which succeeded Nkrumah also attempted to galvanise the people to implement its development programmes. Accordingly, the military regime enlisted the co-operation of the TUC. To ingratiate the TUC with the government, the TUC was once more given the freedom to organise democratically and bargain collectively despite the fact that the problems of inflation, balance of payments and foreign debts remained. Besides, the TUC was once more allowed wider participation on the national decision-making boards that formulated labour policies.

In effect, the NLC government, like the Nkrumah government, viewed the TUC as a communication link to the masses and as a catalyst to the development process. To ensure that the TUC continued to play this mediating role, the NLC government maintained some sort of control over the union movement. Despite the fact that the TUC was allowed representation on various boards, it was under-represented on these boards. This was a controlling device used by the government to restrict it from exerting authority on these boards. Nevertheless the TUC was ready to co-operate with the NLC government to implement development programmes.

The civil servants who became restive and subversive under the Nkrumah regime for being forcibly unionised had to be moved by the NLC to be co-operative. Their co-operation was eventually enlisted with the dissolution of the Civil Service Act, 1960. Not surprisingly, the civil servants rallied around the government and became the bulwark of the NLC regime. Their co-operation and enthusiasm to contribute to the development process were based on their belief that politicians and the army were all transitory; but they also believed that the country had to continue to exist. As a result, they gave their support to the NLC government to facilitate the smooth administration of the country.

The government also continued to work with the Ghana Employers' Association to promote a cordial atmosphere of industrial relations in the country. The unions and the employers still had the legal obligation to bargain collectively.

The general public was shocked by the government reports of the scandals of the Nkrumah regime. Such propagandistic techniques along with the government appeal for public co-operation made the Ghanaians become politically conscious and vigilant, but nevertheless sympathetic to the government. Consequently, the government was able to dissolve Nkrumah's political organs, the Ghana Farmers' Association, the Ghana Women's Association, the Youth Brigade and so on.

Like his predecessors, Busia also used the legislative instrument to coerce and control the TUC. Initially, he tried to use the same strategies as Nkrumah had applied to assert his proprietorship over organised labour, that is, to centralise the unions and impose party men on the leadership. It was therefore not surprising that he declared his support for free trade unionism in Ghana at the inception of his administration. Speaking of union freedom, he wrote, '. . . I believe it is your privilege and right to choose your leaders without interference. We desire a trade union movement that will work in accord, love, and peace; a movement that will unite the workers to serve our Nation's need.'[28]

Such words of friendship and co-operation failed to enlist the support of the TUC for the Busia government because the TUC was no longer prepared to surrender its sovereignty to any political party. After the experiences of the Nkrumah regime,[29] it had learned to be covetous of its independence lest its very existence be threatened.

Since the TUC remained unmoved by his appeal for co-operation, Busia resorted to the legislative instrument to coerce it into line with his national policies. As a result, the Industrial Relations Act, 1971 (IRA, 1971) was passed introducing the 'contracting-in' principle as a way of becoming a union member. Such a stipulation drastically reduced union membership (from an all-time peak of 700,000 to about 300,000 members) and financial strength. The collective bargaining clause of the Act also weakened the union strength. It stipulated that the gains of collective agreements negotiated by the unions were to be enjoyed by all workers, union members and non-members alike; this was indeed a deliberate government policy to demean the idea of trade unionism to the workers.

To Busia, then, the role of the trade unions was merely to implement government policies. When the unions refused to play a role which they considered inappropriate to their interests, the Busia government used the legislative instrument to relegate them to the background and decided to appeal directly to the workers.

However, he knew that he still needed some sort of organised force to implement his development policies. So instead of using the unions, he reverted to Nkrumah's strategy of mobilising the youth into 'youth brigades'. (The main difference between Nkrumah, NLC and Busia is that whereas the first two looked at the TUC as a mediating body, the latter relegated it to the background.)

Since the Busia regime was of a somewhat conservative complexion, it was quite easy for it to maintain a workable relationship and rapport with the Employers' Association. Also the employers' support was enlisted by many concessions given to them by the government. For example, the state farms started under Nkrumah were turned over to private entrepreneurs. The government's liberal economic and investment policies were very much welcomed by the employers.

But the civil service failed to provide the needed support to the Busia regime. The government in an attempt to modernise the civil service fired 580 top-ranking civil servants as being obsolete in their thinking. Their dismissal triggered popular discontent among the civil servants with the Busia regime. Rumours of sabotage by the civil servants became frequent. But the government maintained control over the civil service.

After the abuses of supplier credit contracts that took place under the Nkrumah regime, the TUC and public were now vigilant over foreign investment arrangements, and public criticism or concern was frequently expressed when new contracts were announced. Similar nationalist sentiments resulted in the legislation of 1970 (the Aliens Act) that prohibited foreign ownership of small- or medium-scale retail operations and affected residence permits of non-Ghanaians (mostly Africans) engaged in petty trading, cocoa farming (as labourers) and other street activities.

But even such legislation failed to allay the fears and frustrations of the TUC and the public who felt that the Busia government had connived with private employers to thwart public and union demands. Consequently, the TUC began to exhort its members and the working masses to withhold their labour by 'go-slows'; willy nilly, government development policies suffered.[30]

The NRC government adopted a pro-labour policy, that is, to enlist the co-operation of the TUC. Consequently, it abolished the IRA, 1971 by a decree, re-established the TUC, and gave it back its right to function freely and democratically. Such government labour policy was acclaimed by workers all over the country thereby setting the stage for the enthusiastic welcome of the government programme of 'Operation Feed Yourself', a widely-publicised campaign launched by the NRC government to increase food production and thus cut down the cost of living.

Chiefs do come forward with offers of land, and a realistic effort is being made to rationalise food shortage and distribution throughout the country. Students also volunteer their service in the harvesting of sugar-cane on the state-owned sugar

plantations. Occasionally, the students organise demon-
strations to some foreign embassies in Ghana, denouncing
what they call 'capitalist exploitation of Ghana's resources'.
The trade unions and the unorganised masses voluntarily participate in the digging of channels for irrigation. This is aimed
at making Ghana self-sufficient in local food, e.g., yams, cassava, corn and so on.

The 'Operation Feed Yourself' programme seems to be
working very well, especially with the constant review of the
targets and methods used. It seems that, for the first time,
Ghanaians are beginning to get really interested and involved
in a campaign launched by the government.[31] This is indeed a
healthy sign that they may have now come to realise that the
task of development requires a collective national effort.

In analysing the various means used by each government to
mobilise the population for the implementation of development
programmes, certain features emerge. First, each government
realised the importance of the trade unions in the development
process. As a result, when the trade unions failed to toe the
government line, coercion and intimidation were used by
government to elicit compliance. Often such government re-
pressive measures back-fired – for example, the Busia regime's
unsuccessful intimidation of the TUC.

Secondly, the trade unions and the public seemed to react
more favourably to government programmes that addressed
themselves to the people's most pressing need, e.g., of having
enough food. The success of 'Operation Feed Yourself' is a case
in point.

The question to ask now is what was the impact of these
various government mobilisation techniques on employment?
Were these techniques oriented to the creation of employment,
or not?

EMPLOYMENT

We shall first discuss the general features of the employment
scene in the country before considering government employment policy from Independence in 1957 up to the present.

With regard to the labour force, let us state at the outset that
detailed information on its size is not generally available.
Officially, it has been admitted that 'the statistical information

now available does not provide adequate data on the current size, occupational composition and economic activity of the labor force. Nor does it shed adequate light on the extent of employment, under-employment and unemployment, nor the degree of manpower utilization.'[32]

Table 3.4 summarises the labour force as given by the 1960 census and the ILO Labour Force Projections for 1970. The labour force shows an increase from about 2·7 million in 1960 to 3·5 million in 1970. The yearly increase in the labour force has been put at about 210,000 to 225,000 – most of whom are middle-school leavers. The labour force in 1960 represented 40 per cent of the total population and 73 per cent of the adult population (that is aged 15 and over). In 1970, the proportions were 39 and 72 per cent respectively. Although the 1970 percentages in both cases represented a slight decline from the 1960 figures, there were in absolute terms one-third more people in the labour force in 1970 than in 1960. Out of 2,724,850 in the labour force in 1960, 61·8 per cent were males and 38·2 per cent females. In 1970 males constituted 62·3 and females 37·7 per cent of the total.[33]

As in the case above, the 1970 percentage shares were on the decline but on the increase in absolute terms.

As regards the structure of employment, agriculture employed nearly two-thirds (61 per cent) of the whole employed labour force in 1960, followed by craftsmen (15·5 per cent) and sales workers (13·5 per cent) in the second and third position respectively. Women dominated sales work. In agricultural occupations, males and females were fairly evenly distributed.[34]

But according to *Labour Statistics*, in 1969 42 per cent of the employed were classified as 'craftsmen, production process workers and labourers'. Professional, technical and related workers (14·6 per cent) and clerical workers (13·6 per cent) were second and third respectively, while agricultural workers accounted for only 6·6 per cent of the employed labour force. The latter's low percentage share was primarily due to non-inclusion of cocoa (the artery of the Ghanaian economy) farm workers. It was also a reflection of the NLC government's policy to disband the Nkrumah regime's employment schemes (state farms, co-operatives, etc.). As a result, many workers in

TABLE 3.4 Participation in the labour force, 1960 and 1970

	Total population (All ages)		Adult population (15 and over)		Labour force		Labour force as percentage of: Total population		Adult population	
	1960	1970*	1960	1970*	1960	1970*	1960	1970*	1960	1970*
Total	6,726,820	9,026,000	3,730,680	4,820,000	2,724,850	3,492,000	40	39	73	72
Male	3,400,270	4,562,000	1,889,440	2,482,000	1,682,730	2,175,000	40	48	89	88
Female	3,326,550	4,464,000	1,841,240	2,362,000	1,042,120	1,317,000	31	30	62	56

* Projections

Note: The table also shows the relative shares of the male and female labour force in both the total and adult population for 1960 and 1970.

Sources: The 1960 figures are derived from the 1960 *Census Population Advance Report* and quoted in Birmingham *et al.*, (eds), *Economy of Ghana*, op. cit., p. 121; The 1970 figures are taken from the ILO, *Labour Force Projections, 1965–1985*, pt II, *Africa* (Geneva: 1971) p. 100.

agricultural occupations were made redundant. It should, however, be noted that agriculture still employs more people than any other single sector. Finally, *Labour Statistics*, 1969 showed that a greater proportion (34 per cent) of the female workers was employed in the professional, technical and related groups than elsewhere.

Fig. 3.1   *Ghana: unemployment scene for both male and female, 1957–71*

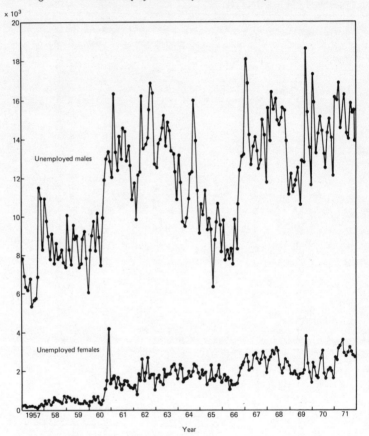

Source: Ghana, Ministry of Labour, Accra

With this synoptic review of the structure of employment in the country, the next relevant question is, what are some of the salient employment problems in Ghana?

First, unemployment and under-employment are considered

'a most serious and pressing problem especially in the urban centres'.[35] The actual magnitude of the problem is not well known. The Ghana Manpower Board's Annual Report put the unemployment rate in 1960 at about 25 per cent of the total labour force. The present situation has not improved. Estimates of those actively seeking employment have been put at between 250,000 and 600,000.[36]

Fig. 3.1 gives a rough picture of the unemployment problem in the country. The graph should not be taken as representing the exact or absolute level of unemployment in the country at any given period. It is based on Employment Office statistics. Since employment offices are usually located in more populous regions (or cities) of the country, registrations are entirely voluntary and neither employees seeking work nor employers looking for workers use the Employment Office services exclusively. The data are thus invariably incomplete and cannot be taken as a reliable indication of the level of unemployment. Nevertheless, they are the best we have got.

From the graph, we can observe that unemployment was acute in 1961–3 and declined to near zero by 1965. The reasons for the acute rate of unemployment in the early 1960s were the expansion of both primary and secondary schools by the Nkrumah government at Independence to make up for the manpower shortages which faced the country then. By the early 1960s the many school leavers entered the labour force and the economy was not modernised enough to absorb them. The government industrialisation programme was not working properly and hence the job opportunities it was expected to create failed to materialise.

But the near-zero unemployment rate in 1965 was not due to any economic boom. With the government's socialist policies, various employment-generation schemes (e.g., state farms, co-operatives, and so on) were created. Such schemes helped to provide jobs for the many unskilled and unemployed masses. Also, in accordance with the government political policy to free the rest of colonial Africa, the Nkrumah government declared war against imperialism and neo-colonialism. Consequently, the economy was put on a war footing, and the Ghanaians were mobilised and made to believe they were at war with imperialism and neo-colonialism. Every able-bodied person was thus put to work to liberate the rest of Africa from these two evils. The result was that there was almost full employment in the country.

But with the change of government in 1966 and the slow down of economic activities that followed, the unemployment problem became much worse. The steadily increasing growth of the labour force further complicated the situation. For example, in 1966 over 80,000 workers were laid off as a result of the stabilisation and retrenchment measures adopted by the NLC government in order to get the economy on a sound footing. This shrinkage of employment opportunities was aggravated by the usual annual additions to the labour force. Moreover, the discrepancies between the types of work available, the skills and the preferences of job-seekers also tended to aggravate the unemployment problem.

A great proportion of the increasing labour force was made up of unskilled, middle-school leavers. This influx of unskilled school leavers into the labour force was attributed to the expansion of middle-school education in the 1960s. Of the more than 65,000 young people who were to complete middle schools in 1970; it was believed that only about 11 per cent would continue at secondary schools. With the One-Year Plan, it was reckoned that assuming 55,000 to 60,000 job opportunities would be available for replacement either because of deaths or retirements, it would still require some 145,000 or more additional job opportunities to find employment for the annual increase in the number of job-seekers.

Other employment problems besides unemployment included a critical shortage of high-level skills,[37] especially such as para-professionals, e.g., medical and dental technicians, research technicians, nurses and so on. In the professional group, the most critical problem was a lack of managerial and administrative skills, according to the 1968 Manpower Survey.[38] The vacancies in this group totalled 1747 compared with 3929 in the para-professional, skilled and foremen categories.

With regard to the shortages in the para-professional group, primary and middle-school teachers constituted 47,866 of the total 68,799 vacancies created, while non-teachers, that is, technicians, electricians, etc., made up the remaining 20,933.

This means that the ratio of teachers to non-teachers is 2·5:1 compared to 1:5 in developed countries.[39]

Another employment problem is under-utilisation of available skills. It is estimated that Ghana spends between 30 and 40 per cent of the annual budget on education. Unfortunately the government fails to make adequate use of the graduates who pour out from the Ghanaian universities and who return from abroad every year. Consequently, the government continues to spend enormous amounts of money without getting any substantial returns.

What are the causes of these employment problems? The reasons vary; some of them are as follows. First, the high rate of population increase (2·4 per cent) tends to compound the problem. There is a lack of comparable growth of employment opportunities to match the rapid population growth which appears to be increasing as a result of modern medicine.

Secondly, Ghana, like most of the other developing countries, experiences excessive rural-urban migration. People are attracted to the life-style of the cities. It is in the cities that they hope to get employment. But rapid growth in urban employment implies a fast increase in the rate of urban unemployment and under-employment. As a result, the reverse could be that life in urban areas is no better than rural life.

Thirdly, the educational facilities tend to be out of step with the manpower needs of Ghana. Education is oriented toward the modern sector. But while it is looked upon by the youngsters as an open-sesame to a better job, better salary and better life, it has limited relevance for the general masses of the population who may not gain access to the modern sector. For example, the 1968 Manpower Survey blames the defects of high-level manpower supply on the lack of adequate and realistic planning of the training and educational programmes. It states that

> there has been very little effort, if any, to relate or gear educational development specifically to the needs of the growing economy. Education has not significantly shifted from its traditional role of providing basic education to its beneficiaries. The focus has been more general in most cases than direct or specific with the result that the economy is not supplied with

its entire needs of trainable persons (out of the schools/ institutions) both quantitatively and qualitatively.[40]

Fourthly, high wages in the modern sector also contribute to the employment problem. A worker in this sector earns fifty to fifty-two times his rural counterpart. The high wages attract urban migration from the rural sectors.

Fifthly, inadequate incentives for productive activity also tend to constitute a problem. In Ghana, as in many other developing countries, urban development and industrialisation are financed by taxes of one kind or another on rural production, especially cocoa production. A substantial proportion of funds for development of the modern sector, therefore, comes from agriculture. But the income of farmers is minimal compared to urban wage-earners. Consequently, the farmers who constitute the bulwark of development lack the incentives to increase their productivity. Indeed, they are taxed to provide privileges for the cities to which they have no easy access.

Finally, the slow rate of economic growth and industrialisation which Ghana is experiencing is also a contributive factor to the unemployment situation. The Ghanaian economy is just not growing fast enough to have an impact on the employment problem: nor is modernisation progressing fast enough. On the other hand, in a dual economy like that of Ghana, modernisation tends to create an *unemployment dilemma*. The causes of unemployment mentioned above are concomitants of the rapid pace of modernisation. As a result, the more rapid the rate of modernisation, the higher the rate of unemployment. So modernisation *per se* is a generator of urban unemployment. This aspect, therefore, constitutes a dilemma in a dual economy – where unemployment is a result of both rapid modernisation and the lack of it.

How did the various governments in Ghana try to solve these employment problems? The Nkrumah government decided to know the dimensions of Ghana's manpower needs before finding appropriate solutions. Accordingly, employment exchanges were set up in urban centres all over the country. For example, in 1958, there were ten employment exchanges of which three were central and seven regional.[41] These exchanges were very successful in placing people and thus became the best medium of disseminating information about work and employment in general. In 1958 and 1959, the exchanges received on average 8463 and 8327 employment requests monthly and were able to place 1399 and 1806 respectively.[42]

Also, to assist in making the labour market more responsive to the needs of the economy, the Nkrumah government launched an extensive education programme in addition to setting up training facilities among the various party organs, e.g., co-operatives, and the Committee on Workers' Organization (CWO), an equivalent of the US Civilian Conservation Corps (CCC). Most of these programmes were designed to stem the rural-urban migration which contributed greatly to urban unemployment.

On the other hand, the NLC government established the Manpower Board in 1968 with the aim of improving the overall manpower planning and human resource development activities in the country. Since its establishment, one of its functions has been the examination of the relationship between formal schooling, vocational training, and the experience gained through practical work in the development of skills and the finding of ways to achieve the most productive economic mix among the possible alternatives.

In the management field, the government supported agencies like the Institute of Management and Public Administration and the Management Development and Productivity Institute, whose activities have been directed to the upgrading of management and supervisory skills in both the public and private sectors. Government support varied from organised courses, in-plant and on-the-job training to special intensive programmes for top-level managers and administrators. The National Vocational Training Institute was established in 1969 with the assistance of the United Nations Development Programme (UNDP) and the International Labour Organisation (ILO). Its functions include the development of training standards and trade testing and organisation of apprenticeship, in-plant training and training programmes for industrial and clerical workers. Also, it intends to consolidate the existing training activities into a national system.

The Busia regime also gave adequate attention to creating employment opportunities for the massive unemployed population. The One-Year Development Plan contained a number of proposals about how the problem was to be tackled. One was the government's instruction to executing agencies 'to give preference to labour-intensive rather than capital-intensive methods wherever such choices are technically feasible and economically reasonable.'[43] Also, the government was prepared to support only industries with employment potential.

Closely related to the labour-intensive projects was the government's encouragement of the use of simple tools in agriculture as well as better methods and inputs, so that productivity could be increased without too much mechanisation. However, the government, realising that the substitution of labour for capital was unlikely to succeed as long as wage increases were unrelated to productivity increases, appealed to the Prices and Incomes Board, the trade unions and management organisations to keep wages rates at appropriate levels.

We have mentioned that one of the causes of urban unemployment is rural-urban migration. To slow down the rate of migration, the Busia government launched a rural development programme aimed at modernising the rural areas as well as agriculture. Government's active encouragement to farmers by means of credits on easy and reasonable terms, the provision of extension services, improved transportation, the construction of feeder roads, better marketing facilities, and the strengthening of the co-operative movement helped to enhance the economic rewards for farming and consequently caused a slow-down in rural-urban migration.

In line with government's employment creation programme, the National Service Corps (NSC) was established 'as a part of the Government's effort to mobilize all available human resources for productive activity.'[44] The function of the NSC was to organise all able-bodied persons in towns and villages who were 'willing and anxious to help the nation to meet pressing needs'.[45]

Ever since its foundation, the activities of the Corps have been mainly in development schemes like the building of community facilities or public conveniences, wells, schools, health posts, markets, incinerators, minor feeder roads, town and village parks, gardens and community centres. The Corps works in close collaboration with both the Ministry of

Youth and Rural Development and several voluntary organisations. Through the latter, about 300,000 people were registered with the Corps in September 1970, 50 per cent of whom were unemployed, 20 per cent students and 20 per cent in full employment.

The existence of graduate unemployment especially among the general degree students in social science (including history and geography, and biological science graduates) was another serious problem facing the government. The government plan was 'to redress the imbalance between the humanities and the sciences generally so that students' choice of courses will conform with the manpower requirements of the country.' To obtain up-to-date information on the careers of university graduates a tracer service was established.[46]

The NRC government is putting much emphasis on its self-reliance doctrine and on rural development to curb mounting urban unemployment. The government also has a policy of controlling wages to enable it to combat employment problems.

What has been the impact on income distribution of all these various government strategies to generate employment?

INCOMES POLICY

Here we shall deal with the general level of income distribution in the country before proceeding to examine the incomes policy of the various governments.

With regard to income distribution, official statistics do not furnish detailed analysis. However, Table 3.5 indicates the nature of income distribution among income-tax payers. Before going into the details of the information contained in the table, its limitations must be pointed out. The table does not cover the whole income earning or gainfully employed population of Ghana. There is inadequate information on those parts of the population earning less than Nc 400 per annum (in both the public and private sectors) who are exempted from tax under the existing income-tax system. The table refers only to those with incomes above Nc 400 per annum who are either civil servants, self-employed or private sector employees. Since the income-tax system in Ghana excludes income from cocoa farming and (from 1969/70 income from all farming)[47] the table also

TABLE 3.5 Ghana: distribution of income-tax payers (no. of taxpayers)

Income group Nc	Civil servants 1960–70	Percentage of total	Cumulative percentage	Self-employed and private sector 1966–7	Percentage of total	Cumulative percentage
Less than 400	37,470	41·3	41·3	—	—	—
401–600	24,428	26·9	68·2	69,203	54·0	54·0
601–800	11,509	12·7	80·9	19,957	15·6	69·6
801–1000	5022	5·5	86·4	12,368	9·7	79·3
1001–1200	2816	3·1	89·5	5680	4·4	83·7
1201–1400	1624	1·8	91·3	3870	3·0	86·7
1401–1600	1173	1·3	92·6	3750	2·9	89·6
1601–1800	1454	1·6	94·2	1864	1·5	91·1
1801–2000	1279	1·4	95·6	1688	1·3	92·4
2001–3000	2525	2·8	98·4	3861	3·0	95·4
3001–4000	619	0·7	99·1	1877	1·5	96·9
4001–5000	525	0·6	99·7	1293	1·0	97·9
5001–6000	525	0·6	99·7	897	0·7	98·6
6001–8000	172	0·2	99·9	814	0·6	99·2
8001–10,000	82	0·1	100·0	436	0·3	99·5
10,001–12,000	18	neg.	100·0	222	0·2	99·7
12,001–14,400	—	—	100·0	201	0·2	99·9
over 14,400	18	neg.	100·0	179	0·1	100·0
Total	90,734*	100·0		128,154	100·0	

* The assessable income of the civil servants in 1969–70 was Nc 60 m. on which Nc 2·9 m. of income tax was collected.

Source: Ghana, Central Revenue Department.

excludes information on the distribution of income among the farming sector. In short, the table gives only a partial picture of the income distribution in Ghana. Finally, it should be noted that the data on the two sectors (civil servants, self-employed and private sector employees) refer to different dates).

With the above caveat in mind, Table 3.5 shows that 80–85 per cent of the income-tax payers in 1969–70 earned under Nc 1000 per annum and that about 90–93 per cent belonged to the income group of less than Nc 1600 per annum.

The urban (civil servants) income distribution as a whole appeared highly skewed with an extremely large proportion of the taxpayers in the income levels of less than Nc 1000 per annum or between Nc 1000 and Nc 1500 per annum.

Among the self-employed and private sector employees more than 50 per cent of the income-tax payers in 1966–7 earned between Nc 400 and Nc 500 per annum and about 80 per cent earned between Nc 400 and Nc 1000. There were more people in this sector earning between Nc 6000 and over Nc 14,400 per annum than the number of civil servants within the same level of income. Civil servants in this analysis include people in government corporations and projects.

A pilot survey of household budgets carried out by the Institute of Statistics of the University of Ghana in 1966[48] estimated the 'subsistence level' for the year 1966 to be Nc 349. With 8 per cent increase in the national income *per capita* during the period 1966–8, the subsistence level was accordingly revised and estimated at Nc 384.

On the whole, some conclusions can be drawn from the above discussion on income distribution. Reasonably enough, income tax is not levied until the subsistence level is passed. Workers with less than Nc 400 are not required to file returns.[49] However, although a substantial proportion (41 per cent) of income-tax payers among the civil servants in 1969–70 did not gain very much above the subsistence level, there was a reasonable margin between the subsistence level and the starting point of income-tax payers among the self-employed and private sector employees in 1966–7.

Secondly, Ghana, like most developing countries, exhibits large disparities in income thereby creating serious socio-economic problems. Consequently, each government devised ways and means of solving or controlling these problems.

The Nkrumah government issued the Minimum Remuneration Instrument in 1960 which applied to all workers whose wages were below Nc1360 per annum but excluded farm labourers, domestic servants, piece-workers, apprentices and part-time workers. It set the minimum at 87c per day on the average. The setting of the minimum wage was intended to induce private employers to follow the government's lead in raising wages. By this government action, the trade unions pledged their co-operation in the development process of Ghana.

To ensure continuous co-operation of the unions, the Nkrumah government, early in 1964, classified most daily-rated wage earners employed on a permanent basis as salaried employees with monthly salaries twenty-six times their former daily rate. The principal supplement to cash earnings was housing.

The normal working week for wage and salary earners was forty-five hours. The Public Holidays Act of 1960 provided nine public holidays for wage earners. Holidays of salaried employees were based on collective agreements (the only time that government collectively bargained with its employees). Overtime work was not limited by law and overtime pay, based on collective agreements, ranged from 125 to 200 per cent of regular rates.

However, wages increased more rapidly than prices from 1956 to 1962 because of the early economic boom and the heavy foreign reserves at Independence. The purchasing power of workers increased by about 10 per cent. From 1962, prices rose sharply due to poor economic policies which, as we have discussed earlier, were adopted while wages were controlled, resulting in a low standard of living for wage earners. Housing was in short supply despite government efforts to improve housing conditions. With all these problems and hardships facing the workers, the unions became restive and strike action was becoming inevitable. But it was forestalled by a military coup which brought the NLC to power.

The NLC government, faced with the problems of acute inflation and foreign debts, decided to hold the minimum wage at 87c even though the salaries of the army were raised.

The Busia regime inherited the legacy of debts and inflation from the NLC government. Faced with workers' strikes and civil servants' clamour for increase in wages and salaries to keep abreast with the high rate of inflation, the government awarded the civil servants an increase in salary. To meet the demand of the workers, the Campbell Commission was set up to review wages and salaries of all employed personnel in the modern sector.

The government, however, did not wait for the Commission to issue its report before adopting an incomes policy. It devalued the cedi, the national currency, as mentioned earlier, and raised the minimum wage to Nc 1 to enable the workers to cope with the inflationary situation. The trade unions protested at such arbitrary government action and asked the government to wait for the report of the Commission before adopting any policy. But the Busia government was outsted by a military coup before it could respond to the union demand.

The NRC government which came to power after the coup revalued the cedi as already pointed out, but left the minimum wage at Nc 1. The six-day working week was reduced to a five-day working week and with it a simultaneous reduction in weekly hours. The unions were happy with this new government policy and pledged their support to rebuild the shattered economy.

Unfortunately, wages have remained rather stagnant over the years despite successive governments' attempts at improving the living standards of Ghanaians. This may be due to the fact that the unions still rely on the colonial technique of bargaining for daily instead of hourly minimum wages. It may be argued, of course, that Ghana is not rich or developed enough to afford the hourly minimum wage. But if the unions hope to get wage increases which are abreast with the rising cost of living they will have to change their bargaining tactics. For example, instead of asking for a daily minimum, they could start by demanding a minimum for a half-day. The government might refuse to comply with such demands on the pretext that they are extravagant. But given the important role which the trade unions play in the development process of Ghana today, and with a little bit of union pressure, the government might eventually give in to such union demands. Once the half-day minimum wage has been established, the trade unions could then proceed to ask for a quarter-day minimum wage. With such a progressive tactic, they could eventually achieve the hourly minimum. Unless the unions begin to think progressively, wages will probably continue to stagnate in spite of the visible signs of development.

THE GHANAIAN DEVELOPMENT PATH

The development path of Ghana, as the above discussion shows, has been anything but rectilinear. It has been punctuated with various ideologies and governments. Ghana has been through more political experience than many African countries: ambivalent experiences of colonialism, the one-party system, military junta, parliamentary democracy, and, again, military junta. As we have seen, each of these governments had its own development ideology and each tried to shape the socioeconomic institutions in line with its development ideology. The result of these many ideological experiences is that the Ghanaian population has become confused as to what ideology to follow. The frequent change of government which entails a rapid change in ideological positions has therefore helped to retard the development process. In short, it seems that in Ghana development ideology has become a 'game of musical chairs'. Several theories, models and ideologies of development have been employed – Western model, socialist model, the trickle theory, the human resource approach, and a host of other theories and models.

Inherent in this 'musical chair' approach to development is the phenomenon we might call *negative competition*. Many Ghanaians, like many other Africans, look at themselves as crusaders who are out to liberate their people from both endogenous and exogenous oppression. They are more disgusted if the supposed oppression is endogenous. By the concept of negative competition, a political leader who succeeds to power tends to do everything possible to obliterate the legacy of his predecessor. Whether anything in that legacy is developmentally sound or not is an irrelevant consideration. The fear that the citizens may tend to compare him to his predecessor who normally is ousted on charges of corruption or economic mismanagement is so great that he prefers to outlaw anything that may remind the population of the past. Besides, since he comes to power rather illegitimately, he expends great effort and national resources in political jobbery and in prestigious projects to get popular support which invariably he misconstrues as a legitimisation of his authority. The resources and capital so committed are usually so great that they become constraints to development itself. As a result, his crusade motive of seeking to liberate his suffering masses is circumvented.

Also, since his tendency is to destroy the legacy of his predecessor, he normally has to start totally afresh with no tradition to follow except his own vague and hazy development notions. Locked in this perpetual morass, it is not surprising that development is never cumulative enough to prepare the ground for an economic take-off. Instead the development path becomes circular with no possibilities for a take-off.

Ghana seems to have been virtually stranded in this quicksand of 'negative competition' throughout most of her independent existence. It is sad, especially for a country that started with so much promise. To pull herself on to firm ground, she is going to need some bold and ingenious device.

First of all, she will need a tough political leadership that knows where it is going. This means that she will need a well-defined and stable development ideology that would be a guide to socio-economic planners. A lack of well-defined ideology has no doubt compounded the problems that result from her cyclical development pattern.

Many development planners thought that Nkrumah attempted to provide such an ideology. But unfortunately, his vision was too global and his development approach too extravagant for Ghana's resources. The present NRC government has yet to make known its ideology, if indeed it has any. But so far, it has shown a willingness and an ability to learn from the mistakes of its predecessors. Its rather well-publicised policy of self-reliance, appropriately dubbed 'Operation Feed Yourself', is certainly a bold step in the right direction.

But for Ghana, like many other African countries, the question still remains which way leads to paradise, the Western way, the Eastern, or the Chinese? Ghana has sojourned through both the Western and Eastern ways. Maybe she has to try the Chinese way. You never know.

4 Kenya: Strategies for Development

FRANCES STEWART

'. . . and is everywhere in chains'

INTRODUCTION

The Kenyan economy cannot be viewed in isolation either from its own past or from the world economy. The past determines not only where it is today, in terms of distribution of industry, employment, technology, trade, resources of manpower, etc., but also the possibility of exercising policy options. Economists tend to regard policy as the autonomous factor to be manipulated by eager, rational decision-makers in the pursuit of declared objectives. Policies too are part of the fabric of social struggle, and are the outcome as well as, in turn, a cause of historical developments. While its history limits and in large part determines current and future possibilities, this history itself is largely conditioned by the impact of events outside Kenya or Kenyan control, what is often termed 'the world system'. Current options are likewise limited by this system. The following chapter aims to emphasise this perspective, so that the current situation may be viewed as a link which simultaneously is part of and joins two chains, one chain to the past, another to the world system. Two questions, which underlie most of the discussion here, are thereby raised. First, in what direction do the chains lead? Secondly, how determined is the system; to what extent do decision-makers today have any freedom of choice?[1]

The historical developments leading to the current situation form two distinct periods: the colonial experience, and the post-independence era.[2] It is impossible to do justice to either of these periods in a short essay: here we pick out some salient facts that have contributed significantly to the present economic situation.

80

THE COLONIAL ERA

The colonial settlers, particularly in the early period, gave agriculture priority. They took over the best agricultural land (the White Highlands) and formed large and prosperous estates, paying extremely low wages to the displaced African population and producing wheat, coffee, tea, sheep, beef and maize. They limited African rights to land and African access to credit and markets.[3]

They introduced the Asian population into Kenya, first to help build the railway linking Kenya, Uganda and the coast, and subsequently to provide the skilled services for which the African population was as yet untrained.

On a relatively small scale, egged on by shortages during the Second World War, the settlers established a small industrial base, concentrating on the production of simple import substitutes and agricultural processing industries (e.g. milling). These industries were generally owned and managed by Europeans, employed Asians as skilled workers and Africans as extremely low-paid unskilled labourers.

The colonial administration kept control of the African population not only by force and regulation, but also by emphasising and exploiting tribal and ethnic differences[4] in a form of divide and rule. The policy ultimately led to the Mau Mau rebellion of the 1950s.[5] The tribal (and racial) distrust which was accentuated, if not engendered, by the colonial power, lives on.

The British administration, much aided by the efforts of missionary societies, introduced British attitudes, institutions and education. Though often on a small scale and with very partial African participation they moulded the aspirations and the institutions of the population in their own image. Thus the structure of government (central and local), the trades unions, educational institutions and educational content, consumption and living patterns among those with comparable incomes, were all, on Independence in 1963, essentially British with little modification to suit local conditions.

This brief account is of course highly selective. The colonial administration introduced medical facilities and communications; it provided the possibility of literacy and life-styles previously not open to Africans. The fall in the death rate and rise in population during the first half of the twentieth century[6] may largely be attributed to the influence of Western technology. The Swynnerton Plan for Agriculture[7] enabled African small-holders to participate in the cash economy and benefit from modern technology. In any case, the intention is not to assess the colonial era,[8] nor to judge those involved who had their own chains linking their actions with their circumstances. This is simply an attempt to pick out the facts of greatest relevance to Kenya's prospects as an independent power.

The Kenya which the Africans 'inherited' in 1963 was thus heavily British oriented. Over one quarter of trade outside East Africa was with the United Kingdom. Even where the ultimate destination was non-British, Kenyan goods generally were exported via London. The economy was dependent on a few primary commodities for exports, and imported most consumer goods and machinery, in a classical imperial pattern.

Access to education and to income was heavily racially biased and self-enforcing, as poor educational qualifications justified

TABLE 4.1   Trading pattern, 1963

Exports		Imports	
Category	Percentage of total	Category	Percentage of total
Food, drink, tobacco	53	Food, drink, tobacco	8
of which		Materials, fuel and oils	13
coffee	23	Manufactures (including	
tea	12	chemicals)	73
Basic materials	31		
of which			
sisal	16		
Manufactures	9		
of which			
natural based			
chemicals	4		
Percentage with the UK	25		31

Source: Kenya Statistical Abstract, 1964.

limited African access to higher paid jobs, and low incomes increased the difficulties of acquiring education. There were also more formal limitations to both jobs and education. Table 4.2 illustrates the position.

TABLE 4.2   Incomes and education

| | Modern sector 1963 | | Percentage of male population (1969) with | |
	Percentage of employment	Percentage of wage bill	no education (or not stated)	secondary education
Africans	89·5	49·3	67	3
Asians	7·1	22·7	30	29
Europeans	3·3	27·9	33	53

Sources: Kenya Statistical Abstract, 1970; Kenya Population Census, 1969.

The figures in the table are for the modern sector only. They thus exclude incomes and employment outside this sector, where the bulk of African economic activity takes place. In 1960, the colonial peak for modern sector employment, the sector employed 622,000 out of a total work force of 3 million. Incomes outside the modern sector are substantially lower – some estimates suggest about one half[9] of average unskilled wages within the modern sector. Thus the table much exaggerates the relative position of Africans, taking the economy as a whole.

At Independence, Kenya was still primarily an agricultural economy with only a small manufacturing sector. In 1962, 92 per cent of the population lived in the rural areas, and the subsistence sector accounted for more than a quarter of GDP. In the modern sector agriculture and related activities accounted for 46 per cent of employment, commerce and services for 18 per cent, the public sector for nearly 30 per cent. Manufacturing and repairs employed 45,300 people, $8\frac{1}{2}$ per cent of total modern sector employment and about $1\frac{1}{2}$ per cent of the total workforce.

POST-INDEPENDENCE

One talks of a newly independent state 'inheriting' a country: they do so only in a curious and limited sense, lacking the resources, of manpower, technology and finance, to take truly independent decisions and facing a world situation which leaves only limited room for manoeuvre. While formal political authority was handed over to the African people in 1963, the civil service, industry and agriculture remained predominantly in European control.[10] The economic strategy adopted since Independence has a number of threads, not always consistent, and has developed over time. However, it is possible to pick out some significant aspects: very broadly the strategy may be summarised as Kenyanisation and modernisation (in particular industrialisation) in a capitalist framework.

One of the prime aims of post-independence policy has been to take over the positions of power and privilege from the Europeans and Asians. The immediate takeover was that of the government itself. By 1967 it was estimated that 90 per cent of the civil service was Kenyanised.[11] The settlers on the White Highlands were rapidly bought out and the land distributed to African smallholders. Subsequently, using a variety of methods,[12] non-Kenyans have been gradually replaced in the army, education and business. The process has been slow, and indeed rather ineffective. With a shortage of qualified people, abundant advice from foreign experts on the dangers of going too fast,[13] increasing availability of foreign technical assistance, and expansion of the economy increasing the need for high-level personnel, nearly ten years after Independence the pyramid of privilege, with Europeans at the top and Africans at the bottom, still looks much as it did in 1963 (see Table 4.3).

In 1968 of the fifty top directors in industry, forty-four were non-Africans (and forty-one were non-Kenyan).[14] The NCCK Working Party concludes: 'Our analysis has shown that African participation in the directorships, top management and shareholding in the major foreign (and local) companies is at present small . . . African participation on the Stock Exchange in Nairobi is minimal.'[15]

Despite the small inroads Kenyanisation made, particularly in the first five years after Independence, it has succeeded in establishing a new class of African sharing some of the privileges previously monopolised by others. These[16] include those who have taken over in government, agriculture and private indus-

TABLE 4.3   Modern sector

	Numbers employed ('000s)		Average earnings (K£)	
	1964	1971	1964	1971
Europeans	16	14	1513	2537
Asians	37	27	570	1010
Africans	535	639	112	191

Note: These figures cover only earnings of employees, not the self-employed· Since a good deal of effort has been devoted to raising the earnings of the self-employed; e.g. in distribution, the inclusion of self-employed incomes might somewhat alter the picture.

Source: Kenya Statistical Abstract, 1972.

try. The new élite does not form a homogeneous group; it includes politicians, managers and directors of foreign corporations, top civil servants and administrators of the parastatal bodies, large farmers, clerical workers and skilled labourers, and smallholders. While there are many relevant differences within the élite – in terms of source and level of income, tribe and power – they share one simple but important characteristic: they have all gained by the post-independence strategy, and are likely to gain more. Their interests may diverge on particular policies, but broadly they have similar interests in maintaining the present strategy and policies, and in maintaining the present power structure. The government, office-holding politicians, members of parliament and civil servants (central and local) are all personally part of this élite. Government policies and their administration reflect this fact.

The political and economic strategy adopted by the Kenyan government since Independence was self-described as African Socialism.[17] In more conventional terms, it may be described as a capitalist strategy,[18] both in domestic policy and in policy towards the world system, modified by the declared intention (not discernibly reflected in policy, as we shall see below), of redistributing some of the gains to the poorer sections of the community. While domestic and foreign private ownership has been encouraged, the public

sector has simultaneously expanded rapidly, as has government intervention in the economy. In this respect, Kenyan
development resembles that of many other economies, in
being one of *managed* capitalism, or a mixed economy, as it is
sometimes described. Domestically the government has favoured private ownership as the mode of production both in
agriculture and industry. In agriculture, land consolidation
and registration has enabled private ownership to flourish, and
land acquired from the White settlers has been settled on Africans on the basis of private ownership. Small-scale entrepreneurs have been encouraged[19] by the provision of credit and
technical facilities. Internationally, the government hás encouraged the integration of the Kenyan economy into the world
capitalist system. Multinational corporations have been offered
favourable terms. The Foreign Investment Protection Act of
1964 provided generous guarantees for repatriation of profits,
guarantees that have been honoured. There are investment allowances of 20 per cent on the value of all fixed assets. The estimated cost to government revenue was 1 per cent of direct
taxation.[20] The free flow of technology has been encouraged.
Tourism has been promoted, so that by 1970 it was the second
biggest foreign exchange earner. Foreign aid and foreign missions have been welcomed. Between 1969 and 1971, 14 per cent
of Kenyan imports were financed by official aid.

The policies favouring foreign investment have had the effect
of encouraging a high rate of investment from abroad.
UNCTAD estimated[21] that 45 per cent of Kenyan investment
(1964–70) in manufacturing was financed from abroad.[22]
Foreign control of industrial investment formed a greater proportion since Kenyan investment in foreign-owned companies
exceeded foreign finance between 1964 and 1969.[23] Among
manufacturing companies employing fifty or more workers, it
is estimated that foreign companies accounted for 57 per cent
of the gross product in 1967.[24] The very large proportion of the
industrial capital stock owned by foreign corporations means
that very high rates of foreign investment have to be maintained to finance the outflow of dividends on current investments. In 1970 the outflow on existing assets amounted to
£8 m: the potential outflow was over twice as great as that since
the retention ratio was 54 per cent. Inflow of new capital at

£9·4 m. exceeded the actual outflow, but fell well below the
potential outflow. In 1971 inflow of new private long-term capital almost exactly matched net outflow of investment income.
This illustrates one of the dilemmas facing an economy pursuing a strategy of encouraging foreign investment from abroad.
Once foreign assets form a sizeable proportion of the total
stock, the potential dividend outflow also forms a sizeable proportion. Hence a high rate of growth of foreign investment must
be maintained to offset the potential outflow. The maintenance
of such a rate of growth leads to further potential dividend outflow and hence the need further to encourage foreign inflow.[25]
Policies of the government therefore have to be continually
shaped so as to attract foreign investment, while foreign ownership of the economy increases. A complete switch in policy,
involving confiscation of foreign assets and/or major restrictions on outflows of profits is a possible way out, since new
foreign investment would no longer be needed with the restrictions on potential outflow. But minor and gradual changes,
involving a gradual diminution of dependence on foreign inves-

TABLE 4.4   Inflow and outflow of capital (K£'000s)

	Profits (after tax and depreciation)	Retention ratio	Dividend outflow*	Inflow of new capital
1963	9843	36	6329	6286
1964	8665	41	5119	7254
1965	8731	35	5713	5782
1966	8750	32	5950	700
1967	9079	53	4267	5934
1968	11,791	65	4127	4428
1969	12,515	54	5757	6147
1970	17,428	54	8017	9447

* These are declared outflow. Real outflow can be very different according
to the use of transfer pricing. The ILO Report estimated that 'the amount
of surplus transferred in the form of dividends and after taxation might
be less than half the total surplus transferred by foreign enterprises in the
manufacturing sector.' ILO, *Employment, Incomes and Equality*, p. 456–7.

Sources: UNCTAD TD/B/C.3/79 Add.2/Corr.1; and ILO, op. cit., p. 136,
Table 37.

tors, are ruled out since they tend to reduce the new inflow, while increasing the outflow on existing assets, imposing impossible balance of payments demands on the economy. Developing countries often appear to adopt extreme policies *vis-à-vis* foreign investment – some providing every encouragement, others imposing wholesale restrictions and following confiscatory policies. These extremes are to be explained, in part, by the impossibility of pursuing gradualist policies where foreign-owned assets are already sizeable. The Kenya government has found itself in this kind of situation. So far, its policies have involved increasing reliance on foreign investment, as Table 4.4 indicates. Whether nationalist feelings and other consequences to be discussed below will make this viable in the long run remains to be seen.

IMPORT REPRODUCTION

Kenya's industrialisation strategy has been largely one of import substitution, on the pattern familiar to observers of the Latin American scene.[26] Import *reproduction*[27] describes the policy more accurately since it consists not just in replacing goods bought from abroad by goods fulfilling similar functions produced at home, but in replication locally of goods previously imported.[28] To achieve the exact replication the policy requires the use of the same technology, which means that the technology has to be imported and with it, very often, the technical skills and managerial resources that go with the technology. The net effect on the balance of trade has not been altogether favourable because of heavy imports of machinery, spare parts, raw and semi-processed materials.[29]

The policy of import reproduction introduces import-biased technical change. Since it is based on the use of advanced country technology (the technology responsible for the previously imported goods that are now being reproduced), its use tends to involve advanced country-type resources. The consequence is that the methods adopted are capital-intensive, require materials that are available in the advanced countries, but often not in the developing country, are skill-intensive and require complex Western-style management techniques.[30] All this arises because the methods are designed in and for the developed countries. The resource use involved is almost totally out of tune with local needs and conditions, and imposes demands on the economy which it is incapable of meeting. The attempts to meet these demands distort the entire economy: the educational system is geared to producing the high-level manpower required;[31] income distribution and tastes are perverted to provide a market for the goods produced; complementary services like roads, banking, accountancy, building, are developed to enable the goods to be produced, distributed and used. Attempts are made to meet the demands imposed by the technology but, because of the different availability of resources and levels of income in underdeveloped economies, they are alien and inappropriate, and the attempts lead to (relative) failure in meeting the requirements. This failure means in the first place that efficiency, in relation to advanced country standards, is low – labour productivity is low, capacity utilisation is low, and unit costs are high so that a considerable degree of protection is needed if the industries are to be viable. In the second place, the failure to meet the demands means continued (and often increased) reliance on advanced-country imports for men, technology and finance, all of which require heavy payments and lead to continued dependence on advanced countries.

The policy of import reproduction is closely tied in with reliance on multinational corporations. There is two way causality. Because the policy requires technology that only the advanced countries possess, multinational corporations are its natural agents. For this reason they have an interest in promoting the policy and in introducing further advanced-country technical change so that they maintain their technological advantage over their local competitors. Reliance on foreign investment to carry out the policy of import substitution almost inevitably transforms this policy into one of import reproduction since this is the area in which the multinationals operate.

The goods produced with a policy of import reproduction are often *inappropriate*, in the sense that, designed for much richer consumers in richer countries, they tend to embody standards in excess of those which poorer countries can afford, and which require an extremely unequal income distribution and imposed tastes if an expanding local market is to be forthcoming.[32] While an initial unequal income distribution was responsible for the import of the goods in the first place (for what sort of market is there if everybody has the income of the average – i.e. £45 per annum in Kenya), once they are produced locally, expansion of local production requires expansion of upper income consuming power. Local producers (including employees) acquire an interest in perpetuating the income distribution which maintains an income for their products, in their capacity as producers, as well as income recipients. Local production using advanced-country technology tends to generate the unequal income distribution required to provide a market for the goods it produces. The shortage of skills – itself in part a result of the unsuitable skill-intensive technology adopted – leads to high relative incomes among those with the required skills. The need to import management and technicians means that pay has to be comparable with earnings overseas. The high labour productivity of the semi-skilled and unskilled, deriving from the capital-intensive technology, permits management to pay (relatively) high wages. Management of advanced technology firms is thus in a position to give in to the demands of trade unions for higher wages; they are encouraged to do so by a number of other factors. First, the low proportion of total costs accounted for by labour;[33] secondly, the tendency for productivity to rise with rises in wages, as nutrition and health improves; thirdly, the desire of foreign firms to keep a clean record and to be seen to be contributing part of their gains to the country in which they are located, by paying wages a little above those ruling; fourthly, government pressure tends to favour higher wages,[34] since they rely on the support of organised labour, and since, as far as foreign firms are concerned, they would like to reduce the potential outflow of profits. The conditions for the creation of a labour aristocracy[35] are thus created.

The pattern and consequences of industrialisation based on import reproduction in Kenya have conformed to this general picture. It is estimated that the capital stock per worker in manufacturing is £2000,[36] or about two-thirds that of the UK. Many industries have developed behind a fairly heavy protective barrier,[37] which has enabled firms to pay relatively high wages and generate high rates of profits despite inefficiency. Real wages among those employed in the modern protected

sector have risen, at first in response to minimum wage legislation and then to trade union pressure. Average earnings
among enumerated employees rose by over 55 per cent between
1964 and 1972. Labour productivity rose by over 3 per cent per
annum in manufacturing between 1965 and 1972. Continued
reliance on foreign management, technology and finance was
indicated earlier. The failure of the Kenyanisation policy to
make a substantial impact on reducing the penetration of the
economy by foreigners can now be seen as one aspect of the type
of industrialisation strategy pursued – one based on the continued import of technology. The policy of import substitution
was accompanied by a continual rise in imports from 1964 to
1971, both absolutely and as a proportion of national product.
The sharp deterioration in the balance of payments in 1971 led
to the imposition of a number of import controls, which (together with rising exports of primary products) produced a
rapid, if possibly temporary, improvement in the next year.

The infrastructural and complementary investment necessary for the industrial technology has been provided; education[38] expanded, particularly at secondary and university
levels. Investment in major roads, offices and banking, in
houses for the better-off workers, in health facilities, again particularly for the better-off urban dwellers can all be seen as
necessary to back up the main industrial strategy and provide
the necessary inputs, human and physical, that modern industry requires. The concentration of government (and other) resources on the better-off parts of the country, and the better-off
members of the community,[39] is often regarded as the consequence of the successful political pressure from the gainers,
and another dimension of unequal distribution of power and
income within the community. While this undoubtedly is one
aspect of the unequal distribution of real income, since most of
these items are consumption goods which do make those who
benefit from them significantly better off, it is their investment
aspect which concerns us here. To the extent that the industrial structure *requires* educated, healthy and strong workers,
modern roads, etc., then the concentrated expenditure on
these items follows from the industrial strategy. In so far as
these are investments in this sense, policies which aim to attack
(significantly) the distribution of real income, while leaving the

industrial strategy unchanged, are almost certain to be ineffective, because the maldistribution of income is a technical requirement of the industrial policy. The argument extends, in part at least, to the distribution of private consumption as well, since private consumption is an essential aspect of the health and efficiency of the work-force.

The industrial strategy has been, broadly speaking, one of import reproduction, but many of the implications of the strategy follow from any industrialisation policy which depends on importing technology, more or less unadapted, from the developed countries. A more export-oriented strategy which also uses advanced country technology, despite some significant differences, will share many of the characteristics associated here with an import substitution policy. In particular, although it is likely to use somewhat more labour-intensive technology, so long as the technology used is among the most recent originating from the advanced countries – a necessary requirement for success in many export markets – it is likely to impose resource requirements, in terms of skills, management, raw materials, scale, investment, more suited to the advanced country for which it was designed than for the developing countries. The distorting and dualistic nature of development based on advanced-country technology – to be discussed more below – arises from technological dependence on the developed countries. Countries like Kenya – relatively small, with a colonial past which left neither opportunity, incentives nor resources for major autonomous technological developments – have little choice: the continued import of advanced-country technology presents the only immediate possibility of industrialisation. In the longer run co-operation with countries in a similar situation might generate an alternative path. In this respect the East African Community is of particular interest.

EAST AFRICAN COMMUNITY

The East African Community was established in 1967, although it had its seeds in earlier collaborative arrangements. Apart from the broader needs for unity, the Community was in the Kenyan interest as preferable to the restrictions likely to be imposed on Kenyan goods by her less industrialised neighbours, particularly since East African countries provided the

main export markets for Kenyan manufactures. A complex differential tax system was introduced to safeguard Uganda and
Tanzania from the full force of Kenyan competition.

TABLE 4.5   Trading patterns with the EAC

| | Percentage increase in trade | | |
	1964–7	1967–70	1970–2
Exports to			
A. Total: outside East Africa	14	34	27
Tanzania and Uganda	4	19	4
B. Manufactures*: outside East Africa	25	51	28
Tanzania and Uganda	−2	20	−14
Imports from			
A. Total: outside East Africa	39	33	25
Tanzania and Uganda	17	19	−16
B. Manufactures*: outside East Africa	48	34	17
Tanzania and Uganda	36	37	0

* Defined here as all exports less food, drink and tobacco, basic materials
and fuel.

Source: Kenya, Ministry of Information, *Economic Survey 1969* (Nairobi:
Government Printer, 1972).

As Table 4.5 suggests, the Community has not transformed
Kenya's trading pattern: trade outside the Community has
risen faster than trade within. Kenya remains in substantial
trading surplus with her community partners. The Community[40] may have been responsible, temporarily, for preventing the more rigid restrictions introduced against Kenyan
exports by Uganda and Tanzania, as suggested by the 20 per
cent increase in trade in manufactures between 1967 and 1970
in contrast to the fall between 1964 and 1970. But since 1970
trade shares with Uganda and Tanzania have fallen sharply.
In the context of Third World industrial strategy the Community has, to date, failed. No agreement has been reached
(despite elaborate co-ordinating and administrative machinery) about the distribution of industry between the three
countries, nor about a co-ordinated policy towards the development and import of technology. Industrial co-ordination
and technological co-ordination are closely related. So long as

the three countries make independent and often duplicative decisions about which industries to introduce, they will remain in a sellers' market as far as technology is concerned. The market is too small in the individual countries for many modern industries, and hence all sorts of inducements have to be offered to attract the required technology. The protective structure which is thus justified enables sellers of technology to exact the price they consider appropriate and to disguise this price in the form of transfer prices, managerial and other payments unrelated to the real costs of the resources.[41] A co-ordinated industrial policy would place the three countries in a much stronger bargaining position *vis-à-vis* international technology and would enable them to avoid paying three times for one technology. Industrial co-operation and co-ordination between Third World countries provides the essential precondition for the development and use of an alternative technology. But by the same token those who currently gain by the unco-ordinated nature of industrial policy would lose – in particular the sellers of the technology – mainly multinational firms. It is apparent that the sellers concerned have encouraged the divisions and duplications between the three partners so as to exploit the resulting situation. They have, in the course of this, acquired powerful allies within the three countries, from those who are conscious of the need to expand employment and production within their own countries, and from those who have gained position and income, licit and illicit, as a result of this industrial strategy. A major difficulty for decision-makers in each of the countries, taken individually, is that the options open to them have been extremely limited. Given that, within each country, policy-makers recognised the need to diversify and to increase employment opportunities, then the policy of encouraging industrial investment, even if it involved duplication and excess capacity for East Africa as a whole, would appear the rational policy for each country by itself. In this respect, the situation is similar to that of oligopoly within a country. The creation of additional capacity may be rational and in the interests of the individual firm – because it gains markets at the expense of the other firms – while being (often) irrational, from the point of view of the economy as a whole. Thus only an *effectively* co-ordinated policy would justify individual decision-makers to avoid duplication in so far as they were primarily concerned with welfare within their own country. But co-ordinated industrial policy requires a very large degree of co-ordination in overall development policies. Differences in philosophical and political approach have thus contributed to the lack of industrial co-ordination among East African countries.

The discussion above has concentrated on the broad industrial strategy. The major omission is the agricultural strategy. The initial task here was the redistribution of the land previously held by the White Settlers in the Million Acre Scheme. The land was distributed privately (on varying scales) with government loans to cover the purchase price and finance inputs. This was combined with a variety of extension schemes, and co-operatives for marketing, provision of inputs and processing. Cash crops, previously confined to plantations, were introduced to smallholdings with (unexpected by many) success.[42] Hybrid maize was also successfully introduced to a large number of farmers. The policy of consolidation and registration of farmland, started by the colonial government, was continued. The net effect of these, and other, measures was the development of a flourishing agriculture based on private ownership, with consequent emerging inequalities as the successful bought out the unsuccessful, and the extension schemes reinforced success, rather than obviating failure.[43]

SOME CONSEQUENCES OF THE STRATEGY

In many ways the strategy adopted has been successful. Both agriculture and industry have succeeded in generating an acceptable – indeed viewed historically, and in comparison with other countries, high – rate of growth of *output*.

Despite a rapid (over 3 per cent per annum) growth in population real incomes *per capita* rose between 1964 and 1970 at around 3 per cent per annum; African participation rose, particularly after 1967. Political stability has been maintained for ten years, combined with a fair degree of freedom. All the normal welfare indicators – statistics on health, medical facilities, housing, nutrition, electrification and education also point in the same direction – to a steady rise in economic welfare.

In both parts of the economy – agriculture and industry,

though most obviously in industry – the output targets have
been achieved by concentrating resources on a small part of the

TABLE 4.6   Rate of growth of output (percentage per annum)

	1960–3	1963–7	1967–70	1970–2*
GDP at factor cost (current prices)	10·6	7·3	8·7	11·3
GDP at factor cost (constant prices)	n.a.	6·4†	6·9	6·7
GDP *per capita* (constant prices)	n.a.	3·3†	2·7	3·0
Manufacturing and repairs (current prices)	10·3	15·5	13·4	12·5
Manufacturing and repairs (constant prices)	n.a.	6·2†	9·0	10·2
Agriculture, forestry and fishing (current prices)	10·6	4·6	6·5	10·6
Principal crops: quantities				
Tea	9·8	6·1	21·8	10·3
Coffee	20·1	4·4	6·7	0·6
Wheat	−4·5	10·1	21·4	7·6
Maize	7·9	4·3	−6·9	n.a.
Sugar cane‡	n.a.	8·3	28·0	−9·0

* 1972 estimates.
† 1964–7.
‡ Maize delivered to the Maize Board.

Sources: Statistical Abstracts, Economic Surveys.

total economy, and to a large extent neglecting the rest. The
major weakness of the strategy adopted has been this dualism
of approach, which is the source of the main problems that have
accompanied and now threaten to overshadow the output successes, in particular the problems of unemployment and under-
employment, of maldistribution of income and of poverty.

There are many dimensions to the so-called employment
problem in developing countries.[44] Broadly, they may be
summed up as dissatisfaction with the employment opportunities available. For those who can afford to be unemployed
this takes the form of open unemployment; for others who
cannot and must work to live, low productivity employment

outside the modern sector provides temporary (and often permanent) refuge for the frustrated job-seeker. This approach to
the question makes it difficult to define precisely who and how
many constitute the employment problem. Nonetheless,
although concepts and measurement are imprecise there are
some indicators of the magnitude of the problem. In Kenya, the
two Tripartite Agreements[45] provided an opportunity for those
who wanted jobs in the modern sector to register. In 1964,
205,000 people registered within two weeks (35 per cent of
modern sector employment). In 1970, over 290,000 registered
within four days, 46 per cent of total modern sector employment, and 6 per cent of the population of working age. On each
occasion the books had to be closed because the authorities
were overwhelmed with applications. Many of those registering
for jobs already had jobs and were trying to improve their positions. Hence the numbers do not indicate numbers unemployed in the economy.

The very large number desiring modern sector jobs is not
necessarily an indication of surplus labour in the economy,
rather an indication of how favourably these jobs are regarded
as compared with the alternatives available. It is thus a function
of two variables: on the one hand of the incomes available to
those who do get a modern sector job; on the other of the
meagre opportunities open to those who do not. Viewed in this
way, the employment problem is thus partly a reflection of the
inequalities in income earning opportunities throughout the
economy. In Kenya, the existence of such inequalities has been
well documented.

Both industrial and agricultural strategy has been directed
to a considerable extent at the first two categories in the table
which accounts for nearly one quarter of the households. Their
real incomes have risen substantially. On average earnings in
the modern sector rose by 5·6 per cent between 1964 and 1972;
overall *per capita* income rose by 3 per cent during the same
period, indicating the worsening distribution of income as between modern sector workers and the majority outside. While
the increase in the incomes among these groups – variously described as the 'modern', 'protected' or 'formal' sector workers –
has increased the incentive to join their ranks, opportunities
open to those outside, i.e. for the remaining three-quarters of

the households, have tended to decline. In part this is because

TABLE 4.7   Household income distribution, 1968–70

Category includes:	Earnings per annum £	Proportion of total households (percentage)
A. Middle and large farmers; industrialists; professional and highly skilled	Over 600	3·4
B. Unskilled employees outside agriculture; semi-skilled	120–600	19·7
C. Employees in formal sector agriculture; better-off in informal sector	60–120	14·1
D. Workers on smallholdings; many in informal sector; smallholders; pastoralists; unemployed and landless	Under 60	62·8

Source: ILO, Employment, Incomes and Equality, Table 25, p. 74.

investment and technology has been concentrated on the modern sector and has neglected those outside – indeed in some cases modern sector investment has destroyed outside alternatives – for example modern technology in maize grinding mills and bakeries destroyed rural employment opportunities in less sophisticated technology. It is also a matter of numbers. Kenya's total working population has been growing at about 2·7 per cent per annum, or an annual addition to the labour force of around 300,000. Modern sector employment was 709,000 in 1972; between 1964 and 1972 it grew by 2·6 per cent per annum. Thus of the 300,000 annual additions to the labour force, the modern sector provided jobs for around 15,000 leaving the remaining 285,000 to find an income elsewhere. The extra people, not provided with extra investment resources with which to make a living, exerted a downward pressure on incomes and opportunities outside the modern sector. In those areas where there was already a land shortage, the extra numbers added to the landless and helped depress the low agricultural wage on smallholdings. The agricultural sector proved incapable of providing livelihood for many who therefore moved to the towns in the hope of getting a modern sector job.

The combination of increasing rewards within the modern sector, and increasing difficulty of finding rural work opportunities led to a rapid rate of urbanisation. A survey of urban migrants found that inability to find work was by far the most important reason given for migration[46] – the reason given by 81 per cent of those questioned. The overall annual increase in the urban population was 7 per cent per annum between 1962 and 1969 but this figure conceals considerable divergencies. Nairobi, which with over one quarter of a million people in 1962 accounted for 40 per cent of the total urban population, grew by nearly 10 per cent per annum during this period, and accounted for 47 per cent of the urban population by 1969.[47]

The massive increase in the population of Nairobi was matched neither by jobs nor by houses. From 1964 to 1969 jobs (modern sector) in Nairobi increased by 14,000, against an increase in population of over 200,000. Even if one assumes that 50 per cent of the additions were not in the work force (a high proportion for migrants) this still leaves 86,000 additions to the work force for whom no formal employment was available, equivalent to nearly 50 per cent of total modern sector employees in Nairobi. There was an even greater gap on the housing front. Between 1964 and 1969 the public sector produced or helped produce 9500 houses and sites. The private sector built about 250 a year. Estimated demand was for 7000–10,000 dwelling units a year.[48] The growing gap between the numbers of people looking for jobs and accommodation and the numbers provided for by the modern sector led to the development of an *urban informal sector*. This imprecise term covers the activities of those who have failed to find modern sector jobs, and provide their own means of livelihood. The sector has been described as the *unenumerated* sector – i.e. activities of those not counted in the official statistics; another term sometimes used is the *unprotected* sector, in contrast to the *protected* sector. All these terms tell us something about the activities of the sector. In general, the sector is outside the law: government regulations of health, hygiene, specifications of standards and minimum wages do not apply. The sector includes shops and catering establishments, construction and food processing which fall well below government official standards. Though it is primarily a self-employment sector, there are some employees who are paid wages well below the official minimum or trade union or trade council determined levels. Some of the activities are more obviously illegal: brewing, prostitution and theft are mainstay activities.[49] Many of the activities are performed for other parts of the same low-income sector – hairdressing, child-minding, house-building, informal systems of administration for example. There are also minor manufacturing units – producing furniture, sandals and crockery. There are links with the formal or modern sector: not just shoeshining, and match-selling, but also transport and entertainment, the sale of goods and the purchase (or theft) of materials and the use of waste materials of the modern sector. People move in and out of the sector as they acquire and lose modern sector employment. In Nairobi one of the most important activities of the sector has been the provision of accommodation to meet the needs of those not catered for by the modern construction industry.[50] Many of those with jobs in the formal sector live in these houses[51] – another link between the formal and informal.

An informal, or unprotected, urban sector of the type described has been a feature of many poor countries in Latin America and Asia for decades. It is perhaps because it is a recent development in Kenya that it has aroused such attention. Its development is a response to the failure of the modern sector to provide income earning opportunities for all who need them. Two questions arise from this development: first, why the formal sector has failed and thus evoked the development of an informal sector; and secondly, whether this development provides an adequate solution to the failure of the modern sector and the consequent employment problem.

The failure of the modern sector was a dual (and related) one: in the first place, employment opportunities in that sector grew slowly, 2·6 per cent per annum as against a rate of growth of output two and a half times that rate. This rate of growth was slightly slower than the natural growth in the labour force so that the proportion of the work force employed in the modern sector fell between 1964 and 1972. Secondly, the strategy adopted raised aspirations which it could not fulfil. Rising real incomes in the modern sector increased people's desire to get work there; the rapid increase in education increased – particularly among the young and those receiving education. Numbers of those receiving education increased faster than the jobs available for them.

Both slow growth in employment opportunities and over-fast increase in incomes within the modern sector are largely due, as argued earlier, to the nature of industrialisation pursued – in particular to the policy of import reproduction based on advanced-country technology. Reliance on foreign technology was largely responsible for the increasingly capital-intensive nature of the technology adopted, while the consequent high labour productivity permitted (and in part required) the rapid rise in wages; this rise justified further moves in a capital-intensive direction, which in turn contributed to rising labour productivity and rising wages.

While it is easy to attribute the employment problem, and accompanying maldistribution of income, to the industrial policy pursued, it is less easy to see what alternatives were open to Kenya. Export of manufactures is not an alternative at a very early stage of industrialisation, and in any case also normally presumes continued use of imported advanced-country technology, with the associated consequences. Technological dependence on the developed countries is the consequence of the world concentration of technological resources in the advanced countries.

Even large developing economies, with abundant and sophisticated scientific and technical manpower and equipment, rely heavily on advanced-country technology. India and Brazil provide examples. Kenya, with virtually no technical resources, was bound to be technologically dependent if she industrialised. The real choice was thus not between appropriate or inappropriate technology, but inappropriate or no technology. To choose none and hope gradually to forge an independent alternative is a possibility that cannot be dismissed out of hand. But the possibility of making such a choice – irrespective of the balance of advantage involved – was severely curtailed by the nature of the situation, and particularly the nature of the decision-makers in newly independent Kenya. The already established foreign interests in commerce and industry, education and the civil service, as well as the expectations and aspirations induced by such interests, made the choice almost out of the question in 1963. The government had neither the power, the discipline, the inclination nor the knowledge given us by hindsight to choose the alternative strategy. Since then interests, shared by government, civil service and other parts of the Kenyan establishment, in the maintenance of the current strategy have grown with the growth of the economy and its increasing Kenyanisation. Corruption has played a part. The Protestant ethic – that to strive for personal gain is morally praiseworthy within certain limits, and morally despicable outside them – is a schizophrenic one. In developed countries, despite the Savanorolas and the Gladstones, practice rarely lives up to the principle. In developing countries – perhaps less schizophrenic or hypocritical – transfer of this ethic is rarely, if ever, successful.[52] Corruption has been used as an instrument by foreign businesses to gain its sway over local decision-makers, further reducing the possibility of resisting trends in the economy.

Given industrialisation based on imported technology, the dichotomy between the modern and traditional, formal and informal, protected and unprotected sectors thus appears unavoidable. The temptation then is to treat the informal sector not only as a response to the situation but also as a solution. This is one aspect of the strategy of the ILO Mission: 'the sector can be a source of future growth as an integral part of an employment strategy.'[53] The informal sector does provide the one element of self-reliant development; it is totally African owned, controlled and financed; its technology is largely indigenous and it uses only locally available resources; it is labour intensive and uses investment resources sparingly. Its products, in nature and method of production, are appropriate to the incomes of the consumers. In all these respects, its characteristics are diametrically opposed to those of the formal sector; those of the informal sector are virtues. But, having said this, and added that the sector provides life-support for many where both modern sector and government have failed, it is also true that it is possible to romanticise the sector and be naively optimistic about its potential.[54] Productivity is extremely low as reflected in the low incomes earned. Of the households living in Mathare Valley Village 2 (lower village), 60 per cent had incomes below 100s a month, or £60 a year for a household (average size of household was four).[55] While the technology employed is largely of local origin, it also lacks scientific and technical expertise, which is one reason why productivity is so low. Technical developments in the modern sector continually threaten to undercut many of the activities of the informal sector, just as the modern sector has undercut traditional industries elsewhere.[56] For example, a small reduction in the price of mass-produced plastic sandals would eliminate the informal sector tyre-sandal manufacturers. Modern methods of making bread are gradually eliminating local small-scale bakeries. So long as the informal sector continues to use a makeshift technology, its productivity will remain low and its market will be threatened by modern sector developments.

As suggested earlier, the urban informal sector is not a new phenomenon in developing countries as a whole; the size and range of activities of similar-type sectors in Latin American and Indian cities[57] far exceeds anything that is to be found in Kenya. Yet in these countries, the sector has generally been regarded as a sponge which sucks up the unemployed and transforms them into the *disguised unemployed*. The history of employment in informal sectors elsewhere – which goes back over decades – does not suggest that they become a dynamic source of self-reliant growth, rather that they remain a form of disguised unemployment relief.

What is new or different about the Kenyan informal sector? Not very much, it must be said, except that it is newer, smaller and does less than many similar sectors in other countries. What is new is the way of looking at it. This new way has three advantages and one disadvantage. The first advantage is that the approach does not assume that anyone who is not employed, or being educated, or governed, or provided with health services, in a strictly developed country way, must therefore automatically be unemployed, uneducated, ungoverned and untreated. It suggests that in all these, and other, fields there are alternative local methods which may be more appropriate than advanced-country methods, and should certainly be examined before being dismissed. Secondly, the approach emphasises the alien character of much modern sector activity and the self-reliant character of developments outside it. The informal sector provides the seeds of development from below, a training ground for local entrepreneurs, and an opportunity for the development of local methods. Thirdly, and perhaps most important, the approach suggests that a major task is to see how the opportunities open to the sector may be improved – by improving its technology, its access to resources and its markets. As the ILO Mission puts it, policy changes are needed so that the development of the sector may be *evolutionary* not *involutionary*.[58] The disadvantage of the approach is that the identification and description of informal sector activities, which correctly suggests that the unemployment problem defined as complete absence of work is much less than might have been supposed in the absence of such a sector, and the unemployment problem defined as complete lack of income is also much less, may be taken to mean that there is no employment problem. But the employment problem defined as frustrated aspirations, and the employment problem defined in terms of relative and absolutely low productivity levels remains. Measures, such as those put forward in the ILO Mission Report, which will decrease the legal restrictions on the informal sector and encourage the modern sector to make more use of its facilities, may somewhat improve the lives of those within the sector (or may moderate the likely reduction in living standards as more and more join the sector), but they will not alone tackle the major problem. For this at least two further conditions must be met. First, a *major* shift of resources into the development and introduction of appropriate technology so that high productivity technology at relatively low cost may be available throughout the economy. Secondly, for such a technology to be effective (once it is available, which for today largely it is not), the resources have to be shifted out of the modern sector; the privileges and the privileged there would need to be attacked. Measures which improve conditions of the informal sector, combined with the continued expansion of the modern sector based on imported technology, do neither of these things: they are therefore likely to be palliatives rather than cures.

FUTURE PROSPECTS

Prospects depend on strategies; these will be discussed below. With current policies it seems likely that the future will resemble the past, only perhaps more so. There are likely to be some differences (that is where the 'more so' comes in). First, the phase of easy import substitution is coming to an end. It is less obvious which industries should be the next candidates, and it is likely that continued import substitution will require increasing levels of protection, giving greater scope for inefficiency and for corruption. As imports of parts catch up with imports substituted for there may well be a chronic balance of payments problem which would give further impetus to restrictions, quotas and tariffs. However, current conventional wisdom is strongly against this pattern of development,[59] and this could lead to the setting up of a tariff-free export zone which would generate countervailing interests, favouring low-cost imports and low protection. Whichever of these strategies is pursued the employment problem is likely to worsen. The increase in population and work force against any reasonable rate of expansion of employment opportunities suggests a massive rise in numbers outside the modern sector[60] – and consequently a massive increase in numbers in the informal sector. The educational imbalance is likely to deteriorate most markedly. An important reason for the expansion of the educational base, particularly at secondary and university levels, was to meet the challenge of Africanisation, but much of this was a once-and-for-all requirement to replace non-Kenyans. Thus the capacity of the educational system exceeds long-term requirements of the economy. At the same time there are great pressures for its further expansion. Rado's explosive model of education[61] is likely to come into play. As unemployment increases (and for every job there are hundreds of applicants) employers tend to select according to educational qualifications. Hence the educational requirements of a job increase in response to excess supplies of job-seekers at any educational level. As soon as there are excess supplies of educated manpower at any level, educational qualifications for the job rise, quite independently of the objective needs of the job. Hence the desire for education increases in order to get jobs and there are tremendous pressures on the system to expand. If the government fails to meet demands people meet it themselves, as with the Harambee Schools.[62] Supplies of educated manpower further increase, and the educational requirements of jobs therefore rise again. The explosive model is in operation. Kenya is at an early stage of this model. Future possibilities are suggested by India where unemployment is rife among engineers,[63] and in some parts bus drivers need M.A.s.

POSSIBLE STRATEGIES
Most observers agree that the current strategy (i.e. continuation of past policies) is not desirable (or even possibly workable) in the long run, because of the growing employment imbalances associated with it. The I.L.O. Mission summed this up in the phrase 'the cost of inaction'. Two alternatives have been suggested: price reform and redistribution through growth.

PRICE REFORM
Neo-classical economists (among whom many distinguished examples find a brief resting place in the Institute of Development Studies, Narobi) see factor price distortions as at the heart of the problems of the economy, and their removal as providing the cure.[64] It is argued that high wages (above the opportunity cost of labour), investment incentives, and protection have been responsible for inefficient use of resources, over capital-intensive investment and hence inadequate employment; and for the emerging inequalities via high wages and artificially high (because protected) manufacturing profits. The strategy suggested following from this analysis – removal of such price distortions – is unrealistic, and would probably be ineffective. It is unrealistic because it fails to recognise that the so-called distortions reflect the power distribution in the economy and are not an incidental development arising from mistaken policies, which may be removed once this mistake is drawn to the attention of the government. The 'distortions' initially developed in response to a combination of technological and power group circumstances – high real wages in the modern sector, for example, being in part a response to the introduction of modern technology, and in part reflecting the political and economic power of organised workers. Once these factors led to the initiation of the 'distortions' they became self-reinforcing, in two ways. First they justified technical and economic developments which led to further 'distortions'; thus the high wages encouraged and permitted further labour-saving changes, which in

turn allowed further wage increases; protection of one industry provided a market for other industries, while increasing their costs and hence justifying an extension of (higher) protection to the secondary industries. Secondly, they created groups within the economy who gained from the 'distortions' and would resist their removal, while the very distortions often increased the power of the groups concerned. The unrealism of a strategy based on the cry for removal of price distortions is indicated by the fact that a policy to control industrial wages has been promised since 1964, yet nothing has happened.

Removal of price distortions would in any case probably be ineffective because prices are only a small part of the story, and very likely a dependent, not independent part – the tail, not the dog. In the absence of an efficient alternative technology, changing prices would be unlikely to change much else.[65] It must be remembered that prices already present a substantial incentive for labour-intensive investment as compared with prices ruling in developed countries, yet the technology adopted is not all that dissimilar. It should also be remembered that even a quite dramatic (and unrealistic) expansion in modern sector employment would only make a small dent in the total situation because of the small size of the sector to begin with. In the major part of the economy, outside the modern sector, there is nothing much wrong with prices from a neo-classical point of view. Here one can see much more clearly that the problem is not prices but absence of an effective technology and dearth of resources. A price policy confined to the modern sector might well be counter-productive in that, by making the modern sector more competitive with the informal sector, it might destroy more employment opportunities than it created.[66]

REDISTRIBUTION THROUGH GROWTH

This is the strategy of the ILO Mission. It is to allow (indeed encourage) the present rapid growth and redistribute the gains from growth in the form of *investment* resources to the have-nots. These investment resources would then allow the recipients to acquire a permanent source of income. The strategy is combined with that favouring the informal sector (discussed above) in that many of the additional resources would go to that sector.

The policy is attractive in two respects; first, it involves no immediate sacrifice of any section of the community since it is a matter of withholding the increase in incomes, not cutting back on existing incomes; secondly, since the redistribution consists of investment not consumption it should have a long run, and not simply once-and-for-all effect. Although in any one year the redistribution would be small, cumulatively it would become large, so that a gradualist or marginal approach would ultimately produce a wholesale change.

Closer examination of this gift horse suggests that it may be too good to be true. Curiously, doubts arise from the same sources as over the neo-classical strategy – realism and effectiveness.

On realism, the argument is very similar to that just advanced for the neo-classical strategy. While it is true that only *increases* in incomes are involved, this was also true of the incomes policy that never happened; the alacrity with which the recommendations of the Ndeewa Commission[67] (recommending large increases in civil service pay) were put into effect, and the failure of the tax system to redistribute income,[68] at a time of *rising* incomes, suggest that the fairly draconian measures put forward by the ILO Mission[69] are not likely to be put into effect. This is more likely to be the case if, in part at least, the maldistribution of income is a function of the technological requirements of the system, as argued above. In so far as high and rising real incomes (relatively, very low by advanced-country standards) are necessary for the changing technology adopted to be used effectively, then employers as well as employees will resist cut backs.

The Kenyan economy – and its rapid rate of growth – are based on free enterprise. The sort of inequalities which have emerged are one aspect of the kind of growth that has occurred, with competition for personnel between public and private sectors, the use of incentives to attract investment and manpower from abroad, and free collective bargaining to maintain good industrial relations and support for the government, in a system which provides very little else in the way of incentives for social behaviour. It is unlikely that the system can be changed in this one way – control over rewards – while remaining unchanged in every other respect.

This leads to the second objection. While the unlikelihood of persuading people to adopt a policy is not a good reason for not trying to (unless it diverts attention from other more important matters), a much more substantial objection lies in the possible inconsistencies of the strategy, of which the one discussed above was a subsidiary example. The major inconsistency arises from relying on a continuance of current growth,[70] while changing, at first marginally but ultimately substantially, the distribution of the benefits, because the distribution of income influences the nature of industrial development and hence the growth path. It is not just that the distribution of benefits arises naturally out of the industrial structure adopted, but also that the pattern of consumption generated by the distribution of income is an essential aspect determining the industrial structure. Kenyan growth has been based on an expansion of the domestic market for Western-style consumer goods; this market has been provided by the high and increasing incomes among the protected workers in the modern sector. Private consumption expenditure has grown at 5·3 per cent per annum in real terms. If the additional incomes are no longer consumed but used as investment resources for the poorer parts of the community, then the pattern of domestic demand will turn away from the type of consumer goods currently being produced towards simple investment goods, and subsequently very low-income type consumer goods. The economy will no longer provide a market for expansion along previous lines; the nature of industrial development will have to change and with it, almost certainly, the rate of growth.

Kenya presents this dilemma, perhaps, in less acute form than many other countries. The type of products on which much of Kenyan industrial development has been based have not been luxury products in the way that, for example, those of some Latin American economies have been. For example, consumer durables have played no part in Kenyan development. Fairly simple products – soft drinks, cigarettes, food processing, nails, paint, shoes – are examples, but then so are high-quality tyres, luxury house and hotel building. Thus it may be that Kenya would be able to switch to a more redistributive path, without a major change in the nature of products produced. But even the existing products have been more suitable for the income levels of relatively well-off urban consumers than for the rural poor. For example, the relatively high-quality food processing, and construction methods and materials[71] have confined their consumption to (broadly) the top quarter of income-earners. Perhaps more to the point, any continuation of rapid growth is likely to be based on a high rate of imported technology, mainly via the multinational companies, and this technology tends to be directed at the richer classes. Thus while some Latin American countries exhibit patterns of production and consumption based on an unequal income distribution, to a greater extent than Kenya, this is probably largely due to the fact that they are at a later stage on a similar development path, having passed through the stage of simple products' import substitution. Many of these economies have maintained relatively fast growth rates as a result of the strategy adopted. The question here is whether an alternative strategy, redistribution through growth, presents a consistent alternative, because redistribution would change the nature of additional markets, and hence would later change the required technological base to meet the additional demands.

One cannot assume a continuation of current rate of growth if one removes the basis on which it subsists. This provides a further reason why the policy may be resisted – because the losers of the policy include producers whose markets may be threatened.

If successful, the strategy will therefore change the pattern of demand. Local producers may respond to the new demands for investment goods and low-income consumer goods; if they did this would provide the basis for a new and more egalitarian industrial strategy. What is being emphasised here is that this would be a new industrial strategy producing different goods for different people; though it might start as redistribution from existing patterns of growth, if effective, it would transorm these patterns. Two questions arise: whether and how the change would affect the growth rate, and other key variables; and whether a policy is workable which involves such a major discrepancy between what happens to the bulk of production and what happens at the margin. It is rather like trying to combine two economies, one capitalist, large scale, capital intensive, producing goods for relatively high-income consumers, like the existing modern sector in Kenya; the other small scale, low income, producing appropriate goods – a sort of poor man's China – and expecting the former not only to finance the latter out of the gains it makes, but to continue to finance it, out of its growing gains, despite the fact that its own engine of growth has thereby been removed.

ALTERNATIVE STRATEGIES
Both the alternative strategies discussed have been criticised for failing to recognise that existing distortions and inequalities arise out of the political and technical characteristics of the economy, and thus cannot be removed without changing these characteristics. The government is not an independent arbiter but itself represents those who have gained by past developments, and is therefore unlikely to provide effective resistance to them. The most likely strategy is therefore one broadly in line with past developments, with some modifications where imbalances have become so acute as to be dangerous, or at least uncomfortable. If Kenya continues to achieve a rapid rate of growth this together with a somewhat greater effort to help (or at least not hinder) the neglected three-quarters of the population might mean rising standards of living among them, as a result of the (much criticised) 'trickle down' strategy.

An alternative is disciplined socialism. Certainly discipline, and not just lip service, is needed to achieve significant redistribution of power and income, but this does not mean that this is a likely development. Even socialist economies are at the mercy of world forces, particularly world technology. Kenya, to break out of her chains, needs to forge an alternative technology and to curtail her trade, financial and technological ties with the developed countries; to do so alone is impossible. Third World unity and self-reliance are needed to provide an alternative. But the comparative failure of even the East African Community suggests that Western economies have too successfully penetrated the economies of developing countries to make this likely in the near future.

5 Sudanese Development Path

ABDEL-RAHMAN E. ALI TAHA

THE SOCIO-ECONOMIC AND POLITICAL ENVIRONMENT

Extending over an area of almost one million square miles, the Sudan is the largest country in Africa. It is a land of widely differing geography and diverse cultures and ethnic groups. The 1956 census[1] showed a population of 10·26 million. At a 2·8 per cent annual rate of growth the population was projected to reach 15·78 million in 1970 and 18·54 million in 1975.[2]

Ruled since 1898 by an Anglo-Egyptian condominium, the country gained independence in 1956 after a relatively peaceful nationalist struggle. The most conspicuous feature of Sudanese post-independence politics is their instability. Since 1954 the country has experienced two four-year periods of parliamentary democracy (1954–8 and 1964–9). Both these periods came to an end as the result of armed forces intervention (the Abboud regime, 1958–64, and the Nimeiry regime, 1969 to the present). However, in the midst of this instability a common thread tying political events in the country could be discerned. This was the continuous struggle for power between traditional and what could be called 'progressive' or 'revolutionary' elements. The former who were represented by the Umma and Unionist Democratic parties were composed of the tribal and religious élites, their rural followers, and their urban allies among the rising business class, Western-oriented intellectuals, civil servants, traders, and marginal urban populations. The progressive elements were represented by an amorphous and shifting coalition composed of the Sudanese Communist Party, the Sudan Workers' Trade Union Federation, professional associations, and student, youth, and women's associations.

The economy of the Sudan, as in most developing countries, is basically agricultural and pastoral. Of the economically active population, 3·33 million or 85 per cent were engaged in agriculture in 1960. This is comparable to the

112

East African average of 87 per cent but higher than the 66·1
average for the whole continent.[4] The occupational distribution of the economically active population again reflects
the predominance of traditional economic activity. In 1956 83·4
per cent of adult males reporting main occupations were classified as farmers, shepherds and animal owners. Unskilled workers accounted for 5·2 per cent, skilled workers, 5·7 per cent,
semi-professional occupations, 4·8 per cent, and managerial
and professional occupations, 0·2 per cent.[5] Another indicator
of the structure of the economy is the percentage contribution of
different economic activities to the gross domestic product.
Table 5.1 shows that for 1960, 1964 and 1968, agriculture and
livestock contributed 57·5 per cent, 47·8 per cent and 38 per
cent respectively, while manufacturing was responsible for only
4·7 per cent, 5·8 per cent and 7·9 per cent for the same years.

TABLE 5.1   Gross domestic product by economic activity for 1960, 1964
and 1968, at factor cost (£S million)

Economic activity	1960	%	1964	%	1968	%
Agriculture	123·3	35·2	115·7	27·4	131·6	25·0
Livestock	77·9	22·3	86·0	20·4	68·3	12·9
Mining and quarrying	0·3	0·1	0·3	0·1	2·3	0·4
Manufacturing and handicraft	16·5	4·7	22·8	5·4	41·5	7·9
Electricity and water	15·0	4·3	16·3	3·9	16·7	3·2
Construction	22·0	6·3	29·0	6·9	24·3	4·6
Commerce and hotels	23·6	6·7	58·0	13·7	108·0	20·6
Transport and communications	26·0	7·4	30·0	7·0	33·8	6·4
Finance and real estate	12·2	3·5	15·6	3·7	19·0	3·6
Miscellaneous private services	2·7	0·8	2·7	0·6	16·1	3·1
Government services	27·3	7·8	41·0	9·7	51·5	9·8
Non-profit services	3·1	0·9	4·3	1·0	13·9	2·6
GDP at factor cost	350·0	100	421·7	100	527·0	100

Source: Adapted from Republic of Sudan, Ministry of Planning, Department
of Statistics, The National Income Accounts and Supporting Tables, 1969 (May
1972) p. 31.

Table 5.2 gives estimates of GDP and GDP per capita for

1955–6 and the decade of the sixties. GDP grew from
£S350.0 m.[6] in 1960 to £S505.9 m. in 1969. The highest rate of
growth, 7·5 per cent, was experienced in 1961 and the lowest,
4·0 per cent, in 1969. The average rate of growth for the period
1960–9 was 4·2 per cent. *Per capita* GNP grew from £S27.7 in
1960 to £S36.4 in 1968 but dropped to £S33.9 in 1969. The average rate of growth in *per capita* GNP for the period 1960–9 was
1·3 per cent.

The above picture reflects the instability and slow growth of
the Sudanese economy. The relative stagnation of the economy
is due mainly to the low productivity of agriculture:

> The large amounts which are invested in agriculture every
> year are devoted to capital intensive projects . . . Despite this
> high and relatively successful series of investments, tra-
> ditional rainland agriculture, using little and locally-made
> equipment is still predominant and currently accounts for
> about two-thirds of the value of agricultural production. Its
> productivity tends to be low, partly because of unreliable
> rainfall.[7]

TABLE 5.2   Gross domestic product at constant prices, 1955/6–1969, at
factor cost (£S million)

Year	GDP	Annual percentage Δ in GDP	GDP per capita	Annual percentage Δ in GDP per capita
1955–6	284·2	—	27·7	—
1960	350·0	—	30·3	—
1961	376·2	7·5	31·6	+4·3
1962	402·6	7·0	32·9	+4·1
1963	408·1	1·4	32·4	−1.5
1964	421·7	3·3	32·6	+0·6
1965	441·3	4·6	33·1	+1.5
1966	456·9	3·5	33·4	+0·9
1967	489·9	7·2	34·8	+4·2
1968	527·0	7·6	36·4	+4·6
1969	505·9	−4.0	33·9	−6·
Average		4·23		1·3

Source: Republic of Sudan, Statistics Department, *National Income Accounts*,
annex 1, p. 31 and annex 3, p. 33.

The instability of income is attributable mainly to the dependence of the economy on cotton. 'Cotton and cotton seed accounted regularly for two-thirds of the country's exports and one-fifth of the income generated within the economy. . . . Wide year-to-year fluctuations in average yields of cotton per acre and in its world price subject the whole economy to considerable instability.'[8]

STRATEGY OF DEVELOPMENT

The present structure of the Sudanese economy owes a great deal to colonial economic policy. During the colonial period (1898–1956), the Sudan had little but agriculture to offer foreign investors. Thus colonial economic policy aimed at developing large-scale agricultural projects to produce raw material for Western markets. The Gezira cotton-growing scheme which started operation in 1925 to become the backbone of the Sudanese economy was the major achievement of this policy. No serious attempt to foster industrial development was made by the colonial government. The modest industrial investment made during the early fifties was undertaken by private domestic and foreign investors.[9]

Following the attainment of independence in 1956, nationalist governments faced with the rising aspiration of the population for higher incomes and better services began to adopt a development policy stressing 'industrialization as a means of modifying the mono-culture of the economy and of achieving higher rates of economic growth.'[10] This was to be achieved through private domestic and foreign investment in industry. The government declared a policy of encouraging 'private enterprise to develop activities which are in the public interest and also to create conditions which attract foreign capital to this country for such enterprises.'[11] To support its policy the government issued the Approved Enterprises (concessions) Act of 1956 extending substantial fiscal incentives and concessions to private investment in industry.

The era of economic planning was ushered in in 1960 with the promulgation of the Ten-Year Plan for Economic and Social Development 1961/1962–1970/1971.[12] The Plan envisaged 'a substantial increase in real income per head'. GDP was expected to rise by 65 per cent over the Plan period, or 5 per

cent annually, and *per capita* income to rise by 25 per cent or
2·25 per cent annually. The Plan also aimed at the 'improvement of social conditions, education and training and increased
opportunities for productive employment', and 'a considerable
increase in exports and import substitution'.

The Plan maintained the traditional emphasis on agriculture. Several large-scale agricultural projects costing £S85m.
or 30 per cent of net public investment during the Plan period
were planned. However, for the first time the government
involved itself in manufacturing. A number of industries including two sugar factories and two vegetable and fruit canning
factories were established during the early years of the Plan. As
a result of this policy public sector total investment in industry
reached £S23.3m. by 1968–9.[13] In spite of the government's
dramatic entry into the industrial field, the Ten-Year Plan
assigned an important role in development to the private sector.
Introducing the Plan the Minister of Finance and Economics
stated: 'Economic development is not a task to be shouldered
by the government alone, but it also entails the participation of
private enterprise, its encouragement and channelling of its
efforts so that public and private efforts may proceed in har-
mony and cooperation in furthering economic development'.[14]

In pursuance of this policy the government established the
Industrial Bank of Sudan in 1961 to assist private industrial enterprises through the provision of medium- and long-term
loans. Also the Organisation and Promotion of Industrial
Investment Act was passed giving more concessions to private
industrial investors than its predecessor the Approved Enterprises (concessions) Act of 1956.[15] As a result of this policy the
average share of the private sector of capital investment in
manufacturing maintained a 62·6 per cent level despite increasing levels of public investment.

Due partly to public pressure in 1968 the government decided to venture into new areas of economic activity which were
traditionally reserved for the private sector. The government
took over the importation of tea and coffee and the wholesale
distribution of salt. It seems that the government was motivated
in this takeover more by 'the necessity for extra Government
Revenue' than by a desire to give the government more control
of the economy.[16] Thus in 1969 as the government's hopes for

high profit proved unrealistic the businesses in question were denationalised.

With the advent of the May regime in 1969 the strategy of economic development was up for a radical though short-lived change. A Five-Year Plan for Economic Development, 1970/71–1974/75, written by Soviet experts, was promulgated. In its preamble it is declared that 'The Five-Year Plan is a comprehensive programme which aims at achieving [the] major goals put forward by the May Revolution that has announced the Socialist way of development of the Sudan, in the sphere of creation of [an] independent national economy, steady growth for prosperity of the Sudanese people, further development of culture, education and health service.'[17] The Plan aimed at, among other things, increasing gross domestic product at an average annual rate of 8·1 per cent, guaranteeing 'full employment of [the] economically active population', and 'providing for priority development of the public sector . . .' In addition, in May 1970 the government announced a large-scale nationalisation programme. All banks, both foreign and national, were nationalised. And foreign-owned and some Sudanese industrial firms were either nationalised or confiscated.

Ironically the government continued to profess its belief in the important contribution the private sector could make to economic development. In a meeting with representatives of the private sector early in 1971 President Nimeiri pointed out that 'the nationalization and acquisition decisions were not meant to detract from the role ideally played by the private sector, or to create an atmosphere of uncertainty and instability for this sector'.[18] Moreover the Five-Year Plan projected a capital investment of £S 23 m. by the private industrial sector and allocated £S 2 m. to enable the Industrial Bank of Sudan to provide financial and technical assistance to private industrial enterprises.[19]

The attempt to build a socialist economy did not survive for long. Both economic and political factors helped to swing the strategy of development back to a more moderate path. The most important factor was the dismal performance of the economy. The growth of the economy since the implementation of the Five-Year Plan is estimated to be negligible (the Plan predicted an 8 per cent rate of growth). This was the result of unrealistic and faulty planning, the lack of foreign capital, the disruption of traditional channels of foreign trade (mainly with the West), transport bottlenecks, the reluctance of the private sector to invest, and the mismanagement of public enterprises, particularly the newly acquired ones. On the political side the ousting of the Communists, who had been instrumental in charting the development strategy, following their abortive attempt to take over the government in July 1972, paved the way for the development of a more pragmatic development path.

Although under the new policy the public sector continues to play its traditional leading role in development, the local private sector, foreign companies and international lending organisations are now all invited to invest in development projects both in industry and agriculture. To allay the fears of private investors both local and foreign, the previous owners of nationalised firms were promptly compensated and the majority of confiscated companies were returned to their owners. Speaking to the World Bank Special Advisory Committee in Paris during June of 1973 the Sudanese Minister of Foreign Affairs stated:

> Our political and economic choices and our past experience compels us to assign a leading role in our development to the public sector. This however should not endanger the private sector which will be given all the opportunities to play a role in all the areas of development in which it has competence. We see the role of the two sectors in development as complementary rather than competitive.[20]

To give credence to the new policies the government passed the Organisation and Promotion of Industrial Investment Act of 1972. The Act authorises the Minister of Industry to extend adequate guarantees against nationalisation. If nationalisation is resorted to in 'a national emergency' the government undertakes to pay just and equitable compensation to the owners. Moreover the government will permit the repatriation of the initial capital invested, in the same currency in which it was imported.[21]

In conclusion it seems that, despite a few oscillations due to political changes, a consistent development strategy has been followed since Independence. The main features of this strategy are as follows: (1) The predominance of the public sector, (2) the important role of the private sector, particularly in commerce and industry, and (3) the development of modern agriculture as the main vehicle for economic development.

One important consequence of this strategy has been the concentration of development efforts largely in a relatively small area of the country, namely in the triangle whose apex is the juncture of the White and Blue Nile at Khartoum and extends about two hundred kilometers to the south. There are also two areas of relative prosperity towards the east in Kassala province and towards the west in Kordofan province. Although sound arguments could be made in favour of such a policy, yet it is possible that it could have serious social and political consequences. What is alarming is that the government does not seem to be cognisant of the unfavourable impact of 'spearhead development', and in fact the policy is continuing unabated. Now we turn to the important problem of mobilising the population for development, or 'social relations' as it is referred to in this chapter.

SOCIAL RELATIONS
A crucial problem in economic development is the mobilisation of the population to contribute to the fulfilment of development objectives. In this section we will consider the efforts of different governments to mobilise the various groups in the country for implementing development policies. Three groups seem to warrant special consideration as their contribution is decisive for the success of development strategy. These are: organised labour, the public service and the unorganised urban and rural population.

The labour movement
In countries where the government assumes a special responsibility for advancing economic development, which is the case in most African countries, the question of the role of the labour movement in society and particularly in development is essentially a question of government–labour relations.

Two patterns or models of government–labour relations have

emerged in post-independence Africa: first, 'There is the attempt to assimilate unions into a centralized structure'[22] with
the labour movement acting as the 'industrial wing of the ruling
party'. Secondly, the labour movement is 'independent of the
ruling *élite*' and is in opposition to it. Such élites normally
'represent elements of traditional rule, the growing bourgeoisie
and possibly the army'.

In the Sudan, early in the nationalist struggle, the labour
movement as represented by the Sudan Workers' Trade Union
Federation (SWTUF) allied itself with the Sudan Communist
Party (SCP) and adopted its political and economic line. This
inevitably set the labour movement in a path of collision with
successive national governments after Independence. Thus the
major role of the labour movement for most of the post-
independence period has been that of political-economic opposition.

As early as 1953, when the first national parliament was
elected, a leading trade unionist and a member of the SCP
wrote: 'All signs indicate that the new parliament has been
designed to safeguard the interests of capitalist and feudal elements and to perpetuate rather than alleviate the present economic crisis . . . The working class, the peasants, the shop-
keepers, and government employees should expect more and
not less sufferings, unless they broadened and deepened their
struggle'.[23]

The SWTUF has always maintained that the basic causes
behind the low standard of living and working conditions of
Sudanese workers lie in the faulty economic policy of governments controlled by the traditional parties, and that these
governments are inherently incapable of correcting the situation. It follows that no real and meaningful gains could be
achieved until a government capable of affecting fundamental
changes in the structure of the economy and society comes into
existence.[24] Thus the constitution of the SWTUF declares that
it is the aim of the Federation to bring to power a 'national
democratic government' which would work to 'liquidate all
neocolonial influences in our economy, particularly the activities of foreign banks, trading and insurance companies which
control the economy, and to direct the economy along socialist
lines'.[25]

Thus during the first (1956–8) and second (1964–5) parliamentary periods, the labour movement engaged in industrial protest and overt political activity to promote the causes of progressive elements within the boundaries of a liberal democratic system. During the Abboud regime (1958–64) the labour movement developed into an important centre of determined opposition to the regime and contributed substantially to its downfall in October 1964.

Under such circumstances the problem of mobilising the labour movement to contribute to development objectives became secondary. It was natural that these regimes should assign top priority to protecting themselves from the threat of the labour movement. The strategy of the traditional parties was to weaken the SWTUF through denying it legal status, creating opposing federations, influencing large unions like the Sudan Railways Workers' Union (SRWU), harassing its leadership, and refusing to negotiate with it on workers' demands.[26] The Abboud regime, because of its different nature, adopted a different policy. The SWTUF was dissolved, Communist elements were purged from the movement and freedom of association was restricted. The aim was to depoliticise the labour movement and turn it into some sort of 'bread-and-butter' unionism. This policy succeeded only in forcing the labour movement to resort to clandestine and, therefore, more dangerous political activities.[27]

However, since the rift between government and labour was caused mainly by ideological differences, it is not surprising that when the ideology and politics of the government happened to be in line with those of the labour movement, government–labour relations registered a sudden reversal. On such occasions the labour movement did not only cease to oppose the government but co-operated in implementing government policies and endeavoured to play a 'productionist' role.

The first such reversal in the role of the labour movement was witnessed when an *ad hoc* coalition of political groups dominated by progressive elements took over the government following the abdication of the Abboud regime in October 1964.[28] For the first time since Independence the labour movement, along with tenant unions and professional associations, was represented in the government. For its part the labour movement offered to: (1) postpone all workers' demands that involved financial appropriations; (2) to donate one day's pay of each of its members to the government treasury; and (3) to resolve all disputes between employees and employers in a peaceful manner.[29] This novel experience in Sudanese labour–government relations was short-lived as the October government soon gave way to the traditional parties.

The second instance of co-operative labour–government relations was witnessed during the first two years of the May regime of General Nimeiry (May 1969–July 1971). From the very beginning the regime proclaimed a socialist policy for the development of the country. With the Communists playing an important role in the new regime, it was not surprising that a close alliance emerged between the government and the SWTUF.[30] The workers were asked to forgo wage demands, to increase production and lend political support to the regime. In return the labour movement was increasingly involved in economic and political decision-making, labour laws were revised to meet the demands of the movement[31] and workers' participation in the management of public enterprises was promised. The labour movement for its part provided political support for the regime at critical junctures in the regime's struggle with traditional elements.[32] On the economic front the workers along with everybody else in the employ of the government not only froze their wage demands but were subjected to a heavy tax burden. Moreover, 'with production we protect the revolution' was the favourite slogan of the labour movement.

The honeymoon between labour and government did not last for long. Following the abortive Communist *coup d'état* in July 1971 the SWTUF was dissolved and Communist elements were purged from the ranks of the labour movement. Since then the Nimeiry regime has been attempting to bring the labour movement under closer political control through the activities of the Sudanese Socialist Union – the regime's political organ. It is difficult to asses the results of this effort at the present time, though certain problems are discernible: first, a sluggish economy and a rising cost of living make the workers less susceptible to ideological exhortations and therefore less willing to endure economic hardship; secondly, it is likely that Communist and other anti-regime elements are still active inside the labour movement. Depending on their strength they could seriously undermine the regime's efforts to enlist the movement's political and economic support. Moreover, since the labour movement has been undergoing important structural changes[33] and the Socialist Union itself is in its formative stages, no clear policy with regard to government-labour relations has emerged. Thus for some time to come the regime will face the classical dilemma faced by many other developing countries, that is, how to reconcile the requirements of nation-building with the economic demands of organised labour?

The public service

The role of the state in managing the economy in the Sudan is a pervasive one. Even before Independence the state completely dominated infrastructural activities and invested heavily in agricultural development. The Gezira scheme established in 1925 and brought under full government control in 1950 is still the largest and most important enterprise in the country.[34] During the early sixties the government invested more than 23 million pounds in industry including two sugar factories, a tannery, and a number of canning and agricultural processing factories.[35] In May 1970, the government embarked upon a nationalisation and acquisition programme of unprecedented scale. Almost the entire industrial private sector, the banking sector and the major commercial firms were all brought under government control. By 1971 cumulative government investment in manufacturing reached £S49.20m. with an annual production of £S25.65m.[36] To manage the various industrial and commercial concerns the Public Sector Corporations Act, 1971 created a huge complex of 'sectoral' and 'branch' corporations. By 1970 employment in the public sector, including the regular employees of agricultural projects, reached almost two-thirds of the 130,000 employees in the modern sector of the economy.[37] Moreover, the government closely controls private economic activity. The Ministry of Industry and the Industrial Bank of Sudan closely supervise industrial firms. The Ministry of the National Economy controls imports through a quota system. The Bank of Sudan not only manages the country's foreign reserves but controls the credit policy of commercial banks. To illustrate the degree and extent of government hegemony, take the example of a local manufacturer who wants to import raw materials. First he has to get the Ministry of Industry to certify his need, then obtain an import licence from the Ministry of the National Economy, and secure foreign exchange from the Bank of Sudan. Thus a few months could pass before he could even place an order with foreign suppliers.

The pervasive presence of the government in the economy does not in itself necessarily hamper economic development. But an inefficient and at the same time predominant public sector could pose serious problems. In the Sudan inefficiency, neglect and gross indiscipline have become permanent features of the public service.[38] Several reasons could be cited to explain this state of affairs. First is the rapid localisation or 'Sudanisation' of the public service. Within fifteen months between April 1954 and August 1955, with the exception of a few technical posts, the government machinery was completely Sudanised. This was apt to result in a serious lowering of standards. Second was the impact of political interference, particularly during the Abboud regime and the second parliamentary period (1964–9). Such interference, 'apart from sometimes involving the civil servants in criminal manipulations, demoralised the service and led to inefficiency and bad budgetary management'.[39] A third factor was the large-scale removal of civil servants following changes in government in 1964 and 1969. The removed civil servants were accused of, among other things, incompetence, dishonesty and ideological unreliability.[40] Although the purpose of these purges was to create an efficient, 'clean', and ideologically committed civil service, the unplanned removal of experienced officials inevitably resulted in serious administrative breakdowns and further demoralisation. A final cause of inefficiency in the public service was the problem of overstaffing. Between 1963/4 and 1968/9 employment in the civil service rose from 25,042 to 39,769,[41] that is to say by more than one-third in five years. A large number of the new entrants were employed under the Employment Relief Fund designed to relieve unemployment among graduates. Thus an increasing number of people were employed, for whom no real jobs or even space in government offices was available. The administrative and even moral damage such a practice could create is obvious.

In a perceptive analysis of the role of the state in the economy in the Sudan the Nigerian political scientist Oluwadare Aguda concluded that

> Since the state's ventures in the industrial and commercial fields have so far been very unsuccessful, and since there is little likelihood that the discipline and efficiency necessary to make them more successful will be achieved in the near future, it seems that the road to a satisfactory rate of economic development and a stable political system is through the promotion of private enterprise.[42]

In effect, he is recommending a different path of development. The broader implication of his conclusion is that developing countries with limited administrative capacity should minimise the state's involvement in 'those functions not clearly essential to the governing process . . .'[43]

Although Aguda's analysis is persuasive, one finds it difficult to share his scepticism regarding the susceptibility of the state machinery to reform and rationalisation. Admittedly, the task of administrative reform, particularly in the case of the Sudan, is staggering but not impossible. The creation of a Ministry of Public Service and Administrative Reform entrusted with the duty of 'organising the administration of the public service and public corporations in a manner conducive to the realisation of development objectives, and modernising the structures and improving the methods of these organisations to increase efficiency and reduce cost',[44] is at least an indication of the seriousness of the government in facing the problem. The government has also initiated or planned a number of innovative measures designed to rationalise and improve the efficiency of the public service. An interesting and novel example is the reorganisation of government ministries. The traditional council of ministers was practically done away with in favour of five ministerial councils dealing with the economy, natural resources, rural development, budget and administration and human resources development. Moreover, to facilitate coordination, ministries dealing with a particular field were grouped under one minister helped by a number of junior ministers. For example, the Minister for the National Economy is responsible for economic affairs, finance, commerce and supply. Under him these junior ministers deal with commerce, supply and the national budget.[45] It is too early to judge the efficacy of such measures but at least they are a step in the right direction.

The unorganised masses

In the celebrated Arusha Declaration President Nyerere of Tanzania declares: ' . . . it would be more appropriate for us to spend time in the villages showing the people how to bring about development through their own efforts rather than going on so many long and expensive journeys in search of development money. This is the real way to bring development to everybody in the country.'[46] Nyerere's message assumes a special importance for a country like the Sudan with meagre economic resources, a small private sector, and a dominant but inefficient public service. Under such conditions mobilising the unorganised masses becomes an imperative for the successful implementation of development strategy.

Before 1969 no conscious effort was applied on the part of successive governments to mobilise the efforts of the unorganised population for development. However, since May 1969 the concept of 'self-help' became the corner-stone of the government policy to spread educational, health and other services throughout the country.

The idea of self-help, or *al-a'wn al-zatti* as it is known in Arabic, is not new to the Sudan. The tradition of *naffier*, where members of village or tribal communities band together to help each other in harvesting crops, building homes, or clearing grounds for camping, has deep roots in Sudanese society. What the government succeeded in doing was to give it a new operational meaning and to employ it as a means of mobilising the people's effort for development. Perhaps the most remarkable achievement in this regard was how self-help was enlisted to construct additional classrooms needed for the implementation of a new educational structure during 1970–2.[47]

The new educational ladder launched in February 1970 required the construction of a fifth and sixth classroom in every elementary school throughout the country. The fifth classrooms were to be ready for the opening of the academic year in

September of the same year. The government launched an intensive publicity campaign to rally the people behind the project. Almost immediately Fathers' Councils and similar organisations sprang up throughout the country to collect donations and supervise construction. By September of the same year 2765 classrooms were built in the nine provinces of the country enabling the academic year to start on schedule.[48] The following year saw the construction of an additional 2731 classrooms. Five out of nine provinces were able to build all required classrooms, two provinces completed above 80 per cent and the remaining two completed above 70 per cent. The average 'rate of completion' for the whole country was 91 per cent.[49] The cost of classrooms and other buildings completed was estimated at £S 50 m.[50] The declared government contribution was £S 17,800. Thus, even when non-monetary government aid was counted, the government's contribution was negligible.

The spectacular success of self-help in the field of education, naturally, encouraged its spread to other services. Village Development Committees in rural areas and Local Popular Councils in urban areas took the initiative in the construction of clinics, the introduction of electricity and a variety of similar projects.

The Sudanese experience with self-help methods in providing local services shows that even under conditions of poverty and under-development the people, if properly motivated, could make a significant and meaningful contribution to development.

THE EMPLOYMENT PARADOX

Data on employment and unemployment in the Sudan is scanty and unreliable. The only sources of information are the Household Sample Survey conducted in 1967–8 and government employment offices.

The survey estimated employment in six northern provinces at 3·1 million. The Labour Department put the number of wage earners in industrial, commercial and public establishments in the northern provinces at about 131,000 in 1970, roughly two-thirds of whom were government employees.[51]

Unemployment statistics are even harder to come by. The Household Survey of 1967–8 estimated urban unemployment at 9·5 per cent of the labour force. However, due to the unsatisfactory performance of the economy in the last few years and an increasing rate of rural–urban migration, in addition to the natural increase in the labour force, the urban unemployed have been estimated by some observers to fall anywhere between 10 and 20 per cent of the labour force.[52] In spite of the absence of reliable figures it is increasingly clear that urban unemployment has developed into a serious economic problem which could have unmanageable political and social ramifications. The concern of the government was manifested in its request for the ILO to send an 'employment strategy mission' under the ILO World Employment Programme.[53]

One aspect of the unemployment problem which has assumed alarming proportions is the problem of educated unemployment. An increasing number of graduates and drop-outs from an expanding educational system enter the labour market every year with slim chances of employment. In recognition of this problem the government has instituted an Employment Relief Fund to guarantee employment for university graduates and high secondary-school leavers. Between 1968/9 when the programme was started and 1971/2 the number of persons employed under the fund stood at 2559. The cost of the programme for 1971–2 alone was estimated at £S2.5 m.[54] Apart from the financial burden of the Employment Relief programme, the practice of placing people on the government payroll without reference to real need inevitably creates serious administrative and social problems. It is reported that as a consequence of this programme 'the civil service has become over-staffed, there is not enough seating accommodation, furniture and auxiliary services for the surplus staff, and their employment with no work weakens the morale of the entire staff.'[55]

The problem of under-employment in public and commercial enterprises which the Employment Relief Fund helped to accentuate was already widespread. The ILO Exploratory Mission observed that 'Banks, retail establishments, transport, hotels, the public service – all gave the impression of numbers of people standing around with insufficient work to keep them busy.'[56] As expected, under-employment is also widespread in rural areas. If the number of days worked in a year and the number of hours worked in a day are accurate measures, 'practically all the agricultural and nomadic labour force have to be considered underemployed'.[57]

It is paradoxical that high unemployment and widespread under-employment in the Sudan exist side by side with chronic labour shortages in both the agricultural and industrial sectors. In the Gezira about half a million workers are needed every year for picking the crop.[58] Although it has always been possible to get an adequate supply of labour it has not been an easy job, as about 58 per cent of the supply has to be imported from outside the scheme.[59] The majority comes from the distant provinces of Kordofan and Darfur in the Western Sudan and a sizeable minority comes from Chad and other West African countries. It should be expected, as the new large-scale agricultural projects are completed in the next few years, that shortages in agricultural labour will become a real problem.

High-level and skilled manpower shortages are also felt in the country particularly in technical and scientific areas. For example, the Ministry of Education has never been able to find enough science and mathematics teachers. Medical doctors, engineers in certain categories, qualified accountants and statisticians are all in short supply. This situation is clearly a result of imbalances in the educational system and the lack of manpower planning. For example the distribution of post-secondary students among the various fields of study in 1967–8 reveals that two-thirds (66·48 per cent) were enrolled in the social sciences, law and the arts.[60]

However, these supply problems do not seem insurmountable. Correcting imbalances in the educational system, introducing manpower planning, and increasing the earnings of agricultural labour which have been practically stagnant, should go a long way towards the amelioration of the situation. But curbing unemployment is a formidable problem. In the last analysis the solution lies in a healthy and fast-growing economy.

INCOMES

The policy of focusing the development effort in a relatively small area of the country, which has been followed thus far, has precipitated wide regional disparities in incomes. Although no recent figures are available, the regional distribution of gross domestic product per head for 1956 is indicative. Table 5.3 shows that in the 'Three Towns' (the largest urban concen-

TABLE 5.3   Regional distribution of gross domestic product and gross domestic product *per capita*, 1956

Region	Population (millions)	GDP (£S m.)	GDP per capita (£S)
1 Khartoum, Omdurman, Khartoum north	0·24	27·5	119
2 Gezira	0·73	51·5	71
3 Gash and Tokar deltas	0·22	9·5	43
4 Nile Valley and desert	0·46	10·5	23
5 Semi-desert	1·28	26·5	21
6 Qoz sand	2·46	68·0	27
7 Central clay plains	2·22	60·5	28
8 Flood plains	1·63	19·0	12
9 Ironstone forest	1·00	12·0	12
Total Sudan	10·25	285·0	28

Source: P. F. M. McLoughlin, 'Income Distribution and Direct Taxation, an Administrative Problem in Low-Output African Nations: a Case Study of the Sudan', *Economia Internazionale* (Aug 1963) 538, reproduced in Gusten, *Economic Growth and Planning* (Berlin: Springer-Verlag, 1966) p. 46.

tration in the country) *per capita* income is approximately £S120, or about four times the national average. The Gezira, the Gash and Tokar deltas, areas with modern agricultural production, boast an average income per head of £S65, or more than twice the national average. In the Central Clay plains and Qoz sand belt, in which 45 per cent of the population subsist on rain agriculture, income per head follows the national average. In the semi-desert areas of the north west, inhabited mainly by camel-owning nomadic tribes, income per head is £S22 or about three-quarters the national average. Finally, in the southern region income per head is £S12 or about half the national average. By the 1970s the regional distribution of income must have become more polarised as most of the industrial development that took place during the sixties was concentrated in the Three Towns, and the new agricultural development schemes (Managil Extension, Khashm El Girba and Guncid) were all located in or around the Gezira area.

Thus it seems that the rich areas are getting richer and the poor areas are getting poorer.

There is no national minimum wage law in the Sudan, but since the government is by far the largest employer (two-thirds of wage employment) its minimum wage level acts as a minimum standard for the modern sector of the economy. Based on the subsistence requirement of a family of five, calculated by the Wages and Terms of Employment Commission of 1968, the minimum monthly wage for blue-collar workers in government employ was set at £S 13.9.[61] Recently it has been raised to £S 15.

The structure and level of wages in the private sector follow that of the government. Most of the large and established firms pay minimum wages comparable to or even higher than those paid by the governmet. However, a large number of the smaller industrial and commercial firms pay wages much below the government level. According to the SWTUF some of these firms pay as low as £S 4.500 a month, which is about one-third of the government minimum.[62]

There are two ways through which the government can influence the level of wages in the private sector. The first is the Trades Disputes Act, 1966 which authorises the Commissioner of Labour to act as a mediator in labour disputes (section 13), and to refer the dispute for arbitration when mediation fails and the parties give their consent (section 16). Due to the fact that most trade unions in the private sector are still weak and that very few industrial disputes seem to reach arbitration where the government could exert some influence, it is doubtful whether the law has had much impact on minimum wages in the small firms of the private sector.

However, the government is able to exert some influence through the application of the Wages Tribunal Ordinance of 1952. This empowers the Commissioner of Labour, either on his own initiative or at the request of one of the parties to the dispute, to establish a wage tribunal in any case in which he is of the opinion that no adequate machinery exists for the effective regulation of wages and condition of employment (section 3). Since 1952 at least ten wage tribunals were formed to set minimum wages in industries with a large number of employers and ineffective trade unions. Although these minima were not as high as the government's they are much higher than otherwise would have been the case.

Table 5.4 gives the level and structure of government wages for 1962. Although the level of wages has been substantially increased since then, the structure depicted in the table still gives a good idea of the present wage structure. The table shows that unclassified employees (manual workers), who make 55·9 per cent of all employees, receive an average basic monthly wage ranging from £S 6.750 to £S 30.500. Clerical employees who represent 9·4 per cent of total government employment receive between £S 11.500 and £S 33.335. Semi-professional and technical employees who account for 27·8 per cent of total government employment get between £S 11.500 and £S 69.165. Finally the administrative and professional employees representing 6·9 per cent of government employees receive between £S 39.500 and £S 165.000.

TABLE 5.4 Level and structure of government wages, 1962

Salary group	Assumed average basic wage (£S per month)	Percentage of all employees
Manual employees		
Group I (unskilled)	6·750	24·1
Group II (semi-skilled)	7·950	13·2
Group III (semi-skilled)	10·300	10·5
Group IV (skilled)	13·415	5·7
Group V (skilled)	19·000	1·8
Group VI (skilled)	27·500	0·3
Group VII (supervisory)	30·500	0·3
Clerical employees		
Junior, class 1	11·500	3·2
2	17·000	0·1
3	18·500	0·0
4	19·000	0·2
5	20·000	4·1
Senior, class 6	22·500	0·0
7	25·000	0·8
8	28·335	0·2
9	30·835	0·8
10	33·335	0·0

Salary group	Assumed average basic wage (£S per month)	Percentage of all employees
Semi-professional and technical		
Scales group 1 (1)	11·500	2·7
2 (4)	17·000	3·1
3 (1)	19·000	5·5
4 (1)	20·000	3·0
5 (3)	23·000	1·6
6 (5)	26·000	1·7
7 (1)	32·000	5·5
8 (6)	33·250	0·4
9 (1)	36·250	3·1
10 (6)	53·750	0·4
11 (3)	69·165	0·8
Administrative and professional		
Scales group 1 (1)	39·500	1·8
2 (6)	56·450	0·2
3 (5)	68·750	2·3
4 (3)	76·250	0·4
5 (1)	91·250	0·8
6 (3)	79·600	0·7
7 (3)	97·540	0·1
8 (1)	106·650	0·2
9 (2)	114·900	0·3
10 (3)	130·270	0·1
11 (3)	165·000	0·0

Note: Salary scales are grouped in this manner for simplicity.

Source: ILO, *Report to the Government of the Republic of Sudan on a Proposed Social Security Programme* (Geneva: 1962) pp. 35–6.

By calculating the average monthly wage for each group of employees we find that that of clerical workers is 1·37 times that of manual workers, that of semi-professional and technical employees is 1·88 times, and that of administrative and professional employees is 4·44 times manual wages. This gives a rough idea of the distribution of income in government employment which is more egalitarian than one would suspect.

CONCLUSION

The Sudanese development path is a meandering one. Under liberal democratic regimes and the Abboud regime the private sector was allowed to grow and thrive with few, if any, restrictions. The dominant presence of the public sector was more a consequence of the forces of necessity and tradition than the result of a conscious and deliberate choice. During the brief reign of the October provisional government in 1964 and the first two years of the Nimiery regime the development path took a sharp swing to the left. Banks and large industrial and commercial enterprises came under government control, the leading role of the public sector was asserted more than ever before, traditional trade ties with Western countries were severed, and the private sector, despite declarations to the contrary, resigned itself to an uncertain existence.

Lately, however, a strategy that could be described as pragmatic-socialist seems to be emerging. Although the public sector continues to play its dominant role, generous concessions and guarantees against arbitrary nationalisation are attracting local and foreign investment, and foreign trade is being redirected toward markets where it can earn badly needed hard currency. The policy of concentrating on agriculture that has been carried on since the colonial era is being augmented with the development of agriculturally based industrialisation. The country is expected to achieve self-sufficiency in sugar and textiles before the end of the decade.

For this path to lead to the desired goal of development, formidable obstacles remain to be tackled. The most important seems to be political instability. What makes political instability a particularly intractable problem is that it is both a consequence of, and a contributing factor to, economic underdevelopment. An immediate and more manageable problem – at least in the long run – is the serious transportation bottleneck that besets the country at the present time. The failure of the railways to cope with an increasing demand for transportation and the non-existence of paved roads does not only hamper the development effort, but, as a result of the inevitable shortages in consumer goods, fosters popular discontent and contributes to the problem of political instability. Finally, there is the problem of mobilising the population to contribute to the realisation of development objectives. A balance has to be struck between the demands of organised labour and the requirements of economic development, the public services have to be goaded into efficiency, and the unorganised masses have to be effectively enlisted in the struggle for development.

These are difficult problems for which no tried prescriptions or easy solutions are readily available. But if the goals of development are to be fulfilled these problems must at least be contained. Does the Chinese experience have anything to offer? This is a question that a later chapter of this book will attempt to answer.

6 The Structure of Zambian Development

CHARLES HARVEY

THE INHERITANCE IN 1964

Zambia inherited, at Independence in 1964, an economy and a social structure which very much reduced the new government's room for manoeuvre. Virtually all the skilled jobs in the economy were occupied by white people[1] whose rates of pay reflected their political power and their chances of working elsewhere. Furthermore, there was a whole infrastructure to cater for their particular needs and to minister to their standard of living, in the form of housing and urban services. Thus white housing was in scattered suburbs, separated from black housing areas. Schools, roads, hospitals, shops and the goods in them, hairdressers, cinemas, newspapers had all been developed to cater to the needs of the white population. In some cases parallel but inferior services existed for black people; but in only a few cases had services been shared in such a way that a mere change in government could make them equally available to both races.

For example butchers' shops now allowed black and white through the same doors and closed the side hatches through which Africans had once been served. Segregation in cinemas ceased as well. But the physical distribution of housing on the other hand could not be changed so easily. Naturally the very small number of Zambians who were able to move into senior jobs also moved into the white housing areas. In doing so, however, they had willy nilly to adopt a great deal of the lifestyle of their white predecessors. Scattered suburbs made car ownership essential, large gardens need gardeners (there are no long summer evenings in Zambia for the amateur gardener, nor a rest period in the winter) and although servants' housing does not 'need' servant occupants, it is natural to fill it.

136

As a result, even if Zambians had been willing to accept significantly lower salaries than their white predecessors it would have been very difficult for them to do so. In fact the very large discrepancy between black and white standards of living before Independence, and in particular the lower pay for Africans in comparable jobs, had been one of the driving forces behind the independence movement. It was therefore very necessary, as well as being plainly just, for the new regime to cease to discriminate in as many ways as possible.[2]

The situation is familiar enough and not unique to Zambia. What made Zambia, as in so many other dimensions, an extreme case was the scale of the problem. Zambia already had in 1964 a very large modern sector, by African standards. And this modern sector was almost wholly in the control of whites. In 1964 there were some 70,000 of them, of whom about 30,000 were employed with a small but significant additional self-employed group – farmers and businessmen.

The relative importance of the Zambian urban sector can be shown in several ways. For example, only 14 per cent of GDP in 1964 came from agriculture, compared with 61 per cent in Nigeria in the same year. Comparable figures for the East African countries (in 1963) were Kenya 43 per cent, Uganda 61, and Tanganyika 60 per cent.[3] Similarly, the African urban population was already in 1963 19 per cent of the total, compared with figures of 9 per cent for Kenya, 7 for Uganda and 5 for Tanganyika in 1965.[4] Similar differences are revealed by figures for the proportion of the population in non-agricultural employment.

Even these indices of urbanisation probably understate the dependence of Zambians on urban income because of the continuing migrancy of much of the labour force. Again, this is common throughout Africa, but is extreme in Zambia. The extent to which rural people depend on non-agricultural employment to supplement their incomes varies considerably with the opportunity to earn a cash income from farming. Thus Deane estimated in 1945 that 70 per cent of men were absent from villages in the Eastern Province, whereas only 15 per cent were absent in the Southern Province with its easy access to markets for agricultural products.[5] Furthermore, rural people are partially dependent on urban areas not only for employment but also for urban amenities, especially health and education which can be reached by visiting relatives in town, or by sending children to visit.

The point is that the sheer size of the Zambian urban sector, even by 1964, meant that both for those who were already living in towns and for most of those still living in rural areas, and for the large number of those who were somewhere in between those two categories, urban income was already an essential part of their total welfare. It simply was not true that the relevant policy for the bulk of the population would have been one that concentrated on a self-help, self-contained development of subsistence agriculture and the village way of life. Such a policy may indeed be the right one, for, say, Tanzania, where the relatively tiny urban sector simply cannot be of any great relevance to the overwhelming majority of rural dwellers; but in a situation where the bulk of men in the remoter areas are already absent in town, it is by no means clear what the right policy should be.

Apart from the already considerable dependence on a comparatively large urban sector, and on a large number of foreign white residents to run that urban sector, there were a number of other ways in which the structure of the Zambian economy limited the ways in which it could develop. Thus virtually all imports and exports had to use the railway line to the South. The line did in fact link up with the Zairean system (and had done since 1909) so that there was in theory a second outlet via Lobito in Angola, but in practice 99 per cent of both exports and imports were transported via Rhodesia.[6] Furthermore, some 40 per cent of imports came from Rhodesia and another 21 per cent from South Africa. Dependence on the white South was even greater than is suggested by these figures since the business sector tended to be run by head offices in Salisbury and Johannesburg, and the biggest group of white residents, most importantly in the copper mines, was Southern African. The links with the South must have seemed indissoluble – everything had pointed that way for so long.

Finally, Zambia's urban sector and thus, as has been argued, the incomes of both urban and rural population, depended almost wholly on copper. The figures that illustrate this dependence vary to some extent with the price of copper, since as the price rises so do the proportions provided by copper of exports, GDP and government revenue. Roughly speaking, though, copper provided over 90 per cent of export proceeds, some 40–50 per cent of GDP and about 60 per cent of government revenue. Figures apart, there is really no way of overstating the importance of copper; without it Zambia would be a backward agricultural country, probably even poorer in financial terms than Malawi and Tanzania, even though there is some case for saying that without copper agriculture would not have been so badly neglected and that the ten damaging years of federation with Rhodesia would not have occurred.[7]

Since so much in Zambia in 1964 depended on the mines it is worth reiterating some of the points already made about the country as a whole in terms of the mining sector. It was foreign owned, by two large groups: Anglo American and Rhodesian (later Roan) Selection Trust, predominantly South African and American respectively (despite their names) but with a full range of links with other international mining groups, finance houses and so on. The industry was dependent on expatriates to a formidable extent: in December 1964 there were 7600 expatriates employed (out of a labour force of about 42,000) and only 704 Zambians employed in comparable jobs.[8] On the other hand, because of the long history of mining compared to other industries the Zambian labour force was both experienced and well organised: over 25 per cent of the labour force had more than ten years' service, and the mining union had already achieved considerable progress for its members. The industry depended on imported machinery, much of it from South Africa, coal from Rhodesia for smelting, and a whole range of other imports including explosives. Up until 1964 royalties were payable to the British South Africa Company, and the bulk of profit after tax was exported.

The need to keep the mines in production, in order to sustain all but the remotest subsistence activity, has always dictated a great deal of the constraints on government policy. In particular there was a need to keep the expatriate miners sufficiently happy for them not to leave the country too fast. Whereas there is considerable scope for replacing expatriates in, say, government service with expatriates from other countries, the mines are dependent on very specific local knowledge which it would be damaging to lose quickly. As a result, the key importance of the mines added a very particular need to tread softly on expatriate toes to the more general wariness made necessary by the country's overall dependence on foreign skills.

THE POST-INDEPENDENCE PERIOD

A number of factors combined with great speed to dictate the way in which the new Zambian government reacted to its opportunities and problems. On the one hand, as explained in the previous section, an exceptionally large part of economic activity (by African standards) was already dependent on the urban sector and therefore on the mines. On the other hand there was the plain and obvious need to replace the very large number of non-Zambians on whom the working of this urban sector depended. The minuscule number of educated Zambians was fully stretched manning those jobs which simply could not be left to expatriates for political reasons – ambassadors, cabinet ministers, immigration officials for example – leaving almost none for the industrial commercial and mining sectors, for education above the primary level, even for government activities such as tax collection and security.[9]

Into this situation was injected quite incredibly large sums of money. Three principle factors combined to produce this effect. First, and most dramatically, the British South Africa Company's royalty was secured in full for the use of the new government. The royalty was a form of tax which was based on production of copper, but on a scale which varied with the price of copper.

Secondly, the drainage of funds from the country under the federal fiscal system ended with the end of the federation. Although the Northern Rhodesian government had managed to secure one-fifth of the BSA Company's royalty in 1950, the federation proved to be extremely effective in one of its main objectives – namely to secure for Southern Rhodesian use the bulk of the revenue from Northern Rhodesian copper. Even the income tax was a federal tax, and the federal common market made it easy for industry to grow in the South and use the North as a market.

Thirdly, the price of copper rose. Its movements were, as always, erratic, but it seemed upwards. There were some relatively bad years: in 1967 and 1968 the price was between K800 and K900 per metric ton, and again in 1971 and 1972 the price hovered around and frequently below K800.[10] But in 1963 it had averaged K461 and in 1964 K693, and these prices were not at that time considered to be particularly bad. Indeed, as late as 1967–8 a sober long-term forecast, on which reasonable men would be sensible but not rash to depend, was K500 or so.

TABLE 6.1   Producer price and LME price of copper, 1964–6

	Producer price (K per long ton)	LME average price
1964 (from Jan)	502	704
1965	574	938
1966 (to Apr)	672	1328

Source: 'Copperbelt of Zambia Mining Industry Yearbook 1966', Copper Industry Service Bureau, Kitwe.

Until April 1966 the companies actually sold, by agreement with other copper exporters, at an agreed producer price which was substantially below the world free-market price. This producer price arrangement was intended to stabilise the price to copper users and to discourage substitution of other materials and research into substitution. The companies chose, of course, what they believed to be a sustainable long-term price, so that this chosen price is concrete evidence of expectations at that time, tempered no doubt by adjustments towards the world price in order to prevent the agreement breaking down. In the end, the difference between the two prices created too great an incentive to abandon the agreement. Zambia took the opportunity to introduce an additional tax, the Export Tax, on the copper mines thus further increasing the government share of profits.[11]

The result of these three factors was a phenomenal growth in government revenue and earnings of foreign exchange. For a while, the Zambian government had enough money, in hard currency, to tackle its problems. This meant that by 1968 current spending by government had doubled, capital spending had risen seven times, and the two combined had more than tripled. Yet in 1968 the government had its first substantial budget deficit since Independence and its first balance of payments deficit. A modest reduction in spending in 1969 combined with a new rise in the price of copper pushed both accounts back into surplus in 1969.[12]

In addition to the tremendous economic stimulus provided by the growth in government spending, Rhodesia's unilateral declaration of independence created an emergency situation, a few days after the first anniversary of Zambia's Independence. The strategic decision to follow the sanctions policy meant drastic reductions in imports from Rhodesia, easily the country's biggest supplier. The oil embargo on Rhodesia forced Zambia to import via Dar es Salaam down the grandiosely named Great North Road – it was barely more than a mud track for hundreds of miles and was quickly renamed the hell-run. Other goods also had to enter the country by new routes because of arguments over use of the railway, and the mines were forced to cut back production for the same basic reason since coal for smelting did not arrive in adequate quantities.

The Rhodesian situation created the most tremendous strain on the new administration. It was in any case suffering from the departure of many of its most experienced expatriate staff, and from the fact that many government functions had been performed in Salisbury during federation, so that some operations had to be built up from scratch; and the disentanglement of federal organisations such as the railways and the airline was lengthy, laborious and costly of high-level administrative time. Furthermore, the administration had to cope with the threefold expansion of total spending already described at the same time as a large proportion of both Zambian and expatriate personnel were new in their jobs.

One result of these circumstances was that the budget was underspent in 1966 and 1967 in spite of heavy emergency expenditure – for example, on petrol subsidies, on building the oil pipeline from Dar es Salaam, on improving the Great North Road – the increase in costs caused by diversion of trade from Rhodesia, and the general inflation caused by transport cost increases, wage increases and the overall situation of excess demand in the economy. Another result was that a disproportionate amount of the time of high-level manpower in the government was absorbed by immediate problems: maintaining efficiency in the large inherited urban sector, presiding over its rapid expansion, coping with UDI.

In one area of structural dependence UDI caused an immediate response. By 1968 imports from Rhodesia had fallen from K62m. to K23m., from 40 to 7 per cent of total imports, during a period when the latter doubled. The achievement was even greater than apparent from the figures since K15m. of 1968 imports from Rhodesia was electricity from the jointly owned Kariba dam and classified as imports simply because the first power station was built on the southern side of the dam.

Independence created, for the first time, an opportunity to protect Zambian industry and this was greatly enhanced by UDI. The immediate impact was a boom in profits and, less acceptably, in profits remitted abroad by non-mining companies, which rose by 84 per cent in 1966 as many companies had their time horizons significantly reduced by UDI. To some extent, too, local profits were being generated out of local borrowing with a relatively small input of equity capital. Certainly the commercial banks were very liquid in 1964 and expanded their lending to the private sector by more than two and a half times between the end of 1965 and April 1968. At the same time value added in manufacturing nearly tripled by 1968.

The Mulungushi reforms, announced in April 1968, tackled some of these problems. A majority holding was obtained in some twenty-six industrial companies, exchange control was introduced on the remission abroad of profits[13] and limitations on local borrowing by non-Zambian companies were imposed. In 1969 the copper companies were also taken over and the system of copper taxation reformed. Further takeovers followed, although the intended takeover of the commercial banks did not in the end take place.

THE IMPLICATIONS OF GROWTH

The combination of short-term crises, the need (both political and economic) to Zambianise the economy in both ownership and personnel as quickly as possible, and the availability of cash to tackle these problems head on, meant that the structure of the economy as it existed in 1964 was quickly and extensively reinforced. By 1971 it was estimated that over 30 per cent of the population was urban, and that by 1978 the figure would be 39 per cent.[14] The 1969 census showed that the female population of the towns had grown faster (10 per cent) than the male (7·6 per cent) since 1963. But the rural areas still have large proportions of their adult males absent in town.

Employment generation during the post-independence period was slower than had been hoped, even though growth was so rapid. Nevertheless, by the end of 1971 there were 339,000 Africans employed according to official statistics. This figure omits domestic servants, who were estimated at 35,000 in 1964 and must have increased rapidly in number with the growth of the economy. Furthermore, the growth of the towns must have generated a large increase in self-employment and in 'informal' sector employment unrecorded by official statistics.

The growth in earnings from employment has been greater than the growth in employment. It is one of the causes of both the rapid rate of urbanisation and of the relatively slow rate of growth of employment. Thus average African earnings from employment rose by more than 150 per cent from 1964 to 1971, and the African wage bill rose from K77m. to K331m. At the same time the non-African wage bill rose from K105m. to K149m. This must be taken as further evidence that the informal sector, mainly devoted to services and petty manufacturing, has grown very fast in response to urban spending power.[15]

Although dependence on expatriate labour has decreased quite sharply in relative terms, the absolute *number* of non-Africans in jobs has only declined from 31,700 in 1964 to 26,550 in 1971. In other words the growth of the economy, in the form it has taken, has generated a disproportionate demand for skilled labour which has very nearly offset the progress of Zambianisation. The latter has progressed most rapidly in mining because of the accumulation of experience already referred to, and in the administrative, executive and technical branches of the civil service. Thus the number of Zambians in mining jobs predominantly held by expatriates increased from 704 in 1964 to 4661 in 1970, while at the same time the number of mining expatriates fell from 7621 to 3774. In central government employment the percentage of Zambians rose from 71 to 84 per cent.[16]

Statistics of Zambianisation conceal, of course, a very complex picture. The difficulties of the newly promoted Zambian have been vividly described by Burawoy: lack of commitment of the new type of short-contract expatriate ('the VC 10-er'), hostility from some of the old-timers. 'By focusing blame on the Zambian and the problems of 'too rapid Zambianisation', the expatriate is able to escape responsibility for his own inefficiencies.'[17] At the same time, it seems clear from casual observation as a resident that some of the pressures, created by large numbers of Zambians moving into new jobs over a very short period, have eased considerably. The delays and irritations of, say, cashing a cheque or passing through immigration are minor now compared to 1967, as employees have achieved competence and thus confidence in their jobs. No doubt the situation varies according to the industry and the attitudes of particular groups of expatriates. In government service the fact that the top posts are held by Zambians must make things easier than on the mines where Zambianisation is almost entirely from the bottom upwards. Even within an industry conditions vary: thus one of the two big banks has an extensive branch banking service in England run by the parent company so that job security is no problem for the displaced expatriate; the other, although it has a head office in London, is exclusively an 'overseas' bank so that with localisation taking place all over the world, the expatriate may be afraid of working himself out of a job, and not just in Zambia.

In dependence on copper, nothing has changed. Growth has been generated out of an increased share of copper profits and a rising copper price, but that growth has not included any growth of alternative exports. Some import substitution has taken place, but like import substitution everywhere it has created import-dependent industries. Between 1964 and 1970 domestic expenditure rose by 153 per cent and imports by 118 per cent, both being measured at current prices; comparison of domestic expenditure at fixed 1965 prices and import volume show a similar picture between 1964 and 1968, but in 1969 real domestic spending fell sharply and import volume remained at the same level, so that it is not even clear that import substitution has had any measurable success.[18]

In another sense, dependence on copper has greatly increased, since the enormously expanded level of government services, indeed the whole greatly enlarged urban sector, is wholly dependent on copper. In other words the country as a whole has achieved a higher standard of living, including that part of it provided by government services, which is almost entirely sustained by the earnings of the copper mining industry. What is more, the urban population becomes much more permanently urbanised over time. In the 1930s when the world depression closed down most of the mining industry, the African labour force was almost wholly migrant and those laid off simply went home. This is no longer possible on anything like the same scale.

New forms of dependence have also been created, although hopefully only temporarily. For example the hundred new secondary schools built after Independence are manned over 90 per cent by expatriates which means that Zambia has a huge demand for teachers from abroad, few of whom stay for more than one contract. The result is that teaching in these and other post-primary educational institutions is overwhelmingly in the hands of people new to Zambia and thus only marginally adapted to Zambia's special needs. The time lags in education meant that this condition was bound to get worse before it got better, but the scale of the problem in Zambia is unusual and it creates fears of being culturally dominated or submerged. Again, the short-term problems inevitable in starting so many new institutions in such a short time, combined with the rapid turnover of staff, meant that little time was available to rethink the objectives of Zambian education.

Yet another aspect of the huge investment in education is that the urge to replace expatriates can lead to over-investment. The rate of production of skilled manpower needed to build up an existing stock of, say, mining engineers is much greater than the rate of replacement that will be needed thereafter. Meanwhile the new short-term expatriates, in education and elsewhere, must be attracted by high wages, send ever-increasing amounts of savings out of the country[19] and perpetuate the structure of income distribution and all its implications.

One particular aspect of the continuing dependence on foreigners is worth further comment. The services which these people demand for themselves and their families, especially in health and education, have to be maintained and even expanded, thus perpetuating the unequal structure that existed for racial reasons before Independence. It is clear from various government moves that there is a considerable political desire to make these services more equal. For example, the very sharp distinction between the scheduled and unscheduled primary schools has been formally abolished. But all this has meant in practice is that the fees for scheduled primary schools have been abolished while the same children attend the same schools, which retain their staff at expatriate level salaries, one shift system, etc. Similarly the government hospitals no longer have fee-paying wings, but in Lusaka at least the private medical insurance scheme's nursing home is being allowed to expand. Less obviously, but just as importantly, the pattern of demand created by the present income distribution continues to influence the way in which production of goods and services develops.

There has thus been a very great degree of inevitability about the way in which Zambia has developed in the nine years since Independence; and although major steps have been taken towards reducing some aspects of dependence, notably in transport, education and the ownership of industry, the failure to develop alternative exports and the increase in dependence on the urban sector means that some structural problems inherited in 1964 have been enhanced.

Not all government policy has been dictated by circumstance. Indeed in its attempts to shift the balance of advantage from foreign investment, new and old, in the Zambian direction the government has been imaginative and successful. There has certainly never been any popular support for the sort of drastic policy proposed by left-wing academics in Dar es Salaam, to close down the mines rather than submit to them being controlled by foreign monopoly capital. Probably the strongest line of criticism of government policy has been in rural development. The facts are greatly obscured by the departure after Independence of about half the white settler farmers, but it is probably true that the loss of production from this cause has been considerably offset by a growth in marketed output by Zambian farmers. It is also right to point out that it is far less obvious in rural development than in other sectors what policy should be and that by their nature the results of rural development efforts take a long time to appear. Nevertheless there have been some well-publicised failures, for example the losses of the Credit Organisation of Zambia and the heavy imports of maize in 1971.[20] Another line of strong criticism has been in wages policy. Certainly the post-independence wage award to the copper miners, which gave an increase of as much as 40 per cent to the lowest paid in one year, preceded a rapid increase in African earnings in the rest of the economy. But between 1967 and 1972 average African earnings in mining have increased by only 18 per cent, so that it can no longer be claimed that this sector is damaging the economy. African wages in the rest of the economy continued to rise rather faster, but according to official figures have risen only 9 per cent in 1970–2. Given the existence of a large expatriate labour force which has to be paid internationally competitive rates, it is hard to persuade even the best paid group, the miners, that they are well off.[21] Probably the relative success of the government's income policy is at least partly due to the tremendous opportunities at the present for social and economic advance, both for the workers and for their children – these opportunities must remove some of the urgency from claims for increases in wage *rates*.

FUTURE POLICY

Given that 1964–73 cannot be relived, it is worth looking at the policy options available after nine years of independence.

The most fundamental points are that Zambia has become even more heavily urbanised than in 1964, and that the urban sector and thus the economy is more than ever dependent on copper. Faced with a choice between continuing to expand by increasing copper production and waiting until alternative exports could be developed, Zambia chose the first, even though it meant a short-term increase in copper-dependence and a greater task in the long term to develop alternative exports. It is the latter, however, alternative exports, which *must* be the long-term objective since the copper will not last for ever[22] and living with the copper price is difficult, not to say nerve-racking.

The urban sector is now large enough in relation to the

population for it to be arithmetically conceivable for enough jobs to be created. It is even arguable that there are too many jobs in Zambia, since some rural provinces actually lost population between the censuses of 1963 and 1969, and the structure of the rural population (more than half the adult males absent from some provinces) must inhibit rural development in the long term if not in the short. On the other hand the very urban nature of the country's social and economic structure makes it certain that *not enough* jobs will be created in the towns. In particular, primary school leavers seek, in the main, wage-paying jobs in the urban economy, and there is no immediate prospect of there being enough jobs, even if one includes the informal sector. The fact that there may be land available is almost wholly irrelevant to those born and brought up in town, and is irrelevant to large numbers of the remainder. At best the government can hope to slow down the rate of urban migration, but only by offering the chance to earn a cash income in the rural areas comparable in both size and certainty to what can be earned from wage employment.

Ideologically, the Second National Development Plan has abandoned the earlier emphasis on production co-operatives and puts its main emphasis on 'family farms' with only relatively minor importance given to state farms. Co-operatives are to continue mainly in the provision of marketing and other services. The Plan draws a slightly odd distinction between family farms on the one hand and Zambian and expatriate commercial farmers on the other.[23] This appears to continue what has always been a slightly curious duality in agricultural policy. Large-scale commercial farming has had to be treated with care because of its contribution to output, and Zambians have not been prevented from buying large farms from expatriates. Yet there has been a reluctance to acknowledge that 'other' farming, which anyway ranges from almost pure subsistence to medium-scale commercial farming, should be anything but a 'family' farm. Yet if family farms are to be encouraged by better credit, marketing and extension services, in what way do they differ, essentially, from 'Zambian commercial farms'?

The explanation lies, I think, in an official reluctance to allow the development of a significant class (or rather larger class than at present exists) of agricultural labourers, whose main

income derives from working for other farmers. The urban
sector is very obviously being developed in such a way that most
people are workers and only a small minority are managers and
self-employed businessmen. The reluctance to admit to the
same principles in rural development comes possibly from very
deep-rooted attitudes to land. Some of these attitudes may
derive from the experience of other countries, where large numbers were *forced* off the land, or have been deprived of land by its
unequal ownership distribution. The point about Zambia,
however, is that land is not in general scarce. So if a man
chooses to work for regular wages rather than to work his own
farm, he does so from choice not compulsion. At the same time,
the prospect of a cash income, ideally a regular one, and an
escape from the risks of farming on one's own account are precisely the factors that induce so many people to migrate to
town.

In practice, both the government's rural policies (especially
credit which must feed on existing success if it is to be repaid)
and the opportunities of the growing urban markets for rural
products have already created enormous disparities of income
and ownership of assets in agriculture. In turn this must
already be leading to a growth in agricultural employment
mainly ignored by the statistics. It would seem worth considering, therefore, a policy of overt recognition and encouragement of this trend, and a less reluctant support of state
farms. If people are prepared to vote with their feet in large
numbers for urban employment, some at least may be prepared
to vote for rural employment.

Certainly it is the rural sector which has the best chance of
producing alternatives to copper for export. The problems of
the last nine years may make this sound unrealistic, since Zambian agriculture has not even been able to produce enough for
the home market. But export diversification is much more
credible in agriculture than in industry, apart from a few inputs
to the copper industry where Zambia may have a local comparative advantage. The potential of industrial development
remains mainly in import substitution, with only very limited
opportunities for further processing of exports. As for international tourism, it barely exists and there is no immediate prospect of it developing.

For the moment, then, the economic policy options remain substantially the same as they have been since Independence. Perhaps not surprisingly the most recent new initiative has been on the relationship between the government and the mining industry. President Kaunda's speech in August, 1973 announcing the cancellation of the 1969 takeover agreements,[24] is another step in the gradual shift in the balance of advantage in Zambia's direction – within the existing framework.

7 Nigerian Development Path

UKANDI G. DAMACHI

The Nigerian development path, like that of Ghana, has been quite rough and thorny. We shall therefore discuss it according to the same headings as those used in analysing the Ghanaian path, namely, (1) socio-economic and politico-administrative aspects, (2) social relations, (3) employment, (4) incomes policy, and (5) the impact of government strategies on the overall development.

SOCIO-ECONOMIC AND POLITICO-ADMINISTRATIVE ASPECTS
Nigeria became an independent state on 1 October 1960. Three years later, on 1 October 1963, it became a republic.

The 1963 census gave the total population of Nigeria as 55·67 million. This represents a great increase over the 1952–3 census figures of 31·5 million, which amounts to an annual growth rate of 5·6 per cent over the decade. The 1963 census figures were considered contraband. Various estimates have put the Nigerian population in 1963 between 41·5 and 45 million. However, a total population of 45 million still represented a high annual growth rate of 2·5 per cent which is closer and more comparable to the 2·5 per cent growth rate recorded for the period between the 1931 and 1952–3 censuses. Such a growth rate also seems to be more in agreement with the experiences of other developing countries in a similar stage of development.

Nigeria is, nevertheless, the most heavily populated African country. The distribution of population is very uneven and characterised by ethnic diversity. There are well over 250 ethnic groups in Nigeria, some of which number less than 10,000 people.[1]

With regard to the economic aspect, Nigeria is basically an agricultural economy. The economy comprises two main sectors, the modern and the traditional. The modern sector embraces manufacturing, mining, electricity and water supply, building and construction, transport, communications, health, education, and other services and commercial estates, e.g. rubber plantation farming. The traditional sectors pertain primarily to village-based agriculture and crafts.

The gross domestic product of Nigeria increased in real terms at an annual average rate of a little more than 4 per cent from 1950 to 1960. In the same period, the population increased at an estimated annual rate of 2–2·5 per cent which amounted to a *per capita* income growth rate of less than 2 per cent.

TABLE 7.1   Growth rates of gross domestic products at constant prices, 1962–71

Year	GDP (£m)	Growth rate (percentage)
1962–3	1315·4	—
1963–4	1425·7	8·4
1964–5	1463·4	2·6
1965–6	1543·0	5·4
1966–7	1583·1	2·6
1967–8	1560·8	−4·8
1968–9	1503·8	−0·2
1969–70	1699·9	13.0
1970–1	1862·5	9·0

Source: Nigeria, Ministry of Information, *Economic and Statistical Review 1970* (Lagos: Government Printer, 1972).

By the middle of the 1960s the national economy appeared to have assumed quite a different course from its impressive growth in the preceding decade and the early 1960s. As Table 7.1 demonstrates, the GDP dropped from its high growth rate of 8·4 per cent in 1963–4 to 2·6 per cent in 1964–5. It improved a bit in 1965–6, rising to 5·4 per cent (although still less than the growth rate obtained in 1963–4). But it declined again to the 1964–5 rate of 2·6 per cent during the 1966–7 period. A contributory factor to this decline was the political crisis in the country, the first rumbling of which occurred late in 1964 and which in 1966 escalated into a civil war which lasted till January 1970. During the early stages of the war, production declined and remained at relatively low levels until the year 1969–70, when there was a marked recovery. The increase in output in 1970–1 of 9·6 per cent, though not as impressive as the

13 per cent gain registered in the previous year, is still substantial. The key factors in the apparent ease with which the national economy had absorbed the strains and stresses of the civil war were the rapid rise in the production of petroleum and the continued high performance of the agricultural sector. Following closely behind these two key factors was the increasing volume of investment. Over N760 m.[2] was invested in the country in the period 1970–1 while in 1971–2 the volume of investment had risen to N930.8 m.[3] (It would seem that there has been a progressive release of resources from wartime needs to normal production requirements and use.)

How have the main sectors of the economy contributed to the composition of the GDP? Table 7.2 gives the major components of the GDP at 1962 constant factor cost and also provides some insight into the structure of the economy.

Agriculture, which includes livestock, forestry and fishing, has consistently accounted for more than 50 per cent of the GDP. It is estimated that about 80 per cent of the total working population in Nigeria is engaged in agriculture and related activities.[4] Before the oil boom, Nigeria had relied almost exclusively on agriculture for subsistence and cash – the major exportable crops being cocoa, oil palm products, groundnuts, cotton, timber and rubber. Recently, emphasis has gradually been shifting to industry and notably the oil industry. Also, the stimulus of growth seems to be slipping away from agriculture. Nevertheless, agriculture is still a vital sector in the country's economic development. As previously noted, it is the main source of employment, providing food for the ever-increasing population, and raw materials for some industries as well as foreign exchange.

In 1962–3, agriculture accounted for 61·2 per cent of the GDP while in 1966–7, real output declined to about 55 per cent of the GDP because of the civil war. Its percentage, however, improved slightly in the following three years (1967–8 to 1969–70) but in 1970–1 it dropped further from its 1966–7 low of 55 per cent, to 53 per cent. The fall in its proportional share of the GDP is likely to continue as economic development progresses, but this is unlikely to affect its dominance as the single most important sector in the economy for quite some time to come. The Federal Commissioner for economic development

TABLE 7.2 Percentages of gross domestic product by sector at constant factor cost, 1962–71

Sector	1962–3	1963–4	1964–5	1965–6	1966–7	1967–8	1968–9	1969–70	1970–1
1. Agriculture, livestock forestry, fishing	61·2	61·1	59·2	56·5	54·9	57·0	58·1	57·3	53·1
2. Mining	2·0	2·2	3·2	5·4	7·2	4·0	2·3	5·1	8·9
3. Manufacturing and crafts	5·8	5·4	6·0	5·9	7·2	7·8	7·8	7·3	7·0
4. Electricity and water supply	0·5	0·5	0·6	0·6	0·7	0·7	0·8	0·7	0·7
5. Building and construction	4·4	4·5	4·5	5·2	5·1	4·8	4·6	4·1	4·9
6. Distribution	12·3	17·7	13·3	13·1	12·7	13·3	13·3	13·2	13·5
7. Transport	4·2	4·3	4·1	3·6	3·4	3·3	3·4	3·1	3·1
8. Communications	0·4	0·5	0·5	0·6	0·6	0·5	0·5	0·5	0·4
9. General government	3·9	3·6	3·6	3·3	3·3	3·2	3·3	3·0	2·8
10. Education	2·7	2·7	2·9	2·8	3·0	3·1	3·0	2·8	2·7
11. Health	0·5	0·5	0·6	0·6	0·6	0·6	0·6	0·6	0·6
12. Other services	2·1	2·0	2·1	2·3	2·6	2·3	2·3	2·3	2·3
Total	100·0	100·0	100·1	100·0	100·0	100·0	100·0	100·0	100·0

Source: Economic and Statistical Review 1970, op. cit.

and reconstruction, A. Adedeji, expressing dismay for the poor performance of the agricultural sector, stated that '. . . of all the sectors, the one that gives cause for concern is the agricultural sector. The rate of growth of this sector is only 2·0 percent per annum during the past two years [that is 1971–2] even though it accounts for over two-fifths of the national income . . .'[5]

The growth of industry (especially manufacturing, building and mining) has been fairly rapid since the 1950s and reached its peak during the civil war. However, the rate of growth has declined from the wartime momentum. Constraints imposed by shortage of staff and lack of feasibility studies account for the fall. This decline, however, tends to vary markedly between different industrial sectors (see Table 7.2).

Mining has become by far the leading growth sector of the economy. Mineral products include the following: petroleum, tin, gold, coal, columbite, lead-zinc, limestone, cassiterite and wolfram. Large natural gas reserves also exist. Nigeria is the world's largest producer of columbite (95 per cent of the world's industrial requirement), the sixth largest producer of tin as well as the ninth largest petroleum producer.

Since 1958 when Shell-BP first began to export Nigeria's crude oil, its export value, and consequently the share of mining in the GDP, has been rising at very high annual rates. The contribution of mining to the GDP in 1962–3 was only 2 per cent. This increased to 7·2 per cent of the GDP in 1966–7. Thus between 1962–3 and 1966–7, mining output grew at a rate of 47·3 per cent per year – the highest of all the sectors.

The history of the oil industry in Nigeria began in the first decade of this century when exploration activity was carried out by the German Bitumen Corporation. In 1937 an oil prospecting licence was granted to Shell-D'Arcy Exploration Parties. In 1955 Mobil Exploration Nigeria Incorporated obtained a concession over the whole of the then Northern Region of Nigeria. But the company abandoned its concession in 1963 after three wells were unsuccessfully drilled.

In the same year, however, the Nigerian government granted ten more oil prospecting licenses on the continental shelf to five companies, Shell-BP, Mobil Exploration Nigeria Incorporated, AMOSEAS, Texaco Mineral Company and Nigerian Gulf Oil. Each license covered an area of 1000 square miles

(2560 sq.km) and was subject to the payment of £500,000 (N1 m.). With these generous concessions, full-scale on-shore and off-shore oil exploration started.

Oil was first found in commercial quantities in Oloibiri well. Further discoveries at Afam and Bomu established Nigeria as an oil producing country. By April 1967, Shell-BP's production in the then Eastern Nigeria averaged nearly 350,000 barrels per day from 135 wells in fifteen oil fields. More oilfields were discovered in Mid-Western Nigeria and production commenced in 1965 on the completion of the trans-Niger pipeline network. By April 1967, oil flow from the Mid-West had reached 145,000 barrels per day.

The first oil-well on the Nigerian continental shelf was struck by the Gulf Oil Company at the Okan field off the coast of the Mid-West. More off-shore wells have been drilled by other companies and production rate rises steeply yearly. The total oil production reached a rate of over 580,000 barrels per day before the civil war.

This impressive growth suffered a set-back at the outbreak of the civil war because the oil-rich sections of the country (the Eastern and Mid-Western states) were the main fighting areas. Production picked up quickly after the war in 1970, raising the contribution of the mining sector to the GDP from 7 per cent in 1966–7 to about 9 per cent in 1970–1.

In response to the structural changes brought about by oil to the country's economy, the Gowon Government intends to increase the total earnings of the nation from the petroleum industry and to use the resources to finance general development, particularly the development of infrastructure for modern agriculture and the manufacturing industries. It was in pursuance of this policy that the Gowon government promulgated a decree in 1971 establishing the Nigerian Oil Corporation.

Manufacturing is another fast-growing sector of the economy. In the decade 1950–60, the most impressive growth rates were recorded in manufacturing; during this period the annual growth rate was about 18 per cent. In the same period its contribution to the GDP rose from 0·6 per cent in 1950 to 3·9 per cent in 1961. In the decade 1960–70, its contribution to the GDP increased from 5 per cent to more than 7 per cent.[6]

Nigeria's manufacturing has been primarily oriented toward

import substitution. Recent trends, however, indicate some developments in the establishment of intermediate products and semi-heavy industries. At the outbreak of war, manufacturing, especially in the Eastern states (which used to account for about one quarter of the country's total manufacturing production), was crippled. With the prolongation of the war, manufacturing in those states ceased altogether; plants and installations were either seriously damaged or fell into disrepair due to lack of maintenance.

At the end of the war, the structure of manufacturing shifted from processing traditional primary products for export to production for the domestic markets. Like the mining sector, manufacturing remains a fast-growing sector.

Other important growing sectors are electricity and water supply, communications, transport, building and construction as well as other services which recorded annual growth rates of 9–16 per cent per year during the periods 1962–3 and 1964–6. The growth rate for the whole economy was 4·7 per cent which compared favourably with the projected growth rate of 4 per cent for the 1962–8 National Development Plan period.

POLITICAL AND ADMINISTRATION

With this synoptic review of the economic structure, we may now consider the politico-administrative aspects from the inception of Independence up to the present. We may divide the thirteen-year span into two main phases, namely: (1) the Balewa phase, 1960–6, and (2) the Gowon phase, 1967 to the present. The Ironsi government, which lasted less than a year (1966–7), was too short-lived to do anything significant. I have therefore considered it not worth discussing.

The Balewa government was a parliamentary democracy. During this era, 1960–6, the Federal Republic of Nigeria comprised four regions: Northern, Western, Eastern, and Mid-Western, and the centrally administered federal territory of Lagos. In 1966, with the military coup, the administration of the country devolved on a Federal Military Government headed for a short while by Ironsi and later by Gowon. The Federal Military Government consisted of (1) the Supreme Military Council, and (2) the Federal Executive Council which comprised both armed forces personnel and civilians. Both councils were and (are still) chaired by the head of the Federal Military Government who is also the commander-in-chief of the armed forces. Civilian members of the council were and still are assigned departmental responsibilities.

In May 1967, as a result of continued political crisis, the four regions were divided into twelve states[7] by Decree no. 14 of 1967, thus giving Nigeria a new federal structure. Except for the East Central State which is ruled by an administrator, each state is ruled by a military governor who presides over the State Executive Council which includes some civilians. The administrative set-up in each of the states is similar to that of the Federal Government, each ministry being headed by a commissioner with the permanent secretary as the administrative head.

At this stage, we may ask what sort of development problems confronted the Balewa and Gowon governments? What attempts were and are being made to solve them?

The Balewa government inherited a whole gamut of socioeconomic problems from the British colonial government. First, Britain left Nigeria with an inherent long-term adverse balance of trade at Independence. Post-Second World War growth resulted in the worsening of the balance of payments situation, and over a six-year period following 1955, the trade deficit increased by fifteen times.[8] Imports generally grew faster than incomes. For example, while the gross domestic product at current prices in the 1950s was growing at an annual simple average rate of 8 per cent, imports and exports were growing at 15 and 6 per cent respectively. While imports remained relatively steady at about 15 per cent of the gross domestic product during the decade in question, the growth in exports declined from roughly 6 per cent in the early part of the decade to about 4 per cent in the latter part.[9] Given this trend, it was evident that with the increasing importation of capital goods, which industrialisation demanded (and continues to demand), added to increasing loans commitments, Nigeria had difficulty in obtaining enough foreign exchange. This invariably imposed severe restraints on the growth of the gross domestic product when Nigeria became independent. In fact, between 1962 and 1967 there was hardly any growth in the GDP (see Table 7.1).

The Balewa government recognised the economic problems

mentioned above and tried to solve them.

To mitigate the economic bottlenecks, the federal and regional governments depended heavily on indirect taxation – mainly duties on foreign trade. The fiscal relations of the former regional governments were set forth in the Constitution, listing permissible sources of revenue and specified activities for which public funds were to be spent by governments. Each regional government had a ministry of finance, independent and dependent (upon the Federal Government) sources of revenue and an annual budget approved by the regional legilsature. Negotiations of loans from foreign governments lay mostly within the jurisdiction of the Federal Government. The proceeds of such loans could be used for federal purposes or could be reloaned to the regional governments. The stability of a regional government's finances and the economy of the region was dependent partly on some mineral wealth and partly on one crop. Thus the former Eastern Region depended on oil palm produce and petroleum; the former Northern Region on peanuts and zinc; the Western Region on cocoa; and the Mid-Western Region on oil palm produce, cocoa and petroleum. On the other hand the equilibrium of government finances and of the economy as a whole was (and is still partially) overly dependent on the world market prices of those crops, namely, cocoa, oil palm produce and peanuts.[10]

The system of regional government marketing boards, however, tended to insulate the economy from fluctuations in world market prices. For example, the boards had an export monopoly on cocoa, oil palm produce, peanuts, cotton and soybeans and by purchasing export crops for a number of years at a price below the world market price, the boards were able to build up reserves which permitted them to pay prices which were more stable than those in the world market. In this way, producer income and the economy as a whole was less subject to disruptive external economic forces.[11]

The second problem confronting the Balewa government was that of the diversification of the economy through industrialisation. Though Nigeria is essentially an agricultural country, the government realised that in order for the economy to attain an accelerated growth and to meet the rising demands of the Nigerian consumer, a bold programme of industrialisation was needed. To attract foreign investments, therefore, the government adopted a deeply liberal attitude to business. This official liberalism was expressed in practical terms in the shape of generous incentives for foreign investors. These included liberal income tax and import duty relief, accelerated depreciation allowances and the imposition of protective duties and import quotas.[12]

The government also acted as middleman between the foreign investor and the indigenous private sector. In Nigeria, as in many developing countries, the resentment against foreign domination of the economy is common, resulting in argument for nationalisation of foreign-owned industries. Such public outcry against foreign investors was common, especially from the trade unions. In response to this outcry, the government called on the expatriate firms to leave the retail trade to indigenous firms. The government's request met with reasonable response and thus helped to alleviate the fear of foreign domination of the economy.

To pursue the problem of industrialisation rationally, the government relied on development planning. In Nigeria, development planning is aimed at effecting a rapid increase in the standard of living of the people. The first development plan was the Ten-Year Plan of Development and Welfare, 1950–60. Following the report of the International Bank for Reconstruction and Development in 1955, a new development plan was launched to cover the period 1955–60. This plan was later extended by two years to 1962. As already stated, the main objective of the plan was to achieve a rate of growth of 4 per cent or more for the economy; to develop as rapidly as possible opportunities in education, health and employment and to open access to these opportunities to the citizens of the country; to achieve a modernised economy consistent with the democratic, political and social aspirations of the people, and to maintain a reasonable measure of stability in the economy. The highest priority was placed on industry, agriculture and technical education. The plan made provision for the capital expenditure of US$270m., roughly 13 per cent of public investment, for the expansion of trade and industry over the six-year period. By March 1968, when the duration of the plan expired, less than one-third of the amount had in fact been committed.

Several factors accounted for this poor showing in the public sector. The objectives of the industrial development programme, though laudable, were not matched with articulated projects and closely defined policies geared towards their achievement. In fact, no well-prepared feasible projects were identified prior to the launching of the plan. The iron and steel project which was supposed to be the corner-stone of the industrial sector had not, by the end of the plan period, passed beyond the investigation stage. Moreover, the incentive measures provided by government to investors and entrepreneurs without any selective criterion succeeded only in enabling certain firms to amass profits at the expense of the tax-payers. Very few of the industrial estates promised in the plan were built, while the record of the establishment of cottage industries was unimpressive.[13]

The impetus to industralise led the government to seek external aid. The apparent success of obtaining foreign aid led to a problem of utilisation. The amount of foreign aid that could be utilised was very much lower than the amount potentially available. This anomaly was caused by a number of factors. Firstly, each donor country had its own requirements, and as a result project documentation had to meet the idiosyncracies of particular lenders. This called for greater versatility on the part of planning officials, and thus accentuated the problems of shortage of skilled manpower.

Secondly, the terms on which the aid was given also discouraged its utilisation. Many donor countries tied their aid to the financing of particular projects in the development plan. These projects were not necessarily those to which the government attached a high priority from the point of view of development strategy. Thus, the government was not prepared to release its limited resources for implementing such low priorities in the early years of the plans. This in effect meant that the foreign aid made available could not be utilised even though there were high priority projects which had been properly appraised and documented and were therefore ready for execution.

Furthermore, there was the practice of lenders providing aid for the foreign exchange component of approved projects while Nigeria had to provide the local cost component. This practice was unsuitable for Nigeria as the problems involved became increasingly apparent. Where local resources were fully stretched, it was difficult or virtually impossible to provide the required local cost. This limited the utilisation of the foreign exchange component guaranteed.

It was in the light of these difficulties that the Balewa administration advocated very strongly a change in conventional practices in the field of external aid. The specified changes called for were more generous local cost finance and programme support.

The first approach implied financing part of the local cost component of projects. But since the overall gap was usually higher than the foreign exchange gap, the elimination of the foreign exchange did not solve the financial problem. The second approach involved an examination of the development programme as a whole in the light of resources expected to accrue from all sources, and subsequently deciding on some degree of financial support for the overall programme. These changes were aimed at increasing both the magnitude and rate of utilisation of foreign aid in Nigeria. Unfortunately, the Balewa government was ousted before the changes could take effect.

The problems of political stability and national unity contributed greatly to the overthrow of the Balewa government. The federal nature of the Constitution helped to guarantee political stability only for the early years of independence. Indeed, the federal structure itself militated against rational, nationwide planning. As already pointed out, while the Constitution reserved to the Federal Government the right to raise long-term loans abroad, only short-term credits could be raised by the regions. The Six-Year Plan (1962–8) was drawn up separately in each region and then formally integrated.[14] A National Economic Council officially presided over a unified economy, but in practice the regions were economic rivals. Each government, indeed each minister within it, faced constant pressure to get industries to be sited in the home territory – pressure which increased in proportion to the ever-rising rate of unemployment.[15]

The Gowon government which succeeded the Ironsi government was confronted with four important problems. The first of these was that of unemployment. One of the paradoxes of the

Nigerian economy is that although it is developing most rapidly, the unemployment situation is still critical. Accurate statistical data are however hard to come by. Nevertheless, the National Manpower Board estimated that about 2·0 million persons were unemployed at the end of 1970. The unemployment problem, particularly in the urban areas, is becoming more acute with the rapid expansion of the labour force due to high population growth rates.

The second problem is the high rate of inflation. The inflationary situation is of course a legacy of the civil war. Investment in industry fell drastically in 1967, the year the war broke out. The import of capital goods and industrial raw materials fell by about US$102m. from the 1966 level. In the private sector, there was a decline of about 5·8 per cent from the 1966 level of inflow of capital.[16]

Faced with this set-back in industrial activity, Nigeria had to rely upon her traditional source of economic strength, agriculture. The high level of groundnut and cocoa production combined with that of internally consumed foodstuffs provided the country with much needed foreign exchange and helped to stabilise domestic prices for a while before fluctuations in the world market for agricultural produce (especially groundnuts) caused a serious foreign exchange problem. An over-supply condition of groundnuts and of close substitutes forced prices down. Besides, evacuation of both groundnuts and cocoa as well as of other commodities to the ports was disrupted by the dislocation of parts of the transport system in the country. The economic blockade of the war areas curtailed the export of palm produce and mineral oil from the Eastern states.

Due to the fall of imports in 1967, the import bill was reduced from US$768m. in 1966 to US$669m. in 1967. The reduction, however, failed to improve the balance of payments that remained in deficit, financed by running down the country's foreign currency reserves. The reserves fell from $214.2m. in 1966 to $109.2m. in 1967.

In the light of these circumstances, the Gowon administration had to review its trade policy. In October 1967, therefore, the government restricted the importation of commodities and items of goods in which the nation is self-sufficient and of such other items of consumption as the government felt to be inessential. Moreover, it raised import duty surcharge from 5 to $7\frac{1}{2}$ per cent, and imposed new modest import duties on a number of raw material items which were then imported free of duty.

These higher tariffs and increasingly stringent import restrictions led to an inflationary spiral which has persisted up to the present.

The third problem facing the Gowon government has been how to diversify the economy through industrialisation. We have noted earlier that the 1962–8 National Development Plan failed to achieve its economic diversification targets. Consequently, the value added as percentage of gross output in most industries, with the conspicuous exceptions of food, beverages and cement, remains remarkably low. Imported raw materials constitute about 45 per cent of the industrial costs in the country. The problem is even worse in the metal production industry where the value added is as low as 7 per cent. At present all the stages of metal production are undertaken abroad except the final stage of metal fabrication.

Another problem facing industrial development in Nigeria is the low level of indigenous ownership and control. The government is convinced that the efforts to attract foreign investment should proceed simultaneously with the drive for greater Nigerian participation in production process on mutually beneficial terms. While welcoming foreigners to invest in the industrial sector, it is now a firm government policy that Nigerians must have a definite and effective role in the ownership and management of each industrial venture.

Finally, the divisive effect on the civil war has to be eradicated in the interest of political stability and national unity. The amnesty offered to all prisoners of war and to the leaders of the then Biafra and the reconstruction and reconciliation schemes have not only helped to bring back confidence in the nation, but have also led to a new kind of political consciousness which hopefully will bring about the sort of political stability and national unity needed for development.

To combat all these problems the Gowon government launched the Second National Development Plan, 1970–4. Its five principal objectives are to establish Nigeria firmly as: (1) a united, strong and self-reliant nation; (2) a great and dynamic economy; (3) a just and equalitarian society; (4) a land of bright and full opportunities for all citizens, and (5) a free and democratic society.[17]

The Plan marks the beginning of the implementation of the nine-point programme of the Gowon government. It contains the policy framework for and the programme of the reconstruction of the war-damaged areas of the country as well as the development of the rest of the country. The Plan involves an expenditure programme of US$5.8 billion over a period of four years. About $2.3 billion is earmarked for the public sector programme while $3.5 billion is to be utilised by the private sector.

The first National Development Plan after Independence, 1962–8, on the other hand, provided for a planned fixed investment of about $3.5 billion. Of this amount, about $1.2 billion was earmarked for the private sector and $2.3 billion for the public sector. Apparently the first plan put more emphasis on the public sector, for with independence there was need to expand and modernise the public sector to meet the new demands of self-government. The second plan puts more emphasis on the private sector which the government considers to be the corner-stone of national development.

It is clear that the industrial policy of the Gowon government in the present Development Plan is designed to check the undesirable trends of the first plan and to lay down a solid foundation for long-term steady growth and development of the industrial sector. The objectives of the new policy are to:

(1) promote even development and fair distribution of industries in all parts of the country: (2) ensure rapid expansion and diversification of the industrial sector of the economy; (3) increase the incomes realized from manufacturing activity; (4) create more employment opportunities; (5) promote the establishment of industries which cater for overseas markets in order to earn foreign exchange; (6) continue the program of import-substitution as well as raise the level of intermediate and capital goods production; (7) initiate schemes designed to promote indigenous manpower development in the industrial sector; and (8) raise the proportion of indigenous ownership of industrial investment.[18]

In pursuance of these objectives, the government hopes to lay down priorities from time to time. Let us then examine how the Balewa government and up to now the Gowon administration have mobilised the people to implement their policies and to see how successful they have been in attaining their objectives.

SOCIAL RELATIONS

Under this sub-title we shall consider government policies toward the following: (1) trade unions; (2) employers and employers' associations; and (3) the unorganised population, e.g. the masses, college and high school graduates.

The Trade Union Act of Nigeria, based on the British System of Labour Law, not only guarantees trade unions the right of protection and freedom of association, but also gives them legal status and exemption from certain common law liabilities. Membership in trade unions is completely voluntary as union shop systems are prohibited. But the unions determine and control their own policies. It is common practice for workers within the same trade in one plant to belong to more than one union. Unionisation is largely confined to the modern sector.

The rapid rate of modernisation which started after the Second World War has been accompanied by similar expansion of the trade union movement. The number of trade unions in Nigeria increased from seven with a total membership of 4337 in 1940 to 551 at the end of 1965,[19] with a total membership of 517,911.

In spite of the rapid growth of trade unions, unionised labour, of which more than half is employed by the government, forms only a small proportion of both the total wage-earning and the economically active population. This poor showing in union membership is due to the fact that union leaders are not motivated enough to carry out membership drives. Their lack of motivation is compounded by the fact that the government has not made any serious effort to have unions play an effective role in the development process. This is evident in the mutiplicity of small unions. Except for a few large unions (e.g. the Railway Workers' Union and the Ports Workers' Union) which are organised on a national basis, the rest are small 'company' or 'house' unions. Between 1947–8 and 1963–4, the percentage share of unions with membership of 50 and under rose from 0·8 to 7·6 per cent while those with membership of 51–250 increased slightly from 6·3 to 7·5 per cent of the total union membership. In the same period, the percentage share of big unions with over 5000 members declined from 63·2 to 45 per cent of the total union membership.

Attempts to establish a single trade union organisation have, from their inception, suffered from unstable alliances and re-alignments. Consequently, many of the past attempts to form a central labour organisation have been transitory. Two main reasons have been responsible for this inability to amalgamate. The first has been union political involvement, or lack of it, and especially the question of international affiliation and financial assistance. Should the central labour organisation be affiliated to the Western bloc of international labour organisations, that is, the International Confederation of Free Trade Unions (ICFTU), or to the World Federation of Trade Unions (WFTU) of the Eastern bloc? This basic problem has been the main source of differences and division among the unions. The second reason for the lack of unification was the fact that the government, for some unspecified reasons, recognised only one trade union (the United Labour Congress, ULC). However, while the government has been reluctant to interfere in these inter-union squabbles, it has not disguised its concern about the poor quality of union administration in the country. It was chiefly because of this concern that the Balewa government amended the labour code (a colonial legacy) in 1961. The amendment introduced a legal provision for the 'check-off' system. Within a few years of its introduction, the unions, with the co-operation of some employers who, although they were not legally obliged to operate it, yet saw fit to help it succeed, were increasingly taking advantage of the system. The 'check-off' system contributed a great deal to lessening the instability of the union movements but it did not bring about the much needed effect. Thus in 1969 the Gowon government, in a bid to end the 'unhealthy rivalry engendered by the multifarious labor organizations in the Country', decided to recognise the four existing central labour organisations.[20]

But the Gowon government has been under constant pressure from development planners and even from some of the union leaders to centralise the four labour centres in the interest of national unity and development. It is therefore not surprising that the government held a referendum among the union rank-and-file members in 1973 to determine which was the most representative central body. The rationale behind the referendum was that the most representative body was to become the only recognised centre and the remaining three were to be amalgamated to it. Unfortunately, the results of the referendum have still not been made known. As a result, the government policy of consulting the four bodies is still in effect, which in turn means the continuous postponement of the advantages of a unified labour movement. The Ghana labour movement has demonstrated the advantages of a united labour front.[21]

Since the four labour centres still exist and the rivalry between them continues, it would be fair to conclude that the Balewa government was not as successful as the Nkrumah government in mobilising the unions to contribute to the development process. The Gowon government has not been much more successful either. But how has the government dealt with the employers' associations?

Unlike Ghana, which has one central employers' association, Nigeria has about fifty. The most prominent of these are the Nigerian Mining Employers' Association in Jos, the Nigerian Plantation Employers' Association in Calabar, and the Nigerian Bankers' (Employers') Association with headquarters in Lagos. All these organisations exist, however, within what is known as the Nigerian Employers' Consultative Association (NECA). The NECA has no strong active role as does the centralised Employers' Association of Ghana. Its position and influence is more comparable to that of the United Kingdom. It is both recognised and consulted on issues and aspects of policy affecting industry by the Federal Ministry of Labour. It thus acts as a national spokesman for private employers.

To encourage the employers to continue to play an important role in the Nigerian development process, the government has very liberal investment policies. As previously noted the Balewa regime extended very favourable investment terms to investors, foreign and indigenous. The Gowon administration is continuing the same, if not more, liberal policies of Balewa. Firstly, the government has stated unequivocally that it does not intend to nationalise or expropriate foreign or indigenous industries. But where nationalisation becomes absolutely necessary, the government will enter into negotiations with the company concerned and will pay compensation in accordance with agreements reached. Secondly, it offers a wide range of inducements to new industries. These include tax holidays, generous capital and depreciation allowances and tariff concessions. A sizeable proportion of profit repatriation is allowed while favourable terms for reinvestment are offered to expatriate firms.

The government has also initiated plans for generating local investment by mobilising domestic sources. One of these sources is the National Provident Fund, a kind of social security fund. The introduction of the National Savings Scheme has made it easy for loans to be floated to small-scale entrepreneurs. Also, the Nigerian Industrial Development Bank has been set up with the sole aim of financing industrial projects and encouraging indigenous investors. In an effort to expand the activities of the bank towards the promotion of indigenous enterprises, the government has provided it with US $6 m. The amount is an initial installment for financing the expanded lending programme of the bank. The bank is a purely commercial enterprise which is expected to follow strictly commercial rules in considering short-term and long-term loans to accredited and genuine indigenous businessmen who must be willing and able to take over and run viable business concerns in the national interest.[22]

One of the four new bodies set up by the government to enable it to implement the major projects in the Second National Development Plan, designed to turn the country into an industrial state, is the Industrial Research Council.

The Industrial Research Council was established by decree to: '(a) encourage, promote and coordinate industrial research programmes in Nigeria; (b) advise the Nigerian Council for Science and Technology and through it the Federal Military Government and the States on national policy on industrial research and its implementation; and (c) ensure the application and development of the results of industrial research in consonance with national scientific economic and social policies.'[23]

In performing these duties, the Council is to keep under review all industrial activities in the country, assess the value and significance of industrial research programmes to the national economy and advise the Federal and State governments through the Council for Science and Technology on financial, organisational and institutional changes necessary to increase the efficiency of industrial research. Furthermore, the Research Council is to encourage general education in sciences relevant to research and to publish or sponsor the publication of results of industrial research which are of national significance. It is also to co-ordinate all industrial activities in Nigeria which are relevant to its functions as well as act as a liaison with international organisations with a view to furthering industrial research and the application of their results.

An Industrial Training Fund has also been set up for the purpose of financing the industrial training of indigenous personnel. All industries are obliged to contribute. Each firm is expected to prepare an articulated programme for increasing progressively Nigerian participation in management at all levels.

With regard to the non-organised sector of the population, little has been done to mobilise it to participate in the development process. During the Balewa regime, attempts were made on regional bases to organise the youth. For example, there was the Okpara Youth Brigade, mainly regional, and the Zikist National Vanguard which was fairly national in scope.

The problem of illiteracy, especially among the adult population, has been plaguing Nigeria since her inception as a nation. The Balewa government sought relentlessly to eradicate illiteracy from the country by initiating a number of adult education activities in all parts of the country, notable among which were those activities in such places as Warri, Calabar, Onitsha and Owerri provinces and in various Native Authority Schools in the Northern states.

The adult education drive has been accelerated during the Gowon regime. The government has adopted ten proposals which are currently being executed and these include:[24]

1 The establishment of a National Adult Education Commission empowered and financed to organise and run adult education courses in the country;

2 the organisation of a National Corps of Adult Education

Tutors comprising all school masters, all students on long vacation, and all volunteers from other fields for the benefit of adult education.

Community development and education clubs are also encouraged by the government. Club activities include leadership training courses, appeal works and other engagements for fund raising, initiation and execution of important community projects such as road and bridge construction and a host of others. Training courses are organised by the staff of the Social Welfare Division of the Ministry of Labour for Youth Clubs; experts are invited to speak on topical matters, like programme planning in youth clubs, the history of youth clubs in Nigeria, public health services, the psychology of adolescence and the behaviour patterns of human beings from infancy to adulthood.

To co-ordinate the skills and expertise of college graduates, the National Youth Corps has been instituted. The Corps is also aimed at promoting national unity since the participants are posted to states other than their own. The salient philosophy in this strategy is to expose the graduates to the life-style of those in other states and tribes.[25]

What is the impact of all these government strategies of mobilising the population on the employment situation?

EMPLOYMENT

Here, we shall discuss the general features of employment before proceeding to analyse government employment policies.

The 1963 national census estimated the labour force to be 18.3 million (that is, about 35 per cent of the population) of which 13.9 million were males and 4.4 million females. There were 344,921 unemployed persons, 272,174 of these being males.[26]

This labour force was shared out among various occupations, with agriculture (including fishing, hunting, loggers and related workers) claiming the largest figure of 10·2 million. The distribution is shown in Table 7.3.

Half the labour force in Nigeria was in the 20–35 year age-group and about 80 per cent of the total labour force was under 45 years old. This is significant in a developing country like Nigeria where there is always the need to have a constantly

TABLE 7.3 Occupational breakdown of the labour force

Occupation	Total	Male	Female
Farmers, fishermen, hunters, loggers and related workers	10,201,328	9,222,448	978,780
Sales workers	2,806,071	1,113,892	1,692,179
Craftsmen, production process workers and labourers	2,190,073	1,676,302	513,771
Service, sports and recreation workers	870,884	641,671	229,213
Professional, technical and related workers	440,613	375,066	65,547
Transport and communications	279,255	273,255	5824
Clerical workers	228,018	206,153	21,865
Miners, quarrymen and related workers	13,856	13,594	262
Unspecified occupations	891,415	55,298	836,117
Unemployed persons	344,921	272,174	72,747

Source: Nigeria, Ministry of Information, *Nigeria Handbook 1973*, (Lagos: Academy Press, 1973) p. 134.

trainable and adaptable pool of labour. Table 7.4 shows the age composition.

It will also be observed that the labour force dropped significantly after the age of 54 years. Most employees in the government service, mercantile houses and other establishments retire from paid service at the age of 55. A breakdown of the labour force showed that the majority of the people employed after the age of 55 are farmers. They accounted for 1,177,084 of the 1,631,101 people employed beyond the age of 55. However, the Labour Force Sample Survey conducted in 1966–7 showed that 40 per cent of the country's population was economically active, and that the number was growing at an annual rate of 2·3 per cent, which is about the same rate as the increase in population. The survey also showed that the labour force participation rate for those aged 15–55 years was 78 per cent, and 76 per cent for those aged 12–14 years.

The estimated gainfully employed were further classified by status. Own-account workers accounted for the largest proportion (63·9 per cent) of the gainfully employed; unpaid

household workers (29·7 per cent) came next, while paid
employees accounted for only 5 per cent. (It should be noted

TABLE 7.4   Age composition of the labour force

Age group	Total	Male	Female
15–19	1,932,252	1,404,183	528,069
20–24	3,666,148	2,704,397	961,751
25–34	6,049,272	4,535,868	1,513,404
35–44	3,333,864	2,597,676	736,188
45–54	1,693,199	1,335,924	357,275
55–64	879,090	699,652	179,438
65–74	405,679	324,216	81,463
75 and over	346,332	284,850	61,482

Source: Nigeria Handbook 1973, op. cit., p. 135.

that the sample survey figures were more reflective of the actual
situation.)

The Labour Force Sample Survey estimated the rate of unemployment in the active labour force as roughly 7·8 per cent.[27]
This comprised 7·6 per cent for all urban areas combined and
about 0·5 per cent for all rural areas combined. The largest
number of the unemployed was (and still is) found in the 18–23
age group, followed closely by the 15–17 and 24–29 age groups
respectively. In short, the under-30s account for over 86 per
cent of the total unemployed.[28]

Primary school leavers contribute to the high incidence of
unemployment, accounting for 59 per cent of all unemployed
personnel.

The structure of employment also reveals a shortage of professional and technical workers at all levels. For example, in
1970 30–40 per cent of those employed as medical practitioners,
architects and town planners and the like were expatriates.[29] Of
those in the senior managerial and administrative positions
expatriates also accounted for about 28 per cent.

Various reasons have been given for the unemployment
problems in developing countries and these countries' attempts
at solution.[30] A few developing countries, with articulate and
dynamic leadership, recognising the magnitude and serious-

ness of the problem, establish comprehensive programmes to tackle it. But many others with less imaginative leadership have failed to provide such necessary programmes. In this category was the Balewa government. The Six-Year Development Plan, 1962–8, launched by the Balewa administration failed to treat unemployment as a national problem.[31] Under the heading 'National Objective', the Plan document stated its aim 'To develop as rapidly as possible opportunities in education, health and employment . . . The creation of more jobs and opportunities in non-agricultural occupations.'[32]

The Western Regional Government Development Programme, which came close to recognising the problem, stated the need for providing 'useful and worthwhile employment for all', but apparently ignored the employment consideration in the subsequent listing of investment criteria. Neither its quantitative assessment nor the probable impact of plan implementation on it was made.

The first time the Balewa government showed any sign of recognising the unemployment problem was not until after the much heralded Development Plan had been launched. It was only then that the Minister of Labour submitted a report of the Symposium on Youth Unemployment held in Tanzania (formerly Tanganyika) in September 1962, to the Federal Government. The government decided, among other things,

1 that the subject of unemployed youth in Nigeria should be dealt with as a matter of the utmost urgency; and

2 that the Minister of Economic Development through the National Manpower Board should give consideration to the problem of youth unemployment, and in consultation with the Governments of the Federation recommended early remedial action.[33]

To implement these recommendations, the National Manpower Secretariat employed the services of employment experts to devise techniques of expanding small-scale industries in order to create employment opportunities for school leavers. The final report submitted by the foreign team of experts to the government failed to state the number of employment opportunities that would have been created by the adoption of the small-scale industry strategy. It only contained labour/

investment ratios for various areas of industrial activity. Consequently, it was not possible to indicate the extent to which
small-scale industry expansion could be expected to reduce unemployment.[34] But full of shortcomings as the report was, any
informed administration would have still salvaged it (at least
since it was on an important programme to which the government purported to attach priority) and implemented it.
Instead, the Balewa administration, either out of administrative incompetence or political manoeuvring, buried the entire report and forgot about it. The Federal Government having
ignored the report, the regional governments now decided to
take individual initiative; thus the Western and Eastern Regions in particular attempted to modernise agriculture by
introducing farm settlements as a way of teaching modern agricultural techniques to school leavers. It was hoped that such
settlements would help ease the unemployment problem to
some extent.

Unfortunately, the impact of this scheme on unemployment
has been marginal. The capital cost of settling each farmer was
colossal. For example, in the former Western Region, after ten
years of the establishment of the farm scheme, there are only a
few thousand settlers in the state farm settlements and each has
been settled at an astronomically high cost of about US $6000.

Beside the fact that the physical transfer of young school
leavers from their various village communities into new and
strange environments of farm settlements meant that amenities
had to be provided where there had only been forests or
swamps, fraudulent over-capitalisation probably contributed
to inflate the costs. But more important, even without corruption, the strategy of the scheme itself was basically inflationary,
involving unrealistic financial calculations and expenditures.
Thus a scheme which, considered purely as an agricultural project, could have perhaps been laudatory, proved ineffective because it could not generate employment, which was one of the
primary objectives.

The Gowon administration so far has attempted in various
ways to correct or eliminate the strategic errors in development
plans of the Balewa regime. Unlike the Balewa administration,
the Gowon government gives the unemployment problem top
priority consideration in the Second National Development

Plan, 1970–4. The Plan devotes a substantial section to the problem of manpower needs and employment. In this regard, the main objectives of the National Manpower policy are to:

(1) contain the incidence of youth unemployment by the provision of more training and employment opportunities; (2) correct existing imbalances in the educational system consistent with the changing requirements of the economy; (3) reduce the proportion of expatriate participation in employment; and (4) meet the manpower requirements for the successful implementation of the Plan and the optimum development of the economy as a whole.[35]

With the expanding trend in primary school education, the Development Plan advocates a policy of employment creation which would accommodate youth employment. It might well be pointed out now that this scheme has its attendant problems. For example, the expansion of the primary school enrolment has necessitated the recruitment of more teachers. This recruitment itself poses a threat to the government capital expenditure for education. When the vast number of newly recruited come to retire at the age of fifty-five, the government will be faced with such a heavy retirement benefits bill that the cost of education, which is already about 30 per cent of the national budget, may double. The doubling may result in a financial crisis for the government. But with the oil revenue, such a crisis could be averted if the money were properly utilised.

Other high employment areas on which the Plan seems to concentrate its attention are the self-employed or own-account workers in the traditional sectors of the economy, which accounted for 60 per cent of employed persons in 1967. The Plan lays emphasis on small indigenous non-agricultural enterprises like mechanic and repair workshops, services, manufacturing and processing as well as petty trading which employed less than ten workers. If the programmes and projects in the Plan were fully implemented, a total of about 3·3 million new jobs would be created.

This optimistic figure is based on the assumption that the Plan would only cater for those who are visibly unemployed and the new entrants into the labour force. In other words, it has been implicitly assumed that the under-employed (in both the rural and urban areas) would not join the ranks of those seeking employment even when the implementation of the planned programmes start generating substantial new wage employment opportunities. But the lessons of Kenya have demonstrated that such an assumption does not usually hold. The government of Kenya once decided that business establishments in the country should increase employment by 15 per cent. After the implementation of this decision, unemployment actually increased because of the exodus from the rural areas once it became known that more jobs were available in the cities.

Also, under the Development Plan, the government is undertaking a special programme for the development of managerial manpower. The estimated annual demand for managerial personnel over the Plan period is put at 3500. The educational system is expected to meet the formal education requirements in job preparation for managerial and supervisory functions.

The main limitation of the Second National Plan on the unemployment problem, however, is that employment is treated as a residual item. That is, after working out the investment implication of the growth targets set for the various sectors, statistical methods are then applied to the investment. Output figures are thus projected for each sector to obtain the employment implications of the investment programmes in all the sectors.[36] With more time, adequate staff and policy guidelines it might have been possible to work out a more satisfactory programme that would optimise the employment and growth objective. The government also needs to reconsider its policy and solutions in the light of current thinking on the question of unemployment. Experts like Blaug and Falae are beginning to challenge some of the shibboleths about the unemployment problem in developing countries.[37]

With limited employment opportunities and the high spiral of inflation, what has been the government's policy towards income? How is income distributed in the country?

INCOMES

Pay claims in Nigeria are based on three main factors: (1) changes in the cost of living which are tied up with the minimum wage argument; (2) wage differentials; and (3) profits earned by employers.[38]

Every wages commission in Nigeria usually considers changes in the cost of living in deciding on final wage awards. The problem always is to determine what could be regarded as a 'poverty datum line' or a 'minimum wage'. For example, the Morgan Commission,[39] set up by the Balewa government in 1964, in identifying certain problems affecting the cost of living indices in Nigeria, pointed out that most indices compiled by the government and individuals, organisations and institutions which gave evidence before it did not make adequate provision for a number of items such as family size and extended family commitments, habits (e.g. smoking and drinking), and ostentatious spending, (e.g., on funeral and naming and housewarming ceremonies). It therefore recommended these items to be reckoned with when computing a 'living wage'.

The Commission's final recommendations included a general upward revision of salaries and wages of junior employees in both government and private establishments, the abolition of the daily wage system, and the introduction of a national minimum wage. The existing structure of wages, conditions of service in wage earning employments, and the machinery for wages review were to be reconsidered. These recommendations which were eventually adopted and implemented by the government failed to solve the 'living cost' problem.

On the other hand, the Adebo Commission appointed by the Gowon administration claimed that 'no previous Nigerian Commission on wages and Salaries was so preoccupied with the incidence of the cost of living'[40] as it was. Despite the claim, the Commission failed to solve the problem of finding an acceptable pattern of the cost of living. Nevertheless, the work of the Commission has resulted in increases in wages ranging from 30 per cent at the bottom to 10 per cent at the top. In addition, the Commission recommended the adoption of the principle of fair comparison with the private sector for determining pay in the public sector. Among other recommendations was one that three levels of enforceable minimum wage be established, and a Public Service Review Commission appointed.

The problem of wage differentials has also featured prominently in wage reviews. Wage differentials are not only a problem between skilled, semi-skilled and unskilled workers, but also between industries, and between wage-earners in the Civil Service, government corporations and the private sector. The problem is due to differences in basic academic and professional qualifications, skills, degrees of responsibilities and the colonial background of the Nigerian labour market. As the Harragin Commission of 1946 pointed out, 'West Africa is still at the stage when an extra bonus has to be paid for an education little higher than literacy. This paradise for the black-coated worker will soon pass, but he is entitled to make what can be of it while it lasts.'[41] It takes time for the supply of labour to catch up with the demand for labour, especially in a rapidly expanding economy. The increasing demand for various skills which could only be acquired by institutional training tends to give some special kinds of labour longer leases of 'wage differentials' bonuses.[42]

The colonial aspect of wage differentials in Nigeria is found on different levels of pay for expatriate officers. The Harragin Commission said that 'so long as it is necessary for the West African Governments to employ persons from overseas, so long will they have to pay an extra amount to induce them to leave their homes and families and spend their lives in less healthy and less congenial surroundings.'[43] Over the years, increasing numbers of Nigerians have qualified for positions formerly held by expatriates but unfortunately they enjoy the same basic remunerations as the expatriates. This has inevitably widened the gaps among various levels of indigenous civil servants.

The problem of wage differentials became more acute after the Gorsuch Commission[44] of 1955 recommended some upgrading of posts in the Civil Service. The recommendation of this Commission led to the creation of the 'executive class' within the Civil Service. The immediate result was that employees in other sectors began to agitate for the bridging of wage differentials which had been created in other semi-professional and professional employments.

The problems of wage differentials were perhaps best summed up by the Adebo Commission which argued that

Wage and Salary differentials are a function of many things. Differentials in a wisely structured pay system constitute useful incentives to greater efforts to acquiring essential basic educational qualifications; greater effort at acquiring skills or improving on them; greater efficiency in the performance of assigned tasks; acceptance and discharge of increased responsibilities. It is important that the differentials should be sufficient for this purpose.[45]

Nigerian experience has demonstrated that whenever workers or trade unions feel that a group of people is remunerated by more than what it contributes they put pressure on the government to narrow the gap.

Basing wage claims on the profitability of business is becoming a growing concern to Nigeria. Although the government continues to absorb the bulk of the skilled and semi-skilled labour, the expansion of industrial production and commerce has increased the proportion of employment in these sectors in recent years. Since 1964, the private sector has operated a flexible wages and salary policy different from the public sector where conditions have been rather stagnant. As a matter of fact, the average remuneration has been higher than that in the public sector.

It should be noted, however, that the private sector cannot perform effectively and may not even continue in business without a reasonable level of profit. In the industrial countries of the West where free enterprise exists, experience has shown the inadvisability of directly relating claims for higher wages to profits because employers would be able to reverse the claims in conditions of declining prosperity. Employers may resort to mass retrenchment of labour.

The main difficulty which trade unions encounter in trying to secure higher wages based on company profits is the variation in the level of profits from firm to firm within an industry and between industries. Hitherto, the private sector in Nigeria has always reacted to the enforcement of wage rates fixed by the government by laying-off some workers or by offering lower rates, both of which have often led to industrial disputes. Through legislation, however, the government has been able to resolve these disputes as well as control wages. The range of legislation extends from the Labour Code (Amendment) Act of 1961 passed by the Balewa government, Trade

Disputes (Emergency Provisions) to the Amendment Decree no. 33 of 1969 promulgated by the Gowon administration. These laws are concerned with the protection of wages, as in the Labour Code Act, 1961, and the settlement of disputes arising from wages and other matters related to employment as in Decree no. 53. Decree no. 21 put out by the Gowon administration has increased the dimensions of government intervention in the administration of wages through the system of depositing collective agreements with the Federal Ministry of Labour. The commissioner has been empowered by the decree to make a part or whole of an agreement legally binding on the parties to whom it relates by issuing an order. Also, the commissioner may, by order, confirm the award of an arbitration tribunal, which makes it binding on the employers and workers to whom it relates.

Despite these government attempts to control wages, legal regulation of wages is still at a minimum. There is no legal national minimum wage of any sort and consequently existing zonal minimum wages cannot be legally enforced. The Adebo Commission has therefore called for the establishment of a legal minimum wage with a view to enforcing the minimum wages that now exist in certain industries and some types of employment such as motor-repairs and catering. The Gowon government has rightly complied with some of these recommendations. It has declared in a white paper that 'until a national legal minimum wage is feasible, the existing machinery responsible for enforcing minimum wages in certain industries and other types of employment should continue to work.'[46]

This government policy has still not addressed itself to the problem of what the legal minimum wage should be. Also government expression of preference for the existing machinery raises the possibility that there may not be any point in introducing legal regulation now or in the future.

Some experts, like Falae, tend to believe that the government needs to formulate a wages policy which takes into consideration the planned rates of economic growth over the projected planned periods. The rationale for this reasoning is that economic growth must be achieved without excessive inflation. Consequently, the government needs to reconsider and solve the problems of rising costs of living and wage differentials.

THE DEVELOPMENT TREND

The Nigerian development path, unlike the Ghanaian, has been rather consistent except that the path is still too narrow. The government has been making attempts to widen this path through development planning. But the planning itself has not been successful because of the way it has been carried out. At first it was what we could call 'suitcase planning'. By this method, foreign experts were brought into the country to plan the economy, of which they had only superficial knowledge. For example, the Ashby Commission on Higher Education was about 200 per cent off target because the foreign experts who made up the Commission were not familiar with the problems they were to advise on; perhaps these were experts who probably had not been to Nigeria before, stayed for the precise duration of the Commission work and disappeared again to their respective countries. Fortunately, those days seem to be gone.

A new method of planning is replacing the 'suitcase' model. We may call this new kind 'prismatic planning',[47] carried on by indigenous experts who are familiar with the economic structure and its problems. As a result of their familiarity with both the country and its problems and perhaps also through an excessive desire to see the country develop fast, these experts embark on grandiose or overly ambitious plans without setting out clear techniques for realising their targets. Instead, they give very detailed descriptions of socio-economic problems thus raising the awareness of the government. But the embarrassing result is that the government becomes aware of these problems without knowing what to do about them because it is not provided with the systematic techniques and realistic programmes with which to tackle or solve them. Such government inability to provide effective solutions usually leads to public frustration and eventually industrial and political unrest, as was witnessed in the General Strike of 1964.[48]

Another reason why these plans always fail to meet desired targets is that the country does not yet have certain basic political and administrative conditions necessary for their success. The three necessary conditions are:

1 The political community needs already to possess a sense of solidarity such that trust exists between its various sec-

tions; and the uneven impact of development or competition for development must not be likely to deepen existing social cleavages.

2 A basic affinity needs to exist between people and Government such that the latter can ask citizens to make sacrifices and the latter will make them without excessively reckoning the cost.

3 A country has to possess a large, skilled and commited public service that strives to serve the population, that has a vivid sense of urgency of economic growth, and that knows how to provide initiative without stifling it.[49]

'Nigeria', O'Connell concluded, 'is not a tight-knit political community; it cannot expect a deep attachment from its people to Government, and it does not possess an exceptionally well-equipped administration.'[50]

Fortunately, however, the Gowon government is beginning to realise that development comes largely from within and not through the charity or benevolence of another nation. This is why the government development policy is shifting more and more from charity to trade. It has articulated this policy in a pamphlet appropriately called 'Trade, Not Charity'.[51] But it needs to do much more than this: there is an urgent need for the government to spell out its development ideology so that friendly nations and trading partners will know how to co-operate in the development process. Such an ideology should embody the conditions mentioned by O'Connell.

Also, development planning should be carried out largely by the indigenous experts by virtue of their familiarity with the situation and the problems. But to prevent the continuation of 'prismatic planning' the foreign expert should be complimentary to the planning process, checking the plan for loopholes and objectivity and for whether or not an adequate organisational set-up has been provided for successful implementation and utilisation of resources, for these are two key problems that still beset Nigeria. The ILO has taken the lead in bringing about mutual co-operation between indigenous and foreign experts. Its World Employment Programme utilises both the foreign and indigenous experts in its search for a full employment formula.

Nigeria has all the human and natural resources she needs (especially the immense scope now afforded by oil, with the quadrupling recently of prices), but they are not properly utilised. Often the economist, the engineer, the chemist and the physicist are forced to become 'blackboard' professionals. Indeed, Nigeria needs to start challenging her professional class so as to make it more responsive to the development process. Also, the revenue realised from the natural resources should be properly utilised so that the benefits of development are visible to all Nigerians, both urban and rural dwellers. Until Nigeria begins to give serious consideration to some of the proposals raised above, her development path will continue to meander uncertainly. This, Nigeria cannot afford if she is to attain a developed status.

8 The Development Path of China

NORMAN B. SCOTT

The People's Republic is now almost twenty-five years old. This is little in relation to China's three thousand years of unbroken, independent civilisation. It is also a very short time – barely the space of one generation – in which to master the problem of economic backwardness. In this chapter an attempt is made to capture the essence of what had to be done to modernise China, what has been attempted and what has been achieved.

THE LEGACY OF BACKWARDNESS

Agriculture
More than twenty years of armed struggle, both of civil war and against foreign invasion, preceded the proclamation of the People's Republic of China on 1 October 1949. The new government inherited a war-torn economy whose finances were in chaos as a result of nearly three decades of inflation (over 30 per cent per month) and flagrant mismanagement. The large-scale disruption caused by war – for example, some 15–20 per cent of crop land was out of use due to flooding or neglect and cotton production was reduced by half – was superimposed on the age-old problem of the poverty of China's peasant masses. That poverty was firmly rooted in the feudal-bureaucratic system of land tenure and taxation, and in the pressure of population in a limited area of agricultural land. (It is noteworthy that only about 15 per cent of China's total area is arable land – the cultivated area is roughly 110 million hectares[1] – compared to some 50 per cent in the United States. In other words, China, which is now virtually self-sufficient in foodstuffs, has to feed about one quarter of the world's population from the produce of only 7 per cent of the cultivated surface of the globe.)

Land ownership was concentrated in relatively few hands in traditional China. Those farm families which were officially classified as poor – about 70 per cent of the total – owned only 22 per cent of the cultivated land. The landlord and rich peasant families accounting for 10 per cent of the rural population possessed 53 per cent of the cultivated land. Over half the farm workers did not own any land at all, and were either tenants or hired labourers. The good and fertile land was for the most part owned by the rich minority, while the masses had to eke out a miserable livelihood by the intensive cultivation of the poor marginal land.

The other great source of pressure on land resources, and resultant fragmentation of holdings, has been the growth of population. The cultivated area *per capita* declined from 0.86 acres in the middle of the seventeenth century to only 0·7 acres at the time of the revolution.[2] Although new land had been brought under cultivation, population had grown more quickly. Moreover, the geography of China is such that only some 20 million hectares of agricultural wasteland exist, of which it has been estimated that about 18 million might be reclaimed by means of (costly) draining and irrigation.

The combination of scarce land and abundant manpower resulted in highly labour-intensive cultivation – reflected in low productivity per man but high yields per unit of land. The central government had always encouraged, from antiquity, large schemes of water control which helped to reduce the risks of flooding (or drought) and thereby increase the output of crops and government tax revenue. The peasants for their part, driven by the economic whip of necessity, brought great ingenuity and industriousness to the cultivation of the overcrowded river basins. (There was nevertheless a considerable untapped labour potential, since farmers were unoccupied for four to six months each year, except in the limited double-cropping areas.)

High density of labour on the land, minute landholdings, low labour productivity and incomes all meant that there was little surplus available over subsistence consumption for savings and investment. Add to that the burden placed on the peasants by their chronic indebtedness (often repayable at usurious rates of interest), high rents and costly transportation and distribution networks. China's agriculture, employing over 80 per cent of the population, was locked in the vicious circle of poverty and social injustice. In such conditions of small-scale farming and unequal landholdings, in a land vulnerable to flooding, water-logging and drought, plant and animal pests, only revolution could create the prerequisites of agricultural progress.

Industry
Small-scale productive units and highly labour-intensive tech-niques also characterised the industry of China. On the eve of the Second World War the traditional, or handicraft, sector of industry is estimated to have produced over 70 per cent of the net value of manufacturing output. The proportion was much higher than this average in food-processing and transport equipment and between 60 and 80 per cent in building materi-als, textiles, paper and printing. Modern industry, which had been implanted for the most part under foreign control in the Treaty Port areas at the end of the nineteenth century, provided the bulk of the output of metal processing, engineering and chemicals. The main characteristics of the fairly small modern sector were the predominance of foreign control (over 40 per cent of industrial capital at the outbreak of war with Japan), geographical concentration in the narrow coastal belt of the treaty ports, and the preponderance of consumer-goods indus-tries (92 per cent of all industrial capital in 1937 and even 85 per cent of the gross value of output in 1933).[3] As a whole, therefore, the position of Chinese industry at the end of the war resembled that of many other developing countries, contributing only about 20 per cent of GNP and employing some 7·5 per cent of the labour force. Agriculture, for comparison, accounted for 45 per cent of GNP and roughly 80 per cent of the labour force, and the service sector 34 per cent of GNP and the remainder of the labour force. The handicrafts sector was of great importance, producing not only necessities such as clothing and footwear, agricultural implements, etc. but also the stone and carvings, lacquerware and other *objets d'art* which contributed a large share of total exports. Statistics on the distribution of employ-ment are not very accurate.

Thus China also had in common with most other developing countries a dualistic structure of manufacturing output, with traditional and modern sectors coexisting, sometimes in a competitive relationship (e.g. textiles), sometimes in complementary relationship. The former took advantage of the abundance of labour and its considerable manual dexterity but suffered the disadvantage of small-scale production and often antiquated technology. The growth of the modern sector was stunted by lack of capital and industrially skilled labour, and its structure was characterised by the pattern of ownership and the commercial interests and tariff privileges of foreign proprietors anxious to cater primarily for the market for consumer goods. Low labour costs in the traditional sector limited the competitive advantage of labour-saving technology in the modern sector. It has also been suggested that the low purchasing power of the Chinese people helped traditional industry to survive.

Transport
The concentration of modern industry in the coastal provinces has already been mentioned. These provinces, occupying only 10 per cent of the total area of the country, produced 77 per cent of the gross value of factory output in 1949. One consequence of this largely foreign-dictated pattern of industrial location was the under-development of China's transport infrastructure. Factories were far from their supplies of raw materials. Up to the outbreak of the Sino-Japanese war in 1937 some progress was made in modern transportation with the construction of metalled roads and railways. These fell far short of the needs of the economy, however, and were badly damaged during the twelve years of war.

Employment productivity
The pattern of employment in China at the beginning of the People's Republic corresponded to the structure of the economy as described above and resembled that of other developing countries. About four-fifths of the working population was engaged in agriculture, $7\frac{1}{2}$ per cent in industry, about 6 per cent in trade and 5 per cent in transport. No reliable data are available on unemployment and female participation rates in the labour force, but some estimates put unemployment in the neighbourhood of 25 million in 1952. Productivity was low on account of poor education and health and generally low living

standards. Illiteracy was widespread, and acted as a drug to technical training. There were only eighty doctors trained in modern medicine for each million inhabitants, while the higher education system produced a surplus of graduates in liberal arts (55 per cent of all graduates). Standards of nutrition were very low: only about 2 per cent of the calories of the Chinese diet were of animal origin. Only 1 per cent of the total crop area was sown to vegetables.

Foreign trade and investment
The history of China's foreign trade is largely a reflection of the attempt – successful for the most part – of foreign powers to achieve positions of economic dominance. Beginning with the Opium Wars in the 1840s, until the Sino-Japanese War (1937–45) and the embargoes on trade subsequently applied during the Cold War, China has had no cause to wish its foreign trade dependence to be greater than it had been. Partly as a result of the great size of the country and its population, China's foreign trade in *per capita* terms – never exceeding $4 – had probably always been the lowest of any country in the world. The composition of exports reflected the predominance of agriculture and the low level of industrialisation – vegetable seeds and oil, eggs, hides and skins, soya beans, cotton goods, silk and tea were the principal export products. By contrast, over one-third of the import structure depended on metals, chemicals, transport equipment and machinery. So far as foreign investment is concerned, the story is the familiar one, common to mot developing countries, of foreign control of one-third of total industrial production, with a dominant position in textiles, urban public utilities, food processing, tobacco and coal mining.

The condition of under-development as it existed in China until 1949 was not, however, essentially different in its economic symptoms from that in Africa. The originality of the Chinese path of development consists in the combination of socialist ideology and economic pragmatism that has constituted China's response to the development problem. The content of the policies pursued has changed periodically, as have the durations of the plans and the broad strategies of development. At the same time, there has been an unmistakable constancy in the vision of the type of society it is hoped to forge through the process of development. Chairman Mao Tse-tung is the author of the vision and has guided and articulated progress towards its accomplishment since the foundation of the People's Republic.

SUCCESSIVE DEVELOPMENT STRATEGIES

The first three years of postwar effort were devoted to short-term emergency measures aimed at the reconstruction of an economy that had been devastated by twelve years of war. By 1962 industrial output or capacity levels had been restored to their pre-1949 peaks, the transport network had been rebuilt and agricultural production had recovered to a normal volume. China's planners were then in a position to turn their attention to medium-term and longer range planning. They drew their inspiration from two sources: their experience of the war economy based on co-operatives which had been installed in the North-West provinces, around Yenan, at the conclusion of the Long March; and the historical precedent of the Soviet Union's succession of five-year plans of industrialisation.

The first Chinese Five-Year Plan covered the years 1953–7. Some of the successes and mistakes of these years determined the subsequent shift in both the priorities and institution of later plans towards a characteristically Chinese strategy of development. This process of experimentation by trial and error has not corresponded to the time-horizons of the four national development plans but has fallen into the following six phases:

1. 1949–52: rehabilitation of the war-torn economy
2. 1952–7: First Five-Year Plan—priority to industrialisation
3. 1958–60: Great Leap Forward—decentralisation of industry, nature of commerce
4. 1961–5: Retrenchment and recovery
5. 1966–9: Great Proletarian Cultural Revolution—a set-back in industrial output
6. 1971–5: resumed planning—the Fourth Five-Year Plan

Each of the above phases of development has consisted of either the introduction of a particular development strategy – for example, the First Five-Year Plan and the Great Leap Forward – or of a period of retrenchment and consolidation, after a campaign of political 'rectification' such as the Cultural Revolution, during which certain economic policy options, such as use of wage differentiation and material incentives to increase productivity came under severe critical fire. The history and main feature of these successive phases or strategies and counter-strategies are well known. All that is attempted in the following cursory account is the identification of those policies or institutions which, singly or in co-ordination, define the distinctively Chinese path of development.

During the first five years of planning Chinese development strategy in many ways emulated the Soviet model of the years 1928–41. A high investment ratio was arrived at, savings to be accumulated largely from the public sector, and nearly 60 per cent of all investment was channelled to the enlargement of industrial capacity, particularly heavy industry. The Soviet Union undertook to design and supply the equipment for 156 industrial plants and water management was to receive only 7·6 per cent of new capital outlays. In reality, investment in the agricultural sector absorbed even less than planned – only 6·2.

There can be no doubt that this approach to development had a certain justification at the time the plan was conceived. Without heavy industry, China's defences were weak at a time when international tension – of which the Korean war was a proof – was great. China therefore 'leaned to one side' in its foreign policy and sought to bolster its small administrative experience and capacity to accumulate by borrowing planning techniques and industrial technology from the Soviet Union. The plan openly recommended that in carrying it out maximum use be made of the 'advanced experience' of the Soviet Union. Soviet assistance took the form of loans (in kind as well as in cash) at low interest rates and equivalent to about 6 per cent of Chinese annual budget outlay in these years. It consisted mainly of the construction of 141 industrial plants, accompanied by a considerable number of advisers and technicians.

The strategy was flawed, however, despite its undoubted success in broadening China's industrial basis, by a contradiction between the agricultural policy that was politically feasible and the rate of extraction of a surplus for investment on the scale required by the Five-Year Plan. Agricultural mutual-aid teams and semi-socialist co-operatives were encouraged on a large scale, but there was nothing comparable to the coercion and collectivisation which had fuelled the Soviet industrial investment drive of the 1928–32 Soviet First Five-Year Plan.

A cautious and gradualist approach to agricultural reform, part of which consisted in land redistribution, may well have been both wise and necessary in these years. It represented a continuation of the Yenan model of encouraging co-operation by the demonstration effect and did not proceed faster than the political indoctrination of the farmers. Nonetheless, there were two unacceptable consequences of this approach. One was the re-emergence of a more prosperous farmer class which put personal gain before collective progress. In the Soviet Union just such a strategy had been advocated by Bukharin as a means of raising the efficiency of agriculture by reliance on the strength of the desire for self-enrichment. On this reasoning the profit motive would propel the kulak class in the direction of more modern and rational farming methods which, in turn, would yield through taxation the surplus necessary to feed the non-farm population and pay for a widening of the industrial base. In China in the mid-1950s, as in the Soviet Union after the abandonment of the New Economic Policy in 1928, it was intolerable to pursue for any length of time a development

TABLE 8.1   The shares of major sectors in national product, 1952–70

Sector	1952	1957	1970
Agriculture	45	37	28
Industry	21	29	37
Services	34	34	35

Source: Alexander Eckstein (ed.), China Trade Prospects and United States Policy (New York: Praeger, 1971).

TABLE 8.2   Output of grain, 1950–72 (million metric tons)

1950	124·7	1960	150·0
1952	154·4	1963	183·0
1955	174·8	1964	200·0
1957	185·0	1967	230·0
1959	270·0	1970	240·0

strategy whose pace depended on the strength of the profit motive amongst members of a class that was potentially, if not openly, hostile to a socialist order. Moreover, in China the necessary surplus was not forthcoming, particularly since the planners had over-estimated the investment requirements of the enterprises in the sectors producing capital goods.[5]

Part of the transformation of the basic structure of the economy during these early years of planning is reflected in the above figures. From being by far the largest sector of origin of national product at the beginning of the period, agriculture slipped back to a position nearer parity with the expanding industrial sector and the stationary service sector.

The crux of the supply-demand problem after four years of the transition to socialism, and the unfavourable projections for the harvest of 1957, was the declining, or at best unchanged *per capita* production of food crops (i.e. grain). Population rose by 12·5 per cent between 1952 and 1957; the value of total farm output rose twice as fast; but the physical volume of grain production is estimated to have increased at roughly the same rate as population.

Open doubts about the wisdom of maintaining the original set of priorities were voiced only when the Second Five-Year Plan, 1958–62, had already been launched. Encouraged by the rapid industrial progress of the preceding period (an average increase of 14 per cent a year), the planners reaffirmed that the 'central task of the Second Five-Year Plan is still to give priority to heavy industry'. On the other hand, some impatience with slavish imitation of Soviet priorities and methods was already being expressed at the CCP Congress at the end of 1956. Certain measures of decentralisation of management and a relaxation of free marketing of certain farm products were recommended then and introduced on an increasingly broad front in 1957 and 1958. Increasing stress was also laid on the merits of small-scale production and the extravagance of over-investment in modernisation and automation of factories.

A reconsideration of the chosen development strategy became urgent. The decision was taken to break out of the rate of growth dictated by a gradual transition to socialism by proceeding at once to a thoroughgoing socialisation and collectivisation of agriculture – by making, in short, the Great Leap

Forward. This decision marked the beginning, proudly and openly avowed, of the distinctive Chinese path of development.

From February 1958 onwards a nationwide campaign swept the country with slogans calling for dramatic increases – in many cases a doubling or trebling – of the relatively high rates of growth already included in the plan. The new targets for the output of local industries were particularly high and this was one of the hallmarks of the new economic rationale. The intention was to mobilise completely the productive potential of those under-employed, seasonally or otherwise, in the agricultural sector. Through labour-intensive techniques – of making iron and steel in backyard furnaces, of coal mining, power generation, water conservation and control – a new sector of industry manned by an agro-industrial proletariat would come into being alongside capital-intensive larger scale industry. This policy was referred to as 'walking on two legs'. It meant that industrial progress would become less lop-sided as between town and country, large-scale and small-scale production, heavy industry and light industry, and between capital-intensive and labour-intensive techniques.

Agricultural organisation

The launching platforms of the Great Leap were the newly created People's Communes – a bold and lasting experiment in administrative and industrial decentralisation which also represents an original approach to agrarian socialism. Mao Tse-tung foreshadowed already in 1955 'a new upsurge in the socialist mass movement throughout our countryside'.[6] By the following year the process of consolidating the peasants mutual-aid teams (of up to ten families each), of which there were ten million, had extended to 96 per cent of all peasant families, who were grouped in 750,000 agricultural producers' co-operatives. The majority of these co-operatives, which had become the basic economic unit in the countryside, grouped together between 100 and 300 families and therefore contained whole villages. They had brought to agricultural organisation the well-known advantages of collective work in water-control and other infrastructural improvements, to the benefit of all members of the co-operative, while at the same time overcoming the uneconomic fragmentation of the land in miniscule holdings that had characterised the traditional Chinese farm landscape. The co-operatives also made it easier to concentrate surplus production and convert part into on-the-spot investment while another part went to the central state budget.[7] In the most common 'higher' form of co-operatives all land, draught animals and larger implements were held in common. Remuneration was based on a scale of 'work-points' related to the amount of work performed and how arduous or skill-intensive it was. Private plots were, however, permitted on a small scale, mainly for the cultivation of vegetables and the up-keep of pigs and poultry. The co-operatives thus had much in common with the Soviet *Kolkhozes* or collective farms.

The people's communes were much more than the mere merger, which took place in 1957–8, of the co-operatives into some 24,000 communes. 'The co-operatives were agricultural units, where the communes were multifunctional.'[8] They meant not only the absorption of the co-operatives' principles of production and distribution but also the intensification of the socialist or collective dimension of rural life. The commune became both the basic economic unit and the nucleus on which governmental control and the prism of welfare and social security services were centred. It was (and remains) largely responsible for education, health and civil defence. Within the commune, families were divided into production brigades and production teams, one or the other of which has responsibility for accounts, planning and distributing incomes. The commune itself, however, retained responsibility for the organisation of larger scale collective construction works by a system of unpaid collective labour not only in cultivation but also in water conservation and irrigation. This ability of the communes to mobilise labour on a large scale for land cultivation against non-wage payment has undoubtedly made a major contribution to the reconstruction of China's rural economy. To illustrate this in terms of the *amount* of work performed it is sufficient to compare the number of days worked on average under the old system of private ownership of the land and under the communes: in 1930, 190 work-days; in 1960, more than 250 work-days for able-bodied men and 120 for able-bodied women.[9]

Further advantages of the communes for accelerated development have been the integration under their auspices of local agricultural and industrial activity. By setting up numerous small-scale industrial and manufacturing works which provide wage-goods, the relative attractiveness of migration to the cities has been reduced and a lesser burden placed on the country's transport system.

The people's communes have been the most permanent of the innovations introduced by the Great Leap Forward. They have survived as the basic economic-administrative unit of China, regulating the work, education and political activity of over 600 million people. Their conception and functioning, together with the rural-based path of development which they represent and implement, are probably the most original features of China's road to socialism.

The economic results obtained from the Great Leap Forward matched neither the expectations of the party leadership nor the requirements and hopes of the population.[10] This was partly due to the massive reorganisation of administration, economic management and education, all of which was attempted in so short a lapse of time that some disruption of the economy was inevitable. Another cause of economic setbacks in the years 1959–61 was disastrously bad weather. The year 1960, which saw the worst harvest weather conditions for a century, was also the year when the Soviet Union ceased to provide economic or technical assistance and abruptly withdrew all its experts. Whatever the respective weight of these two factors, the excessively ambitious targets for food-grain and cotton production and various basic industrial products which had been set for 1959 were drastically scaled down. For example, the target for food-grains had been set at 525 million tons, compared with the 250 million tons produced in 1958. After two years of natural calamities the Great Leap Forward was abandoned, and a new, more cautious and gradual approach to development was inaugurated. The scales of influence between 'red' and 'expert' tipped back once more towards the latter and more balanced growth was sought between agriculture ('the foundation'), and industry ('the leading factor'). As for the pace of development, the aim was stated to be 'the building of an independent, comprehensive and modern economic system within not too long a historical period.'

The commitment to and subsequent retreat from the economic and political philosophy of the Great Leap Forward left a profound mark on China's political life and the contours of its path to development. Looking back to that experience from the vantage point of a fifteen-year perspective, and with the benefit of hindsight (particularly since the Cultural Revolution), it now appears that the Great Leap Forward mapped out the essential ambitions of the Chinese leadership, articulated by Mao Tse-tung, as it struck out on a different path of development from the one traced by the Soviet Union. These ambitions consisted in subordinating the role of the cities, the educated élite and heavy industry to the economic mobilisation, re-education and activation of the rural population. Here was the genesis of an approach to development where the rate of growth began to count for less than egalitarianism and the forging of a socialist collectivity. In Marxian terms, this meant attaching more importance to transforming the 'relations of production' than to augmenting the productive capacity of the 'forces of production'. Put differently, this philosophy represented a different combination of socialist objectives from those pursued in the countries of eastern Europe. 'Socialisation' of the economy outweighed its 'modernisation' as a goal of policy, and did not consist merely in nationalisation.[11] Egalitarianism was accorded higher priority than growth, possibly because there was not the same historical urgency that had forced the Soviet Union to opt for maximum growth *despite* the inertia of the peasants (and consumers) in the years 1928–41.[12]

When the retreat from these objectives dictated by natural calamities (the crop failures of 1959–61), excesses in decentralisation and reorganisation, and the withdrawal of Soviet assistance went further than called for by tactical considerations, the Great Proletarian Cultural Revolution (1966–9) was launched. Its threefold objective, as defined (by Mao) at a Plenary Meeting of the Central Committee in August 1966, was to be the overthrow of 'all in authority taking the capitalist road, the repudiation of bourgeois academic authorities and the ideology of the bourgeoisie, and the transformation of all parts of the "superstructure" that did not correspond to the economic base.'

What had happened in the five preceding years (1961–5) to

warrant the affirmation, implied in the above objectives, that capitalist, bourgeois and other non-socialist contradictions had reappeared in China?

It seems clear that the policy of economic retrenchment and recovery pursued during the years 1960–4 relied heavily on the reintroduction of market mechanisms and the appeal of material incentives. This course was so different from the preceding economic development strategy that it has sometimes been referred to as the New Economic Policy – by analogy with the liberalisation of policies in the Soviet Union in the 1920s, between the abandonment of War Communism (1921) and the launching of the First Five-Year Plan (1928). During these years in the Soviet Union the scope for private ownership and initiative had been enlarged and the prices of many consumers' goods and staple foodstuffs were determined by the market. At the same time a spirited public controversy took place about alternative strategies of industrialisation and their 'socialist' integrity. In China, in the early 1960s, there was a similar slackening in the tempo of the drive to socialise the economy and increased emphasis on profitability. There was a major difference, however, in the fact that the new phase of Chinese economic policy had to be introduced and defended under the highly critical eye of the Soviet Union, with which a harsh ideological dispute was taking place.

Between 1961 and 1965 China's economy was managed by a system of orderly planning under which more faith was placed in the combination of expert management, technical training and responsiveness to financial incentives as an engine of growth than in the highly decentralised, austere and party-controlled formula of earlier years. Economic profitability, technical efficiency and 'expertness' were at a premium: moral or non-material incentives, payment according to 'needs' rather than according to 'work', and ideological 'redness' were relegated to second place. The pragmatism of this new approach was summed up by Teng Hsiao-Ping, a member of the Politburo,[13] as follows: 'so long as cats, black or white, catch mice they are good cats.'

So far as the instruments of economic policy are concerned, they may be summed up as follows. In agriculture, the right to own private plots and to market their produce was restored to members of the communes. As a result, the share of private-plot production in total agricultural output rose steeply, reaching as much as half of the total in some provinces (e.g. Yenan) in 1962. At the same time the administrative planning and regulation of prices was relaxed, and limited black-markets were tolerated in the cities. Within the communes there was a decentralisation of planning, accounting and distribution to the level of the production brigade (corresponding often in size to the earlier collectives and co-operatives). None the less, the basic structure and administrative role of the communes were preserved. In industry, similarly, the decentralisation of control during the Great Leap Forward was maintained. The following figures show the change in the percentage of industry subordinated to central control:

	1957	1958	1959
Central control	46	27	26
Local control	54	73	74

At the same time, the priority in industrial investment allocations shifted away from producers' goods to the consumers' goods sector, and agriculture also received a larger share. Within industrial enterprises take-home pay became increasingly differentiated on account of the number of bonuses (for innovation, for over-fulfilment of the plan, for savings of materials, for length of service, etc.) and piece-rates which were introduced. Profitability, rather than the volume of output, became the most widely applied test of a factory's performance. This implied a responsiveness to prices and market forces which has led some observers to suggest that during these years China was in substance, if not in form, closer to Yugoslavia's pattern of 'market socialism' than the sharp Chinese criticism at that time of Yugoslavia's 'revisionism' would suggest.

The economic record of these years, 1961–5, was satisfactory in quantitative terms: investment and production recovered and record levels were attained. Not all the economic progress of these years can be attributed to the new economic policy. Much of the gains was the fruit of the investment and educational effort of the 1950s. But if the economic record was statistically satisfactory, there was nevertheless a deep undercurrent of doubt in party circles about the scope these policies afforded for the 'spontaneous tendency to capitalism'. In short, one section of the party, led by Mao Tse-tung, feared that the distinctive Chinese vision of the constant regeneration of revolutionary socialism was being sacrificed to neo-capitalist technocratic efficiency. It was decided to launch a campaign to prevent the reappearance of a 'bourgeois' mentality in the party, the administration, the economy, and in education: the Great Proletarian Cultural Revolution was launched in November 1965 and continued until mid-1969.

As just indicated, its primary objective was more ideo-logical–political than strictly economic. The reduction and 'purification' (rather than purge) of the bureaucracy, and the reaffirmation of the value of moral rather than material incentives to higher productivity ranked high amongst its aims. Moreover, the sweeping changes in outlook and organisation that it sought to achieve and the intense political activism which accompanied it inevitably resulted in a certain disruption of current production, which was reflected in a temporary decline in some branches of industrial output and foreign trade.

In drawing up a balance-sheet of the economic consequences of the Cultural Revolution it is easy to exaggerate its disruptive effects on production. In fact, agricultural output was virtually unscathed. Some industrial production was lost on account of the switch-over to management by revolutionary committees and new principles, as well as on account of the time lost in political meetings. None the less, determined attempts were made to limit the extent of the setback to production, even when the Cultural Revolution was at its height in 1967, by the issuing to all factories of directives for 'grasping the resolution and stimulating production' or 'persisting in the eight-hour workday'. Defence industries, financial institutions and economic planning agencies were safeguarded by being declared out-of-bounds to even Red Guard intruders.

In addition to the ideological regeneration which was its chief purpose, the Cultural Revolution produced a number of changes in the methods and principles of managing the development of the economy whose effect may be long-lived. Three of these may be singled out. Foremost, there was the reinforcement of workers' participation in management, and the simultaneous 'rectification' of the administrative, managerial and technocratic bureaucracy by the establishment of revolutionary committees as the principal organs of management.[14] Second, there was the reaffirmation of egalitarianism and a spirit of austerity by means of the abolition of material incentives. Third, self-reliance and innovation at the factory bench were encouraged. The economic results of these changes are difficult to capture statistically.

PLANNING: CHOICE OF STRATEGIES, PROCEDURES AND INSTRUMENTS

The economic progress of China owes more to the drive and determination of its political leadership, and to the utilisation of popular support for its economic aims, than it owes to the techniques of planning as a means of managing the economy. Planning has none the less done much to translate socialist economic principles into the realities of adequate supplies of food and clothing and the creation of a broader industrial base. Chinese economic planning differs in many respects from that of other socialist or developing countries, and this increases its interest in the context of a comparison of development paths. Its salient features are considered below.

As in other socialist countries where market forces are allowed only very limited scope in influencing the allocation of resources, China has a whole constellation of plans. Besides the national five-year plans for the development of the economy (the fourth of which covers the years 1971–5), there are plans for each province and industrial sector, for each commune and municipality, and for each factory. There are also plans for various time-horizons – the five-year plans being as a rule much less inspirative or mandatory, and much less detailed, than the highly operational annual plans. It is not very clear how consistency and coherence were obtained amongst, say, provincial and sectoral plans. It appears, however, that it is more accurate to regard them as a 'constellation' of plans rather than a hierarchy where the values and targets of one are subordinated to those of another. For example, as far as is known, the Fourth Five-Year Plan consists essentially of a summary statistical image of the year 1975, accompanied by indicative growth targets for the principal sectors of the economy. When the provinces or ministries draw up their annual plan targets they are not obliged to respect those of the medium-term plan.

There can be little doubt that the provincial plans, drawn up by provincial planning bureaux, are the cornerstones of Chinese planning. This is scarcely surprising, when it is remembered that most of the provinces outnumber in population all but the very largest European states. Planning on the larger scale of the national economy as a whole tends to be confined to a number of key indications for broad sectors and to the preparation of more detailed targets only for major enterprises which are administered from the centre. The scale of the country, the weakness of the transport infrastructure, and the vast amount of time and effort that would have to be invested in achieving a detailed and coherent national plan established at the centre, all make for decentralisation.

The provincial planning bureaux draw up in early summer of each year forecasts for the next year of the value and volume of final output, of exportation inputs from other provinces, of the origin of production by branches of the economy. These forecasts or 'shadow targets' are submitted around September to the National Planning Commission which scrutinises and revises or confirms them by reference to the global preparations of the national development strategy and the draft plans submitted at the same time by the central ministries. The penultimate stages of this 'dialogue' of planning are a national 'plan conciliation' conference held in November, when representatives of the Planning Commission, the provincial planning bureaux and the ministries negotiate together the detailed annual plan targets. These are then transmitted to the basic production units in the communes and factories for possible revision (apparently only upward revisions) and discussion of the most economical means of their achievement.

The bases on which the salient targets are set have not been described in any detail.[15] It appears that target-setting at the provincial level proceeds by reference to six key growth-ratios. These ratios, whose values (which are not made public) are determined by the National Planning Commission, are differentiated from province to province. The following ratios relate to development priorities:

i   Growth rate of agriculture: growth rate of industry
(The value of this ratio for the economy as a whole was
said to be 1:4 in 1973. It is obviously a key ratio for the
balanced growth of the two sectors.)

ii Heavy industry: light industry
(This ratio would be expected to reflect the 'law of the
planned, proportionate development of the economy'
encountered in the planning textbooks of the socialist
countries of eastern Europe according to which a constant planned priority is given in the 'take-off' years of
socialist economic development to the production of the
means of production, i.e. the output of investment
goods. The national value of this ratio was reported to
be only 1:1 in 1973, in marked contrast with the ratio of
nearer 2:1 of the Soviet Union at a comparable stage of
industrial development.)

iii Construction of the economic base of socialism: needs of
the population
(This is the ratio relating productive investment to
household consumption and hence determines the rate
of savings. Its national value in 1973 was said to be 1:7.)

The second set of three ratios related to the 'consist-
ency-checking' within these to the target-setting requirements
of planning. They are:

iv Accumulation: consumption
(This ratio reflects both the scale of the provincial
investment effort and of the level of inventories held by
the province, which is particularly important for bread
grains.)

v   Increase in output: increase in employment
(This ratio reflects the labour-intensity of the technology embodied in new investment, as well as target
gains in labour productivity.)

vi Disposable income (or purchasing power): consumers'
goods

Besides these highly aggregated and straightforward ratios,
the planning system also makes use of more sophisticated
accounting and programming techniques, including input–
output tables and linear programming. Some of these technical

procedures of planning came under criticism during the Cultural Revolution as part and parcel of the technocratic 'economism' which was held to be out of touch with the needs of the people. During these years the National Planning Commission ceased to function.

Two final questions may be raised about Chinese planning experience. The first is the status of 'maximal growth' as a policy objective. The second is the use of prices and market forces as an instrument of or supplement to administrative planning by directives. As regards the growth objective, Chinese economists like to quote Mao Tse-tung: 'The objectives of the planned socialist economy are – quantity, quality, rapidity and economic efficiency in the use of resources.' In planning terms, these four goals can be represented by quantity indicators (e.g. national accounts), quality indicators (indices of technical progress), rapidity indicators (time necessary for construction or manufacture) and economic efficiency indicators (cost-reduction indices). The Chinese regard planning as being an instrument for adjudicating between these indicators when they are incompatible. In the short term, for instance, priority may well be given to quantity and rapidity as compared with economic efficiency and quality.

To some extent, the results of this policy are apparent in the range of consumer goods available to the population. Most visitors to China are struck by the uniformity of clothing, for instance, and the rather narrow assortment of consumer goods available in the shops within the communes. On the other hand, such a policy makes sense in terms of concentration of effort on essential tasks such as the provision of basic necessities in adequate quantity and of acceptable quality rather than the proliferation of non-essential consumer gadgets and household appliances. Austerity, in short, is visible but not excessive in relation to previous standards of consumption.

Planning policy as regards the volume and assortment of consumer goods appears to be more closely attuned to changing requirements, and to make greater use of market research, than in some other planned economies.

CAN OTHER DEVELOPING COUNTRIES LEARN FROM CHINA?
The Chinese have always regarded their civilisation as being unique. It is certainly true that theirs is the only great indepen-

dent civilisation of antiquity – with a continuous written record stretching back over 3000 years – to have survived into the contemporary world. In large measure this uniqueness has been due to China's traditional isolation and limited contact and exchanges with the outside world. For the past two decades China has engaged in a historically unprecedented drive to reshape the material and ideological conditions of progress of the largest population of any country of the globe. The sheer scale of this endeavour is unique. No other government has ever been in a position to attempt to mobilise and modernise the resources, and convictions, of over 750 million inhabitants. Imagination, inventiveness and a willingness to experiment have had to be brought to this task, for there were no adequate historical precedents from which to trace the Chinese path of development.

True, the experience of other socialist countries was available and has served as a blueprint from which lessons were drawn and later adapted or rejected. But, in retrospect, it seems clear that the Soviet model was not tailor-made for Chinese circumstances and could only have been transplanted successfully to China if the Chinese leadership had been prepared to accept a quite different conception of the type of socialist society they wanted. For one thing, the Soviet model has evolved in a country where the ratio of resources to population was (and remains) much more favourable than in China, and where the urban proletariat, not the peasantry as in China, had won the revolutionary struggle. For another, the Soviet model relied on highly centralised administrative planning, attached unequivocal priority to heavy industry, and made extensive use of material incentives and income disparities to raise productivity. In short, the different scale and nature of the development problem in China, and the different set of socialist values which has guided China's leadership, almost inevitably led to its differentiation from earlier models. These factors also account (in part) for the uniqueness of the development path which it has hewed for itself during the long years of imposed isolation as a 'socialist developing country'.[16]

The two questions of burning interest to many developing countries throughout the world, and not least in Africa, are, first, has the Chinese path to development succeeded, and, second, what elements of the Chinese experience can be incorporated in the development policies of developing countries elsewhere?

The answer to the first question has already been sketched earlier. China is still materially a relatively poor country, where the austerity of day-to-day life is an inescapable necessity. But it is a country which has broken out of the shackles of backwardness: famine, squalor, illiteracy, endemic disease and corruption have all been virtually banished. Of course, that is only the beginning of the task of removing the mountainous inheritance of economic under-development.[17] However, the very fact that so much has been accomplished in creating these preconditions for economic growth and diversification, while at the same time achieving virtual self-sufficiency in foodstuffs, amply justifies the conclusion that the Chinese path to development is proving successful. It is important to add that this success is more *real* than merely statistical because it has included achievements such as equality of income distribution or the social emancipation of women, which are not reflected in conventional indicators of economic performance such as the growth of GNP.

In the light of the evidence presented in this book, the answer to the second question – can other developing countries learn from China? – would also appear to be affirmative, although it is, of course, for the reader to judge by reference to those developing countries which he knows most intimately. It would be an exaggeration to claim that the Chinese prototype of development could simply be shipped, lock, stock and barrel, to any given African country with a guarantee of successful results in different conditions. The Chinese themselves would be the last to claim so much, for – as pointed out above – they have had their own keen disappointment with the introduction of a virtually unadapted foreign development model during the 1950s. Moreover, stress has been laid earlier on the 'uniqueness' of this Chinese path, which certainly owes some of its characteristics – for example, the collective approach to work and welfare, particularly health – which characterises the people's communes – to peculiarly Chinese traditions. Already in the nineteenth century, when China – confronted with Western military technology – had to decide what to accept and what to attempt to reject, an important school of thought advocated importing 'Western tools' of modernisation, while preserving the 'Chinese essence'. In considering the relevance of Chinese experience for the development problem in African countries, it is therefore essential to bear in mind degrees of similarity and difference, not only in particular problems – such as export dependence on a narrow range of products, as in the case of Zambia – but also in the resources and institutions available for tackling them.

Some of these differences are so important that they should be recalled here. First, and most obviously, there is the matter of scale. China is the third largest country in the world after the Soviet Union and Canada, and with an area of 3·6 million square miles is roughly the same size as the United States. The problems of administration, transport and communications are consequently radically different from those of, say, Tanzania, or even Nigeria. The massive scale of the territory and of the population of China have implications – advantages and disadvantages – both for its internal economic policy and for its external economic relations. In common with other very large countries, for example, only a rather small proportion of China's national output passes through the foreign trade sector. Nor does it permit foreign investment. Far from receiving any foreign aid, it provides assistance to many developing countries. So far as technology is concerned, the size of the domestic market is such that the establishment of even the largest plants can be justified simply to supply domestic demand, whereas many of the other developing countries considered in this book would not be able to cross the 'threshold' of the minimum scale of economic operation if they relied on the national market alone. The sheer size of China also means that its agriculture stretches from temperate to sub-tropical zones and permits a greater diversity of crop production (though more vulnerable to devastating flooding and drought than many other developing countries). To take a more technical perspective, the sectoral origin of gross national product and the transformation it has undergone, also differentiate China from many other developing countries.

Examples could be multiplied of physical and historical factors which differentiate China from African developing countries and which may affect the 'transferability' of elements of the Chinese development model. It is a wise precaution to bear such differences in mind in drawing comparisons and conclusions. Conversely, it would be unjustified to insist too much on these differences. In a great many vitally important respects – low average incomes, an under-developed modern industrial sector, demographic pressures, an inheritance of social and economic immobility and colonial pre-emption of trade structures and policies – China has had to grapple with the same problems.

The salient features or key elements of the Chinese development path are summarised in ten points below. Each of them has made its contribution to the accomplishments described above. Together, they make up a mutually reinforcing set of policies and priorities. While most of them, as argued above, might have to be adapted in some ways if introduced into the development paths of other countries, it is doubtful if a successful transplant could be achieved if some parts (e.g. the easiest, or those with the widest immediate political or popular appeal) were to be selected and the others rejected. An integrated approach seems indispensable. The ten key elements are listed below, not necessarily by order of importance, and briefly commented on in the following paragraphs.

1 Mass mobilisation of resources and a sense of moral purpose for development.
2 Egalitarianism in opportunities, income distribution and social emancipation.
3 Agriculture as the base, and industry as the leading factor in development.
4 A balanced economic partnership of town and village.
5 The encouragement of intermediate technology.
6 Population policy; control and redistribution.
7 Controlled urbanisation.
8 Flexible, decentralised planning and self-reliance.
9 'Grass roots' participation in economic decision-making.
10 Pragmatism in policies for education and health.

The bare listing of the 'strengths' of China's development path is not meant to convey the impression that there have been no pitfalls and no false turnings. There have, indeed, been several. More important and impressive, however, has been the readiness on the part of the leadership to change course and abandon potentially sterile directions of development – such as bureaucratic planning procedures, or unqualified priority to heavy industry – before they become entrenched dogma. In general, despite the highly ideological (and often personalised) way in which development options and issues have been presented in China, an underlying pragmatism, at once flexible and experimental, has prevailed.

Mass mobilisation of resources: the sense of moral purpose
No very complicated accounting is needed to demonstrate that the existence of unemployed and under-employed resources, whether of manpower or of land or of other natural resources, means a loss of potential production and welfare. The creation of opportunities for useful employment on a scale that will harness the potential of the unemployed is therefore a paramount task in any development strategy. One of the first accomplishments of the Chinese leadership during the early postwar year of reconstruction was to sweep away the privileged idleness of the numerous landlord, merchant and bureaucratic classes and to create new employment by the drive to increase output on the farms and in the factories, and by large-scale public construction schemes. As the experience of other countries has shown, however, the mere abolition of open unemployment and waste is not enough in itself to achieve and sustain a development momentum. A strong sense of collective purpose, and a guarantee of distributive justice, is a prerequisite. Otherwise, in the absence of coercion and the profit motive, there will be a tendency to view the State as a remote tax-farming agency in opposition to the interests of the workers. In China, overcoming this attitude was a major problem. As a result of centuries of tax-exploitation by landlords and their frequently corrupt officialdom, the peasant masses deeply mistrusted the exactions of the State and many had become prone, from dire economic necessity, to deep-seated personal acquisitiveness.

To sum up, mass mobilisation of resources has been achieved on a scale necessary to obtain an investible surplus from agriculture by a combination of policies. It is unlikely that the great flood-control schemes of the Yellow River basin, or the Nanking bridge over the Yangtze, or the countless land-melioration transport or neighbourhood industrial works could have been accomplished if exclusive reliance had been placed on any one element of the policy mix. The main lines of policy were as follows: (1) an intensive campaign of political and ideological education or re-education (and inculcation of a spirit of development as a patriotic duty and challenge);[18] (2) egalitarianism in income distribution. In combination, these policies demonstrated that even unskilled labour, if well organised and supplied with able leadership, can achieve great increases in output and transform the material conditions of agricultural work if, at the same time, an assurance is provided that the economic benefits of such work will be distributed equitably. Hence, the next element of policy has consisted in (3) the decentralisation of a large proportion (up to 40 per cent) of national investment to the local level (commune, production team, or – in towns – municipal and neighbourhood committees). The final element has been (4) the activation of periods of the year or groups of the population not previously employed. This has been achieved by such means as concentrating agricultural infrastructural and terracing works, etc. during the quiet season and by channelling certain types of light work towards older age groups. In this connection, the social emancipation of women and the practical bias of education have also made a major contribution.

Egalitarianism in income distribution and social opportunities
A distinctive feature of contemporary Chinese society, and one that makes a profound impression on every visitor, is the policy of reducing visible differences in standards of living as between different groups of the population. Similarly, indeed, virtual uniformity of clothing is the symbol of this egalitarian approach, which is reflected in policies of income distribution, the social emancipation of women and equality of educational and career opportunities. So far as incomes are concerned, the wage scale in the manufacturing industry is concentrated in a narrow range (between 50 and 120 yuan per month in 1972) with gradations by degrees of skill and seniority. Even the manager of a large enterprise (e.g. the engineering works employing over

5000 workers visited by the author in Sian in late 1972) will, at most, earn only twice the average wage in his plant. Accordingly, his life-style – type of accommodation, transport, clothing, personal possessions – will not differ markedly from that of his fellow workers. The abandonment of time- and piece-rates and other material incentives during the Cultural Revolution narrowed further the possibility of differentiation of earnings in industry, as material incentives to increased personal effort were replaced by moral incentives – in other words, a work ethic which relates additional effort and successful innovation to the satisfaction of participating in the socialist reconstruction of China.

In agriculture remuneration is more directly tied to actual output (results) than in industry. This is inevitably so, inasmuch as the amount of surplus crops or cash available for distribution to members of the production teams of the people's communes, after payment of taxes and provision for investment and reserves, is linked to the volume and value actually produced by a system of work-points which depend on the type and amount of work performed. This can result in differentiation between production teams on the same commune, and to still wider differences between communes located in more or less prosperous farming regions. In addition, by marketing the produce of their private plots, the peasants have an opportunity to increase their income which is not available to factory workers. It is very likely that this ostensible departure, though small, from the principle of equality of income distribution is deliberate government policy to reduce the town–countryside differential which had widened during the years leading up to the Cultural Revolution. At one point the rate of the average factory worker's earnings to those of a commune member was more than 2:1, thereby acting as an inducement to farmers to migrate to the towns. This ran counter to the more general policy of achieving a reverse migratory flow. On the other hand, the more attractive prices available for the produce of their private plots has acted as an incentive to peasants to raise their output and thereby contribute to the improved supply of foodstuffs to the towns. In short, the general policy of equitable income distribution has been observed as between town and country, as well as between skills within each sector.

Departures from this general line have usually been occasioned by the pursuit of other policy aims such as mentioned above.

Reliance on moral rather than material incentives to higher output and productivity distinguishes the Chinese path of development from that of other socialist countries. The successful continuation of this policy depends greatly on the degree of conviction on the part of the population that it is both just and necessary. That, in turn, depends on maintenance of a revolutionary *élan* by means of the mass mobilisation and sense of moral purpose in development considered earlier.

Agriculture the base: industry the leading factor

There is a delphic quality about the distinction between agriculture as 'the base' and industry as the 'leading factor'. It is easy to dismiss it as a tautology, or to read too much into it. In common with many other slogans current in China, however, its purpose is to epitomise the party line, the gist of which is conveyed in a few words that can be readily assimilated and memorised by the broad mass of the population. The slogan in fact adequately reflects the balance of the policy that has been pursued since the post-1958 departure from the Soviet model. Agriculture is treated as the supply basis not only for foodstuffs but also for many industrial raw materials. The surplus generated in agriculture is ploughed back in part into the auxiliary industries of commerce and it also fuels material investment. Agricultural organisation, too, is the basis of the economic management of the country, through which 80 per cent of the Chinese people experience and participate in the development of agrarian socialism. The role of industry is that of a leading factor because it is the source of technological advance – some of which flows towards agriculture to raise its productivity. Industry is also less vulnerable to the vagaries of nature and is therefore better able to sustain a high rate of growth of output. As a result, agriculture still employs some 80 per cent of the working-age population, but produces only one-third of the value of national production.

Town and village in economic partnership

This partnership takes two main forms. So far as the towns are concerned, the policy is to encourage the modern sector to be geared to the requirements of the villages. Thus, industry is supposed to be turned to face the villages by producing largely for the villages' requirements agricultural machinery and implements, pumping equipment, chemical fertilisers and pesticides, etc. At the same time it is hoped that the villages will become technology-conscious within this partnership and, as their income rises, devote increasing resources to acquiring modern capital equipment. (The educational system, as pointed out below, helps to cement these ties by including agricultural work as a regular part of the practical curriculum of town schools, and, correspondingly, technical-industrial classes in village schools.) The second form of the partnership worth noting is the close linkage in retail trade between suburban communes and the complete supply of foodstuffs to their nearest towns, on a district-by-district contract basis.

Intermediate technology
Part of the policy of industrial progress by 'walking on two legs' consists in favouring the widespread utilisation of labour-intensive techniques of manufacturing. It has already been noted that the abundant labour power available is employed in labour-intensive farming, construction work and transport. In these sectors this policy makes sound sense, for otherwise the capital- and skill-intensive techniques used in advanced industrial countries would have a labour-displacement effect, creating unemployment and a migratory drive of the jobless to the towns in search of work. Industry is another matter. There are fewer techniques available which are both labour-intensive and efficient means of production. Hence, there is great scope for innovation at the workshop level within factories. Many examples could be given of how factories have themselves developed techniques of using spare materials or existing equipment to produce new tools and by-products within their existing allocation of materials and investment funds. In the people's communes the new brigade workshops serve as a kind of permanent 'technical school' through which the villages are encouraged to experiment with the nuts and bolts of technological progress. This kind of self-reliance can lead to duplication of effort and innovative drive, but it also reduces the strain on the transport

system and kindles and encourages the inventiveness of the workers.

Population policy: control and redistribution
China's population problem is bigger than that of any other country. It grows at a rate which is the equivalent of adding the entire population of Great Britain every three years because its absolute size (now probably over 800 million) means that even a low rate of growth still means the addition each year of a great many mouths to feed. Official policy towards limiting demographic pressure has varied over time – swinging towards and away from family planning during the past two decades. Indeed, a certain ambivalence of approach to the question seems to persist, even though the government has for some years actively encouraged smaller families. For example, it is often pointed out that each new birth is 'not only a new mouth to feed but also two new hands that can in time add to production.'

Prime Minister Chou En-lai has told visitors that the rate of population increase in the 1960s had been brought down to 2 per cent a year – which would be a rate distinctly lower than most other developing countries have been able to achieve. This reported success is the more remarkable when it is remembered that improved health care and reduced infant mortality have greatly increased the proportion of young people in the population – and therefore potential fertility. What means have been used to limit population growth? This is another sector where the Chinese government has given proof of originality. Since the early 1960s there has been a campaign for postponing marriage until the age of at least 25 for men and 23 for women. In demographic terms late marriage can result in a very large drop in fertility rates. At the same time there has been a nationwide campaign advocating that young couples should limit their family size to two children. Neither of these campaigns of persuasion could have been effective if the masses were not imbued with a spirit of collective, patriotic self-sacrifice akin to the acceptance of the austere way of life that is also unique to contemporary China. One traditional feature of Chinese society which has made it easier for this policy to succeed than might be the case in other developing countries is the deep-seated tendency to subordinate individualist preferences to conformity with the standards of belief and behaviour acceptable to the collectivity – be it productive team, street committee or university cell. None the less, it is no mean task to achieve population control by persuasion and the pressure to conform, particularly in the villages. Contraceptive advice and assistance is accordingly provided at all levels of society, notably by the clinics in the communes and even by the 'barefoot doctors' in remote villages.

A final aspect of population control which differentiates China from other developing countries (but less from the socialist countries of eastern Europe) has been the ability of the government to relocate large cohorts of the population (particularly young people) by transferring them to the underdeveloped provinces of the interior. For example, Heilungkiang province in the far north-east doubled its population from 11 million in the 1950s to 21 million at the end of the Cultural Revolution. At least half of that increase must be due to deliberate encouragement or direction of migration. Mobility as between the villages and the towns is also very carefully regulated and an attempt has been made to reverse the natural pressure of urbanisation by actually assigning large numbers of young people from very large cities like Shanghai (probably the largest city in the world) to a number of years of work in underpopulated agricultural regions. Occupational mobility is also closely regulated.

CONTROLLED URBANISATION
China's revolution was a peasant revolution and part of Maoist political-social philosophy has been to insist that the towns should serve the villages instead of being the dominant partner as a result of the equation of industrialisation and urbanisation. Hence the attempt to create the balanced economic partnership of towns and villages (or communes) referred to above. One prerequisite is to remove the conditions under which there will be a spontaneous drift of distressed rural populations from the neglected hinterland to the towns. As was seen, this can be done by narrowing the income differential between the two, thereby removing one incentive to urbanisation. The provision, often by small-scale industry located in the communes, of an

adequate supply of wage-goods (consumers' manufactured goods) removes another inducement. The policy of relocating industry and decentralising economic management is in the same direction. It is not possible, however, to control the pace of urbanisation solely by economic levers. Consequently, the general powers vested in manpower policy to direct the mobility of labour after the conclusion of middle schooling are also used to limit the growth of towns and even to reduce the size of some of them, as already mentioned. In particular, young people are directed often to spend the early part of their working career in regions far from their birthplace. This policy has resulted in a degree of labour mobility quite unknown previously in Chinese history, when the only exception to general immobility was a gradual and undirected drift from north to south, and towards the cities of the coastal provinces.

Decentralised planning and self-reliance
Decentralisation and self-reliance are two sides of the same coin. The purpose of both is to encourage local economic initiative by making recourse to the 'centre' for additional resources more an expedient than a regular practice. If a factory, or a commune, or a municipality, or a province turns first to the next higher level in the planning hierarchy with the question, what new resources or equipment can we expect you to provide? there is little chance that local inventiveness will be brought fully into play in raising production. Of course, in a country of the scale of China there are also good practical reasons for not overburdening either the administrative or the transport system by centralising too many allocational decisions.

From 1957 onwards decentralisation and increased self-reliance right down to the level of innovation in factory workshops, has proceeded in stages. In that year 80 per cent of the previously State-controlled enterprises were transferred to the control of the provinces. In practice, this meant that the central government retained control over the producer-goods heavy industries while the light, consumer-goods industries were transferred to the authority of the provinces. A flood-tide of decentralisation and local initiative was moving during the Great Leap Forward; it ebbed towards the centre in the years

1959–65, when the national motto became 'all the country is a single chessboard' and emphasis was placed on 'expertness' rather than 'redness' as credentials for economic decision-making. The tide of decentralisation was again in full flood during the Cultural Revolution to such an extent that it appeared possible that the remaining moorings of central control would snap. Since then a better balance between local initiative and central control seems to have been restored.

Pragmatism in education and health
The enormous size of China's population multiplied the prevalence of illiteracy and disease at the time when the proclamation of the People's Republic confronted the revolutionary government with a daunting challenge. To sustain the Revolution, the political education of the masses and the creation of a 'social mentality' was essential. At the same time, the industrial progress of the economy could only proceed rapidly if engineering, scientific and technical training was provided quickly, efficiently and on a large scale. From the outset, therefore, there was a latent contradiction between the political and economic objectives of education which was bound to be reflected in both the content of education and in the structure of the educational system. In fact, this tension or competition between conflicting educational goals has been accompanied by a parallel tension dictated by the educational needs and *traditions* of the towns, on the one hand, and the villages on the other. These parallel contradictions were already present, and their nature recognised, during the revolutionary years 1937–45 when different approaches were given a trial in the liberated provinces around Yenan. The imperatives of party control and industrial progress seemed to call for a certain élitism and insistence, by means of stringent entrance requirements and periodic examinations, on the capacity to assimilate theoretical knowledge. On the other hand, the revolutionary need to remould traditional attitudes into a socialist consciousness, and to activate and train the rural masses of the population, militated against the view that the city-based intellectual élite should play the dominant role in re-educating the new China.

In short, the control of China's education, and the system through which it has been administered, have frequently changed during the past two decades *pari passu* with changing development strategies and the intensification or relaxation of ideological and rectification campaigns.

Thus, in the early years of economic planning, the educational system closely resembled that of the Soviet Union and made very extensive use of Soviet instructors in teacher-training schools as well as of Soviet textbooks. Then, in 1957 just before the Great Leap Forward, the campaign of the Hundred Flowers represented a reaction against the over-politicisation of education and its over-emphasis on specialisation. The Great Leap Forward marked a radical new departure in that it decentralised the control of education and instituted part-work, part-study schools in the countryside, under local control, whose aim was to reduce the costs of education both to the State and to the students while at the same time placing emphasis on the practical orientation of education and attempting to break down the traditional scorn of intellectuals for manual labour. This approach, which was not actively pursued during the early 1960s, was reaffirmed during the Cultural Revolution. Indeed, one of the main reasons officially advanced for the Great Proletarian Cultural Revolution was the need to destroy the re-emergent élitist and intellectual-aristocrat distortion of education that was said to have taken place during 'the bitter years' 1959–61, and the subsequent period of retrenchment.

Notes

CHAPTER ONE

1 *The Wealth of Nations*, bk. I, ch. VIII (1776; Everyman ed., 1910, p. 72).

2 Ibid., bk. IV, ch. II, pp. 400–1.

3 Ibid., bk. I, ch. IX, pp. 84–5.

4 Gunnar Myrdal, *Asian Drama, an Inquiry into the Poverty of Nations* (New York: Pantheon Books, 1968) p. 8.

5 The economic literature on growth is reviewed by F. H. Hahn and R. C. O. Matthews in American Economic Association and Royal Economic Society, *Surveys of Economic Theory*, vol. II, *Growth and Development* (London: Macmillan; New York: St Martin's Press, 1965). Other surveys are in Walter Elkan, *Development Economics* (Harmondsworth: Penguin, 1973) chs 4 and 5; H. Myint, *The Economics of Developing Countries*, 3rd ed. (London: Hutchinson, 1967); S. K. Nath, 'Balanced Growth' in I. Livingstone, *Economic Policy for Development* (Harmondsworth: Penguin, 1971).

6 Myrdal, *Asian Drama*, pp. 19–20.

7 Colin Leys and Peter Marris, 'Planning and Development', in Dudley Seers and Leonard Joy, *Development in a Divided World* (Harmondsworth: Penguin, 1971) p. 273.

8 Pearson, Lester, *Partners in Development: Report of the Commission on International Development* (London: Pall Mall Press, 1969) p. 358.

9 Hans Günter explores the philosophical implications of this change in 'Social Policy and the Post-Industrial Society', *International Institute for Labour Studies*, bulletin no. 10 (1972).

10 See David A. Morse, 'The World Employment Programme', *International Labour Review*, vol. 97, no. 6 (June 1968).

11 'New Approaches Suggested by the Colombia Employment Programme', *International Labour Review*, vol. 102, no. 4 (Oct 1970) 13–14.

12 *Matching Employment Opportunities and Expectations: a Programme of Action for Ceylon* (Geneva: ILO, 1971).

13 *Employment, Incomes and Equality, a Strategy for Increasing Productive Employment in Kenya* (Geneva: ILO, 1972). For an assessment of the achievements of the reports and the problems that they revealed see *Strategies for Employment Promotion, an Evaluation of Four Inter-Agency Employment Missions* (Geneva: ILO, 1973).

14 See the list of team members, ILO, *Employment, Incomes and Equality*, pp. xiii–xvi.

15 Chapter 4, p. 80.

16 See Chapter 7, p. 154.

17 Below, p. 87.
18 Below, p. 139.
19 Below, pp. 140–1.

CHAPTER TWO

1 *Freedom and Socialism (Uhuru na Ujamaa)* (Oxford: Oxford University Press, 1968) p. 303.

2 J. A. Hobson, *Imperialism* (London: Allen and Unwin, 1902); V. I. Lenin, *Imperialism* (Moscow: Foreign Languages Publishing House, 1951).

3 One of the popular European apologia for the slave trade was that since Africa was not Christian, all its inhabitants were predestined to eternal damnation, from which their transportation to America and conversion to Christianity could save them. It is only in the last half-century that the riches of African culture have been revealed to the Western eye. See e.g. Basil Davidson, *The Growth of African Civilisation, East and Central Africa to the Late Nineteenth Century* (London: Longman, 1967).

4 See Gideon S. Were, 'The Western Bantu Peoples from A. D. 1300 to 1800', in B. A. Ogot and J. A. Kieran, *Zamani, a Survey of East African History* (Dar es Salaam: East African Publishing House and Longmans, 1968).

5 See John Iliffe, 'Tanzania Under German and British Rule', in Ogot and Kieran, op. cit.

6 See e.g. A. G. Frank, *Capitalism and Underdevelopment in Latin America* (New York: Modern Reader Paperbacks, 1967).

7 *Comparative Development Strategies in East Africa* (Nairobi: East African Publishing House, 1972) p. 5.

8 See Ogot and Kieran, op. cit., p. 295.

9 William H. Friedland, *Vuta Kamba: the Development of Trade Unions in Tanganyika* (Stanford: Hoover Institution Press, 1969) p. 20.

10 E. A. Statistical Department, Tanganyika Unit, *Statistical Abstract*, 1960.

11 Friedland, *Vuta Kamba*, pp. 14–15.

12 Since 1965, TANU candidates have stood against each other in each constituency so that the general electorate has been able to exercise a choice at the polls, a factor that must no doubt encourage members of parliament to try to serve their constituents well.

13 See *Statistical Abstract*, 1965, p. 22.

14 See the *Report of the East African Royal Commission* (1955) and the *Report on Methods of Determining Wages in Tanganyika* (the Jack Report) (1959).

15 The Board was appointed in August 1961, in terms of the Regulation of Wages and Terms of Employment Ordinance, with D. P. Chesworth as Chairman and Michael Kamaliza, subsequently Minister of Labour and General Secretary of the National Union of Tanganyika Workers, as one of the members.

16 There were twenty East African shillings to a £ sterling in those days; now there are seventeen.

17 In 'Statutory Minimum Wage Fixing in Tanganyika', *International Labour Review*, vol. 96, no. 1 (July 1967) 3.

18 See ILO, *Year Book of Labour Statistics*, 1966 and 1968.

19 *A General Theory of Trade Union Development: Some Lessons from Tanzania*, University of Dar es Salaam, Economic Research Bureau paper 27.3 (July 1972).

20 Tanzania, Ministry of Information, *Report of the Presidential Commission on the National Union of Tanganyika Workers* (Dar es Salaam: Government Printer, 1967); and *Proposals of the Tanzania Government on the Recommendations of the Presidential Commission of Enquiry into the National Union of Tanganyika Workers (N. U. T. A.)*, Government Paper no. 2 – 1967, (Dar es Salaam: Government Printer, 1967).

21 Though it is subdivided into nine industrial divisions, each with a fair degree of autonomy.

22 The United Republic of Tanzania, *Background to the Budget, 1968–69* (Dar es Salaam: Government Printer, 1968) table 62, p. 81.

23 Ibid., p. 18.

24 A similar situation was created in Britain by the establishment of the Department of Economic Affairs by the Labour Government that was returned to power in 1964. Their Economic Plan was abandoned almost as soon as it was made. The Department was in due course dissolved and the Treasury returned to its undisturbed rule.

25 So called because it was in Arusha that the TANU meeting was held from which the declaration was made.

26 See Nyerere, *Freedom and Socialism*, pp. 231–50.

27 The Goans, distinguished by their Portuguese names and Catholic religion, and Jesuit education, had played a key role as administrators and managers.

28 United Republic of Tanzania, *Tanzania Second Five-Year Plan for Economic and Social Development, 1st July 1969 – 30th June 1974* (Dar es Salaam: Government Printer, 1969) vol. i: General Analysis, pp. viii ff.

29 Discussed below, pp. 24–9.

30 *Tanzania Second Five-Year Plan*, op. cit., p. xvi.

31 The United Republic of Tanzania, *The Annual Plan for 1972/73* (Dar es Salaam: Government Printer, 1972).

32 Ibid., p. 47

33 See L. Berry, D. Conyers and J. McKay, *District Plans? A Review of Aims and Attainments in Tanzania*, paper presented at the 1970 Universities of East Africa Social Science Conference, Dar es Salaam (Dec 1970).

34 Thus the quarter with the lowest cash income averaged less than Shs. 286 per year, and the quarter with the highest, more than Shs. 2412.

35 And the wants, in some as yet undiscovered way, prevented from becoming the grabs.

36 *Agricultural Change in Modern Tanganyika: an Outline History*, 1970 Universities of East Africa Social Science Conference, pp. 30–1.

37 Nyerere, *Fredom and Socialism*, p. 344.

38 Ibid., p. 351.

39 *Annual Plan for 1972/73*, op. cit., p. 51.

40 In J. H. Proctor (ed.), *Building Ujamaa Villages in Tanzania*, University of Dar es Salaam Studies in Political Science no. 2 (Dar es Salaam: Tanzania

Publishing House, 1971).

41 Ibid., p. 4.

42 It is noteworthy that the local MP not infrequently plays the role of champion of the common man against the Regional Commissioner whose power has not changed much since colonial times. Members of Parliament not infrequently play an honourable role in countering the regional bureaucracy.

43 Procter (ed.) *Building Ujamaa Villages*, p. 6.

44 *Annual Plan for 1972/73*, op. cit., p. 7.

45 International Labour Office, *Report to the Government of the United Republic of Tanzania on Wages, Incomes and Prices Policy*, Government Paper no. 3 – 1967. The Government's policy is elaborated in *Wages, Incomes, Rural Development, Investment and Price Policy*, Government Paper no. 4 – 1967 (Dar es Salaam: Government Printer, 1967).

46 By the Permanent Labour Tribunal Act no. 41 of 1967.

47 The maximum penalty for an illegal strike or lock-out is Shs. 1000 or 6 months' imprisonment or both, while for incitement to illegally strike or lock-out it is Shs. 3000 or 15 months' or both.

48 And by proportionally smaller amounts as the salary scale was descended.

49 The Union, through the Workers' Development Corporation, did in fact establish dispensaries and ran a highly successful farm near Dar es Salaam. But its most conspicuous investments were, surprisingly, in bars.

50 I draw these details from M. A. Bienefeld, 'Workers, Unions and Development in Tanzania', in Richard Sandbrook and Ronald Cohen, *The Development of an African Working Class* (London: Longmans, 1975).

51 *T.A.N.U. Guidelines 1971* (Dar es Salaam: Government Printer, 1971).

52 *The Daily News*, Dar es Salaam (3 January 1973).

53 This philosophy is beautifully enunciated in the evidence of the Gold Producers' Committee to the Commission on Native Mine Wages in South Africa, 1944.

54 D. Chesworth, 'Statutory Minimum Wage Fixing in Tanganyika', *International Labour Review* (July 1967) 43.

55 *Tanzania Second Five-Year Plan*, op. cit., vol. 1, General Analyses, pp. 203–5.

56 *Report on visits to 23 local employment offices . . . in Tanzania* (in the course of an ILO mission. Geneva: ILO, 1967) p. 11.

57 *Arusha Declaration, 1967.*

58 Jolly *et al.*, 'The Pilot Missions under the World Employment Programme', paper delivered to the Meeting on Evaluation of Comprehensive Employment Missions, ILO, Geneva (7–9 Mar 1973).

CHAPTER THREE

1 For details, see UN, *Demographic Yearbook*, 1971 (New York UN Publications, 1971).

2 Eleazar C. Iwuji, *Employment Promotion Problems in the Economic and Social Development of Ghana* (Geneva: International Institute for Labour Studies, 1972).

3 Ukandi G. Damachi, *The Role of Trade Unions in the Development Process: With a Case Study of Ghana* (New York: Praeger, 1974) p. 16.

4 G1 = US $2·80.

5 W. Birmingham, I. Neustadt and E. N. Omaboa (eds), *A Study of Contemporary Ghana*, vol. I, *The Economy of Ghana* (London: Allen and Unwin, 1966) p. 54.

6 Birmingham *et al.*, *Economy of Ghana*, ch. 3.

7 Damachi, *Role of the Trade Unions*, pp. 63–4.

8 Ibid., p. 63.

9 P. Robson and D. A. Lury, *The Economies of Africa* (London: Allen and Unwin, 1969) p. 86.

10 We shall not discuss the colonial rule in detail. The main focus is on the development paths after independence, i.e. when Ghanaians became responsible for their own destiny.

11 For an elaborate discussion of the various types of government, see David E. Apter, *The Gold Coast in Transition* (Princeton, N.J.: Princeton University Press, 1955); Dennis Austin, *Politics in Ghana: 1946–1960* (London: Oxford University Press, 1964); also 'Return to Ghana', *African Affairs* (London) LXIX, 274 (Jan 1970) 67–71, and Damachi, *Role of the Trade Union*.

12 *Ghana News*, vol. 3, no. 1 (Jan 1965) 1.

13 Damachi, *Role of Trade Unions*, p. 62.

14 *Ghana News*, op. cit., 3.

15 According to one definition in 1960 by the Convention People's Party's Bureau of Information, African Socialism meant providing the means for correcting the inequitable distribution of food and other basic material necessities of life that are the legitimate right of all people. It was opposed to capitalism, demanding its vigorous and systematic elimination from society. It was also based upon purely African factors, particularly Pan-African unity and a truly African socio-cultural renaissance produced by a synthesis of the best of traditional Africa with the best drawn from other parts of the world.

16 Ghana, Ministry of Economic Development, *Seven-Year Development Plan, 1964–70* (Accra: Government Printer, 1965).

17 World Bank, *Trends in Developing Countries* (March 1973).

18 Irving Kaplan *et al.*, *Area Handbook for Ghana* (Washington, D.C.: US Government Printing Office, 1971).

19 *Ghana News*, vol. 4, no. 3 (Mar 1966) 7–8.

20 Ghana, Ministry of Labour, *National Employment*, Employment Report (1971).

21 Damachi, *Role of Trade Unions*, chs 5 and 6.

22 Ibid., p. 3.

23 Ibid., p. 3.

24 Ibid.

25 Ibid., p. 5.

26 Some of the problems faced by the unions during the colonial rule were (a) the lack of a central body since most unions were 'house union' weak in structure and organisation; (b) financial insolvency; and (c) the lack of clear objectives.

27 From the speech of the Minister of Labour and Cooperatives to Ghana

Parliament in 1958 as quoted in Birmingham *et al.*, *Economy of Ghana*, p. 142. For an elaborate discussion of the Acts, see Douglas Rimmer, 'The New Industrial Relations in Ghana', *Industrial and Labor Relations Review*, vol. 14, no. 2 (Jan 1961) 210, and Damachi, *Trade Union Role*.

28 K. A. Busia, *The Way to Industrial Peace* (Accra: Ghana Publishing Corporation, 1969).

29 See Damachi, *Role of Trade Unions*, for details.

30 Ibid. See ch. 5 for details.

31 The Ghanaians had opposed similar government campaigns during the Nkrumah regime and Busia regime. On the two occasions, the trade unions went on strike in protest at the development levy imposed by the two respective governments. For an elaborate account, see ibid.

32 Ghana, Ministry of Economic Development, *One-Year Development Plan, July 1970 to June 1971* (Accra: Government Printer, 1970).

33 The percentages are calculated from Table 3·4.

34 Iwuji, *Employment Promotion Problems . . . of Ghana*, p. 13.
Source: Ghana, Ministry of Labour, Accra.

35 Ghana, *One-Year Development Plan, 1970–1*, p. 146.

36 Ibid., p. 146.

37 Examples of critical skills include engineers, civil, electrical, mining, mechanical, chemical, architects, surveyors, doctors, scientists, geologists, managers, etc.

38 Ghana, Ministry of Economic Development, *High Level and Skilled Manpower Survey in Ghana, 1968* (Accra: Government Printer, 1971).

39 Ibid., p. 7.

40 Ibid., p. 11.

41 International Labour Office, *African Labour Survey* (Geneva, 1958) p. 125.

42 Ghana, Ministry of Labour, *Employment Market Report* (Accra: Government Printer, 1959).

43 Ghana, *One-Year Development Plan, 1970–1*, p. 158.

44 Ibid., p. 149.

45 Ibid., p. 150.

46 For a perceptive analysis of 'tracer service' see Frederick H. Harbison, *Human Resources as the Wealth of Nations* (New York: Oxford University Press, 1973) pp. 149–53.

47 The reason is that the existence of cocoa export duty forms a large burden on the cocoa farmer while the income tax exemption on all income from farming is aimed at the diversification of Ghanaian agriculture and the provision of incentives to non-cocoa farmers.

48 D. K. Dutta Roy and S. J. Mabey, *Household Budget Survey in Ghana*, Technical Publication Series no. 2 (Legon: University of Ghana, 1968).

49 It should be noted that the *per capita* annual income in Ghana is approximately $230. This makes the Ghanaian citizen one of the wealthiest in Africa.

CHAPTER FOUR

1 This chapter draws heavily on the facts and analysis contained in the

ILO Kenya Mission (see *Employment, Incomes and Equality, a Strategy for Increasing Productive Employment in Kenya*, Geneva: ILO, 1972), headed by Richard Jolly and Hans Singer, of which the author was a member. That Report is essential complementary reading. It contains much valuable detailed information and analysis not repeated here; its overall view is somewhat different as will become clear later in the discussion. I am very grateful for comments on a previous draft from Michael Stewart and Paul Streeten.

2 This is not to deny the existence of pre-colonial history which determined the situation the colonials found, and which is responsible for many of the institutions, customs and attitudes today.

3 For a brief description of the colonial impact on Kenya up to the Second World War see L. Woolf, 'Kenya: White Man's Country?', Fabian Publications, Research Series, no. 78 (1944). See also G. Bennett, *Kenya: a Political History, the Colonial Period* (Oxford University Press, 1963) and C. Rosberg and J. Nottingham, *The Myth of Mau Mau: Nationalism in Kenya* (New York: Praeger, 1966). For a more comprehensive history see the *History of East Africa*, ed. R. Oliver and G. Mathew, vols I and II (Oxford University Press, 1963, 1965).

4 'This concern to preserve the tribe turned into something near alarm when it later appeared that its alternative might be a xenophobic Pan-Africanism rather than a leaderless mob. During the first world war the Kenya government viewed with foreboding the intertribal contacts formed in the armed forces and the exposure to Islamic culture in German East Africa. The governor put forward a "definite policy of encouraging strong and isolated tribal nationalism" as a possible antidote . . . Any contact between tribes was held to be morally unnatural as well as politically dangerous.' J. M. Lonsdale, 'European Attitudes and African Pressures: Missions and Government in Kenya between the Wars', *Race*, vol. x (1968–9).

The use made of racial division is described by N. S. Carey Jones, *The Anatomy of Uhuru* (Manchester: Manchester University Press, 1966) p. 88. 'The emphasis upon communal (as opposed to common roll) voting had the effect of playing up a consciousness of difference and self-interest on the part of the three main races.' See D. Rothchild, 'Citizenship and National Integration: the Non-African Crisis in Kenya', *Studies in Race and Nations*, vol. 1, study no. 3 (1969–70) which discusses problems of Asian non-citizens.

5 See Rosberg and Nottingham, *Myth of Mau Mau*, and J. M. Kariuki, '*Mau Mau' Detainee* (Oxford University Press, 1963).

6 Estimated population was $2\frac{1}{2}$–3 million in 1912, $5\frac{1}{4}$ million in 1948: *History of East Africa*, vol. II, p. 337, op. cit.

7 R. J. M. Swynnerton, *A Plan to Intensify the Development of the African Agriculture in Kenya* (Nairobi, 1954): the date at which the first serious attempts to aid African agriculture were made – only nine years before Independence – must be regarded as significant.

8 Any assessment must involve some view of what would have happened in the absence of colonialism, the extent to which colonialism destroyed a self-reliant and developing society and an assessment of the desirability of different patterns of development. For one interesting view see W. Rodney, *How Europe Underdeveloped Africa* (Dar es Salaam: Tanzania Publishing House,

1972).

9 This was D. P. Ghai's estimate for 1966 in 'Incomes Policy in Kenya: Need, Criteria and Machinery', *East African Economic Review,* vol. 4 (June 1968).

10 See *Who Controls Industry in Kenya,* report of a working party, National Christian Council of Kenya (Dar es Salaam: East African Publishing House, 1968) for a fascinating and detailed description of the structure of power and the identity of decision-makers in Kenya in 1967.

11 Ibid., p. 257.

12 See *Kenyanisation of Personnel in the Private Sector, a Statement on Government Policy relating to the Employment of Non-citizens in Kenya,* White Paper of Government of Kenya (1967); and D. T. Asup Mol, *Statement on the Application of the New Immigration Act in Relation to 'Work Permits' and Kenyanisation,* Republic of Kenya (Feb 1968); V. Cable, *Whither Kenyan Emigrants,* Young Fabian Pamphlet (1969) ch. 1.

13 See e.g. 'The Economics of Kenyanisation', *East Africa Journal* (Mar 1968) written by a group of mainly ex-patriate economists at the University of Nairobi; and M. N. McWilliam, 'Economic Viability and the Race Factor in Kenya', *Economic Development and Cultural Change,* vol. XII, no. 1 (1963), who emphasises the dangers to the economy of Africanisation of the Civil Service; and also McWilliam, 'Notes on "The Economic Development of Kenya"', *East African Economics Review,* vol. 10, no. 1 (June 1963) where it is suggested that Asians should be encouraged to diversify into industry.

14 See *Who Controls Industry,* p. 145.

15 Ibid., p. 260.

16 There has been considerable discussion as to whether those falling into this sort of category should be described as 'the élite' or in terms of class-concepts. In so far as the use of 'the élite' implies homogeneity where there is little and masks important differences in interests, arising from differences in the relationships to the modes of production, a class analysis is to be preferred. See G. N. Kitching, 'The Concept of Class and the Study of Africa', *African Review,* vol. 2, no. 3 (1972). Colin Leys in 'Politics in Kenya: the Development of Peasant Society', *British Journal of Political Science* (July 1971) and 'The Limits of African Capitalism: The Formation of the Monopolistic Petty Bourgeoisie in Kenya', mimeo (1972), has shown what fruitful use may be made of a class analysis in the Kenyan context. In the discussion here the concept 'élite' has been used, not to imply homogeneity of interest, but as shorthand where the differences in class interests do not seem important.

17 *African Socialism and Its Application to Planning in Kenya,* sessional paper no. 10 (1965). The document which defines African Socialism as requiring no extensions of public ownership was, it is widely believed, drafted by a Ford-financed American economist.

18 B. Van Arkadie, Institute of Development Studies, Sussex, Communication Series no. 57, has criticised the description of Kenya as 'capitalist', arguing that small-scale farming is 'pre-capitalist' or 'quasi-capitalist' – an argument which he would presumably extend to small-scale businesses; while industry being generally under foreign domination may be part of the world capitalist system, but does not form a 'national capital'. Accepting both

these strictures, it remains true that the Government has favoured private ownership and integration with world capitalism.

19 See P. Marris and A. Somerset, *African Businessmen: a Study of Entrepreneurship and Development,* (London: Routledge, 1971) for a fascinating survey of some African entrepreneurs in Kenya. ILO technical paper no. 18 describes services provided by the government for small-scale businesses.

20 See ILO technical paper no. 16.

21 L. Needleman, S. Lall, R. Lacey and J. Seagrave, *Balance of Payments Effects of Foreign Investment: Case Studies of Jamaica and Kenya* (UNCTAD doc. TD/B/C.3/79/Add.2/Corr.1).

22 Overall gross fixed investment as a percentage of GDP at factor cost rose from $13\frac{1}{2}\%$ in 1964 to 25% in 1972.

23 According to estimates of B. Herman, *Some Basic Data for Analysing the Political Economy of Foreign Investment in Kenya,* Institute of Development Studies, Nairobi, discussion paper no. 112 (1971), foreign finance for foreign-owned companies amounted to K£6·9m. and local finance (share capital and loans) to £7·9m., 1964–9. Restrictions have now been imposed on local borrowing rights of foreign companies.

24 ILO, *Employment, Incomes and Equality,* p. 443.

25 Paul Streeten, 'New Approaches to Direct Private Overseas Investment in Less Developed Countries', in *The Frontiers of Development Studies* (London: Macmillan, 1972) p. 209, has succinctly presented this dilemma, in a formula. In fact the formula he presents (that the rate of increase of new foreign investment must exceed the rate of return on old investment) should be modified to allow for local borrowing by foreign firms, which with non-equity borrowing will further increase the potential outflow if the rate of return exceeds the interest rate on the locally borrowed funds.

26 The policy of import substitution has been combined with expansion of exports to her immediate neighbours, largely within the East African Community (discussed more below).

27 A term invented by K. Marsden, of the ILO.

28 An extreme example in Kenya is the substitution for imported blackcurrant juice, of domestically produced blackcurrant juice which involved importing blackcurrants from the UK since they do not grow in Kenya. Import substitution would allow replacement of imported goods by goods produced locally with similar function – in this case substitution of pineapple or orange juice for the imported blackcurrant juice. Import reproduction does not: blackcurrant juice must be substituted for blackcurrant juice, irrespective of resource use.

29 Extra imports are also generated by any additional consumption resulting from additional employment with the industrialisation.

30 A particular technology requires a package of complementary inputs from skill and management requirements, quality and nature of parts, extending to the nature of banking and infrastructure. Thus the influence of the nature of the technology adopted extends far beyond its immediate and apparent implications.

31 Charles Cooper, 'Science Policy in Developing Countries', *World Development* (Mar 1974) has argued that the apparently inappropriate nature of the

engineering education in the University of Nairobi is a response to the requirements of local industry for this type of engineer to service advanced country technology.

32 This point is expanded in F. Stewart, 'Technology and Employment', *World Development,* op. cit.

33 Typically wages form a lower proportion of total costs in developing countries than in advanced countries; the substantially lower wage rates are not completely offset by lower labour productivity. In Kenya the wage bill in the modern sector accounted for 42–6% of the monetary GDP, 1964–70.

34 For example, in 1962 the Ministers of Labour of the three East Africa countries agreed to pursue a high wage policy. The trade unions played a key role in securing independence – see T. Mboya, *Freedom and After* (London: Deutsch, 1963).

35 A concept developed by G. Arrighi, see 'International Corporations, Labour Aristocracies and Economic Development in Tropical Africa', *Essays on the Political Economy of Africa,* ed. G. Arrighi and J. Saul (Monthly Review Press, 1973).

36 ILO, *Employment, Incomes and Equality,* p. 446. Pack has argued that industry in Kenya is more labour intensive than in advanced countries. While this is almost certainly true, the magnitude of Kenyan adaption of technology in a labour-intensive direction is small in relation to the divergence in resource availability between Kenya and advanced countries; and the trend is towards increasing capital intensity over time. H. Pack, 'Employment and Productivity in Kenyan Manufacturing', *Eastern Africa Economic Review,* vol. 4, no. 2 (Dec 1972).

37 See M. G. Phelps and B. Wasow, 'Measuring Protection and Its Effects', Institute of Development Studies, Nairobi, staff paper no. 86 (1970).

38 Between 1963 and 1970 primary school enrolments expanded by 56%, secondary by over 300% (though from a much smaller base). But it is not simply a question of numbers; the nature of the education provided is determined in large part throughout the whole system by the needs of those who will ultimately be employed in modern industry, despite the fact that these are only a small proportion of the total employed and of the total going through the schools, particularly at primary level. As the ILO Report argues: 'the central weakness of the certificate of primary education is its almost exclusive orientation towards selection for secondary school', p. 236. Similar complaints are made at most levels.

39 The concentration of public expenditure in Kenya on health, education, roads, houses regionally, in the urban areas, and within the urban areas on a subset of 'modern' workers has been widely documented. See ILO, *Economy, Incomes and Equality,* pp. 78–9, 215, 301, 383, 512, 514, 475.

40 For more detailed assessment of East African trade, see A. Hazelwood, 'Inter-State Trade in East African Manufactures', *Economic and Statistical Review* (Sep 1971). It seems to be the case that the initial advantage Kenya gained from the Community is now being offset by reactive policies of the two partners – see ILO, *Employment, Incomes and Equality,* p. 287.

41 See ILO, *Employment, Incomes and Equality,* pp. 453–7 for a description of the methods used for repatriation of the surplus, and some estimates.

42 See N. H. Stern, 'Experience with the Use of the Little-Mirrlees Method for an Appraisal of Small-holder Tea in Kenya', *Bulletin of Oxford University Institute of Economics and Statistics,* vol. 34, no. 1 (Feb 1972).

43 'In the past greater attention has been paid by extension staff to the big progressive farmers, and there has been a tendency to neglect the smaller, less responsive and less progressive farmers. Moreover, a few years ago it was deliberate policy not to give advice to women farmers, even though it was known that a very large number of small holdings in Kenya were worked and possibly managed entirely by women.' ILO, *Employment, Incomes and Equality,* p. 153.

44 The question of the definition and magnitude of the employment problem in developing countries forms the basis of a vast literature. See e.g. D. Turnham and I. Jaeger, *The Employment Problem in Less Developed Countries: a Review of the Evidence,* OECD (1971); see also ILO Reports on Colombia and Ceylon (*Towards Full Employment,* ILO, Geneva, 1970, ch. 1; and *Matching Employment Opportunities and Expectations,* ILO, Geneva, 1971, ch. 2) and ch. 5 of ILO, *Employment, Incomes and Equality.*

45 The effects of the Tripartite Agreements are described in technical paper 26 of the ILO Report.

46 H. Rempel, 'Labor Migration into Urban Centers and Urban Unemployment in Kenya,' unpublished Ph.D. thesis, University of Wisconsin (1970).

47 But this high figure for Nairobi is partly due to a boundary change.

48 Kenya, Ministry of Information, *National Development Plan, 1964–69* (Nairobi, Government Printer, 1964).

49 See Keith Hart's pioneering description of activities in this sector in Ghana: 'Informal Income Opportunities and Urban Employment in Ghana', *Journal of Modern African Studies,* vol. II, no. 1 (Mar 1973).

50 Described in *Uncontrolled Urban Settlements Case Studies for Nairobi,* Kenya, Royal Academy of Fine Arts, Town Planning Department, Copenhagen (1971).

51 According to the Nairobi Survey among fringe squatters in Kairiobangi over 40% had jobs outside the fringe area; in Mathare Valley Village 2 (lower village) 38% had jobs in the city centre outside the village, 10% were unemployed, and 52% were self-employed in the village. Among the self-employed in Mathare village 2 (lower village) the following breakdown of activities was given. Percentage of self-employed in village: sell illegal liquor, 37; sell vegetables or run shop, 37; rent rooms, 13; live off subsistence farming, 8; engage in resale activity, 6.

52 Countries which seem to have been most successful in combating corruption are also those which have reduced the role of profit and income maximisation in their economic strategy – e.g. Tanzania and China. On the other hand though this may be a necessary condition for eliminating corruption, it is clearly not sufficient.

53 ILO, *Employment, Incomes and Equality,* p. 229. It is easy though to exaggerate the role given to the informal sector by the ILO Mission because of the novelty of this aspect of the Report.

54 Colin Leys, 'Interpreting African Underdevelopment: Reflections on

the ILO Report on Employment, Incomes and Equality in Kenya', *African Affairs* (1973) has also accused the Mission of romanticising the sector by ignoring the *exploitative* aspect of employment in that sector.

55 *Uncontrolled Urban Settlements*, op. cit., pp. 5. 04–05 and 5. 06–08.

56 K. Marsden has shown how modern methods of shoe production have destroyed employment opportunities in shoe manufacturing. For India see J. P. Ambannvar, 'Changes in the Employment Pattern of the Indian Working Force: 1911–1961', *Developing Economies*, vol. XIII, no. 1 (Mar 1970).

57 See e.g. Heather and Vijay Joshi, *Labour Markets in Bombay* (forthcoming); and B. Dasgupta, 'Calcutta's "Informal Sector"', *Bulletin of Institute of Development Studies*, vol. 5, nos. 2/3 (Oct 1973).

58 ILO, *Employment, Incomes and Equality*, p. 505.

59 A very good example of the expression of this view is I. Little, T. Scitovsky and M. Scott, *Industry and Trade in Some Developing Countries* (Oxford University Press, 1970).

60 See the calculations of O. D. K. Norbye, 'Long Term Employment Prospects and the Need for Large Scale Rural Works Programmes', in *Education, Employment and Rural Development*, ed. J. R. Sheffield (Nairobi: East African Publishing House, 1967) especially table 2, p. 249.

61 E. Rado, 'An Explosive Model of Education', in *McGill Newsletter* (Nov 1973).

62 Described by J. E. Anderson in 'The Harambee Schools: The Impact of Self-help', in R. Jolly (ed.) *Education in Africa: Research and Action* (Nairobi: East Africa Publishing House, 1969) and J. E. Anderson, *The Struggle for School* (London: Longman, 1970).

63 See M. Blaug, R. Layard and M. Woodhall, *The Causes of Graduate Unemployment in India, 1945–1966* (Cambridge: Cambridge University Press, 1969).

64 See e.g. J. Harris and M. P. Todaro, 'Wages, Industrial Employment and Labour Productivity in a Developing Economy: the Kenyan Experience', *East African Economic Review*, vol. 1 (1969); J. Power, 'The Role of Protection in Industrialisation Policy', IDS Nairobi, working paper no. 32 (1972); S. Lewis, 'The Effects of Protection on the Growth Rate of the Economy and the Need for External Assistance', IDS working paper no. 34 (1972).

65 Harris and Todaro, 'Wages, Industrial Employment', have shown a positive correlation between changes in labour productivity and changes in wages in private industries and services in Kenya, and have argued that this shows a reduction in wages would increase employment significantly. However, their correlations do not show the *direction* of the causal nexus. It is equally likely that the increases in labour productivity brought about the increase in wages. In any case their correlation analysis is open to doubt being highly aggregated and using current not constant prices.

66 See F. Stewart and J. Weeks, 'The Employment Effects of Wage Changes in Poor Countries', discussion paper no. 8, Department of Economics, Birkbeck College (1973).

67 The Commission on Public Service Structure and Remuneration.

68 M. J. Westlake, 'Tax Evasion, Tax Incidence and the Distribution of Income in Kenya', IDS Nairobi, staff paper (1971) shows that tax paid in

Kenya at the end of the 1960s was broadly proportionate to income.

69 Proposed changes in incomes were: 3% p.a. for persons earning less than £200; 0–3% p.a. for persons earning £200–£700; and nil for persons earning over £700 (see ILO, *Employment, Incomes and Equality*, p. 267).

70 'A continuation of this (i.e. the past) rate of expansion is essential for our strategy', ILO, *Employment, Incomes and Equality*, p. 106.

71 For example, M. Radezki showed for Tanzania how expansion of milk production was chiefly related to the consumption of upper income groups. In Kenya, recent investment in roller mills for maize grinding has produced a more expensive product consumed by urban wage earners. In construction, until recently the minimum cost of houses produced by the Nairobi City Council was £1000 producing high-standard accommodation beyond the means of all those without steady and (relatively) high incomes.

CHAPTER FIVE

1 A second population census was conducted during April 1973; however, its results have not yet been published.

2 ILO, *Labour Force Projections*: 1965–1985, pt II, Africa (Geneva, 1971) p. 153.

3 For a comprehensive account of Sudanese political history, see P. M. Holt, *A Modern History of the Sudan* (London: Oxford University Press, 1962) and 'Sudan Democratic Republic', in Colin Legum and John Drysdale, *Africa Contemporary Record, Annual Survey and Documents, 1969–1970* (Exeter: Africa Research Ltd, 1970) pp. B47–B68.

4 ILO, *Labour Force Projections*, op. cit., p. 94.

5 UN, Department of Economics and Social Affairs, *Population Growth and Manpower in the Sudan* (New York, 1964) p. 69.

6 £S is roughly equivalent to US $2.7.

7 Omar Osman and A. A. Suliman, 'The Economy of Sudan', in Robson and Lury, *Economies of Africa*, p. 442.

8 Ibid.

9 Osman H. Saeed, 'Industrial Development Strategy in the Sudan', mimeo, p. 5.

10 Ibid., p. 6.

11 Ibid.

12 Republic of Sudan, Ministry of Finance and Economics, *The Ten-Year Plan for Economic and Social Development, 1961/62–1971/72* (Khartoum, Mar 1962).

13 Saeed, 'Industrial Development Strategy', p. 13.

14 Ibid., p. 12.

15 Ibid., pp. 13–15.

16 Oluwadare Aguda, 'The State and the Economy in the Sudan: from a Political Scientist's Point of View', *Journal of Developing Areas*, vol. 7, no. 3 (Apr 1973) p. 433.

17 Democratic Republic of the Sudan, *Five-Years Plan of Economic and Social Development, 1970/71–1974/75* (Khartoum, 1970) p. 1.

18 Saeed, 'Industrial Development Strategy', p. 20.

19 Ibid., p. 19.

20 *El Ayam*, Khartoum (July 1973) p. 24.

21 Saeed, 'Industrial Development Strategy', p. 22.

22 Ioan Davies, *African Trade Unions* (Baltimore: Penguin, 1966) p. 138.

23 Gasim Amin in *El Saraha* (14 Aug 1953).

24 Abdel-Rahman E. Ali Taha, 'The Sudanese Labour Movement: a Study of Labour Unionism in a Developing Society', unpublished Ph.D. thesis, University of California, Los Angeles (1970) p. 193.

25 Constitution of the Sudan Workers Trade Union Federation, article III, section 10 (a).

26 See Ali Taha, 'Sudanese Labour Movement', chs IV and V.

27 Ibid., pp. 107–17.

28 K. D. D. Henderson, *Sudan Republic* (London: Benn, 1965) pp. 203–28.

29 *El Rail El Aam*, (24 Nov 1964).

30 See 'Sudan Democratic Republic', in Legum and Drysdale, *Africa Contemporary Record*, pp. B47–B68.

31 The Consolidated Labour Code of 1970 provided substantial benefits for workers in almost all areas of the employment relationship.

32 For example during the regime's armed confrontation with Imam El Hadi El Mahdi, the leader of the Ansar religious sect, at Aba island.

33 The Trade Union Ordinance, 1971, reorganised trade unions on an industrial basis and provided for the creation of a new workers' federation.

34 See Arthur Gaitskell, *Gezira: a Story of Development in the Sudan* (London: Faber, 1959).

35 See Saeed, 'Industrial Development Strategy', p. 9.

36 Ibid., p. 20.

37 ILO, *Report to the Government of the Sudan on the Development and Implementation of a National Employment Policy* (Geneva, 1973) p. 22.

38 For details see Aguda, 'State and Economy in the Sudan', pp. 342–6.

39 Oluwadare Aguda, 'The Sudan Civil Service, 1964–1971', *Quarterly Journal of Administration*, vol. VI (Apr 1972) 335.

40 Ibid., 336.

41 Ibid., p. 345.

42 Aguda, 'State and Economy in the Sudan', p. 347.

43 Ibid., p. 431.

44 Sudan, Establishment of Central Ministries, *Republican Decree Number Four* (Khartoum: Government Printer, May 1973).

45 *Republican Decree*, nos 4 and 5.

46 Nyerere, *Freedom and Socialism*, p. 246.

47 The new system, which is composed of six years' elementary, three general secondary and three high secondary, replaced a 4+4+4 system.

48 Democratic Republic of the Sudan, Ministry of Education, *Self-Help in the Field of Education* (Khartoum, Jan 1973) p. 24 (in Arabic).

49 Ibid., pp. 44, 50.

50 Ibid., p. 68.

51 ILO, *Report to the Government of the Sudan*, p. 22.

52 Mohammed El Murtada Mustafa, *Manpower and Employment Problems in the Sudan*, IEME 3052, International Institute for Labour Studies, Geneva

234 NOTES

(1972) p. 7.

53 An exploratory mission was sent in July 1972 and a full mission is planned for 1974.

54 ILO, *Report to the Government of the Sudan*, pp. 81–2.

55 Ibid., p. 83.

56 Ibid., pp. 26–7.

57 Ibid., p. 24.

58 Ibid., p. 140.

59 Ibid., p. 142.

60 Mustafa, *Manpower and Employment Problems*, pp. 12–13.

61 Sudan Government, *Wages and Terms of Employment Commission's Report* (Khartoum: Government Printer, 1968) pp. 35–9.

62 Ali Taha, 'Sudanese Labour Movement', p. 217.

CHAPTER SIX

1 It is more accurate to use 'white' than the euphemism 'European'. The latter term is used all over Southern Africa for white; in Zambia it can be seriously misleading since the country was settled mainly from Rhodesia and South Africa, only the colonial administration being predominantly European in the more usual sense of the word.

2 In fact there remained, and remains to the present, some difference between local and expatriate salary terms in many jobs, but the difference is one of degree rather than one of kind.

3 Figures from Scott R. Pearson, *Petroleum and the Nigerian Economy* (Stanford: Stanford University Press, 1970) and B. Van Arkadie and C. R. Frank Jr, *Economic Accounting and Development Planning* (Nairobi: Oxford University Press, 1966).

4 UN, *Statistical Yearbook 1972*. The figure for Nigeria in 1965 was 20%, but Nigerian population figures are unreliable even by African standards.

5 P. Deane, *Colonial Social Accounting* (Cambridge: Cambridge University Press, 1953) pp. 21–2.

6 M. Bostock and C. Harvey (eds), *Economic Independence and Zambian Copper* (New York: Praeger, 1972) Table 5.2.

7 See R. E. Baldwin, *Economic Development and Export Growth: a Study of Northern Rhodesia, 1920–1960* (Los Angeles: University of California Press, 1966) pp. 16ff., for a description of the economy before the development of copper mining; see also J. Fry and C. Harvey, 'Copper and Zambia', in J. Cownie and S. R. Pearson (eds), *Commodity Exports and African Economic Development* (Boston, DC Heath: Lexington Books, 1974) section 1.

8 Zambia, Ministry of Labour, 'The Process of Zambianisation in the Mining Industry' (Lusaka, 1968) p. 9, quoted by N. Kessel in C. M. Elliott (eds), *Constraints on the Economic Development of Zambia* (Nairobi: Oxford University Press, 1971) p. 265.

9 See Richard Hall, *The High Price of Principles: Kaunda and the White South* (London: Hodder and Stoughton, 1969) ch. 12, especially on the security problems created by half the whites at Independence having relations or business contacts in Rhodesia or South Africa.

10 Copper prices are quoted in Kwacha per metric ton, except where stated. Until November 1967 the Zambian and British pounds were equal. In November 1967 Britain devalued by 16% but Zambia did not follow. In January 1968 Zambia decimalised her currency thus: Zambian £1 = Kwacha 2. Copper statistics are variously quoted in short tons (2000 lbs), long tons (2240) and metric tons (2204 lbs).

11 See Bostock and Harvey (eds), *Economic Independence and Zambian Copper*, ch. 6, 'Tax reform in the mining industry'.

12 C. Harvey, 'The Control of Inflation in a Very Open Economy: Zambia 1964–1969', *East African Economic Review* (June 1971) tables 2, 4. There was a small (K21m.) budget deficit in the second half of 1967.

13 Profits remitted abroad rose by a further 15% in 1967 and fell by 59% in 1968 – estimates by M. Bostock in 'The background to participation', ch. 5 in Bostock and Harvey, *Economic Independence and Zambian Copper*.

14 Zambia, *Second National Development Plan* (Lusaka: Government Printer, 1971) p. 50, table 1–11.

15 The figures in these two paragraphs are taken from various issues of the Zambia *Monthly Digest of Statistics* (Lusaka: Government Printer, 1960–72). Employment and earnings figures include agriculture, but the overall impression would be enhanced if agriculture were excluded since recorded agricultural employment has actually fallen since 1964, because of the departure of half the expatriate farmers.

16 Zambia, *Second National Development Plan*, p. 13. The figure for administrative and executive personnel rose from 47% to 87% and for technical from 45% to 67%. Teachers and professional staff were static at 83% and 18% respectively.

17 M. Burawoy, *The Colour of Class on the Copper mines: from African Advancement to Zambianisation*, University of Zambia, Institute for African Studies, Zambian papers no. 7 (1972) pp. 33ff., 'Pressures on the successor'. The quotation is from p. 38.

18 All figures from *Monthly Digest of Statistics*, op. cit., various issues.

19 The debit item 'personal remittances' in the balance of payments has grown from K9m. in 1964 to K97m. in 1972; in the latter year it actually fell (from K108m.) for the first time since 1964. *Monthly Digest*, various issues.

20 The final humiliation was the purchase of large quantities of maize from Rhodesia. Maize pricing policy will never be easy. Because maize is a low-value, bulky commodity, too low a price can lead to expensive imports, too high a price to an unstorable surplus for which there is no external market. The weather can also be perverse.

21 See Robert Bates, *Unions, Parties and Political Development: a Study of Mineworkers in Zambia* (New Haven: Yale University Press, 1971) *passim*.

22 The medium term seems fairly secure in terms of *quantities* of copper, since in all but one of the big mines current reserves exceed known reserves at the time the mine opened – in other words the rate of discovery has been greater than the rate of production; see Alan Drysdall, 'Prospecting and Mining Activity, 1895–1970', in Bostock and Harvey, *Economic Independence and Zambian Copper*, p. 69, table 3.4. In addition, technical progress and a rising price tend to add to the reserves, at least until a major substitute is found.

23 Zambia, *Second National Development Plan*, pt I, ch. II, especially the following quotation on policy (p. 62): 'to promote the long-term development of family farms as the basic unit of production, supported by viable marketing and supply co-operatives; at the same time to give every encouragement to the growing number of Zambian commercial farmers and to the expatriate commercial farmers'.

24 Address by His Excellency the President, Dr K. D. Kaunda, at the press conference on the redemption of ZIMCO Bonds, State House, Lusaka, 31 August 1973.

CHAPTER SEVEN

1 Nigeria, Ministry of Information, *Nigeria Handbook 1973* (Lagos: Academy Press, 1973) pp. 130–3.

2 Nigeria changed to decimal currency on 1 January 1973. The unit of the currency is the Naira represented by the symbol N. The naira is the major unit of the new currency and is divided into 100 kobo, represented by the symbol K. N = US$1.50.

3 *Nigeria Handbook*, op cit., p. 50.

4 *Nigeria Handbook*, op cit., p. 59.

5 A. Adedeji, *Foundation for Sound Development: an Address at the Press Conference on the Second Development Plan 1970–1974* (Lagos: Academy Press, 1973) p. 13.

6 Eleazar C. Iwuji, *Employment Promotion Problems in the Economic and Social Development of Nigeria* (Geneva: International Institute for Labour Studies, 1972) p. 4.

7 The twelve states are as follows: Lagos; Kwara; Kano; North-Eastern; East Central; North-Western; North-Central; Benue Plateau; Rivers; South-Eastern; Mid-Western; and Western State.

8 C. C. Onyemelukwe, *Problems of Industrial Planning in Nigeria* (London: Longman, 1966) pp. 33–4.

9 C. Aboyade, 'Some Implications of Nigerian Imports Structure', *Nigerian Journal of Economic and Social Studies* (Mar 1962) p. 53.

10 The oil industry has replaced agricultural produce in contributing to the GDP. Payments by the industry accounted for about 7% of federal government revenue in 1971–2.

11 Ukandi G. Damachi, *Nigerian Modernization: the Colonial Legacy* (New York: Third Press, 1972) pp. 75–6.

12 Ibid., p. 91.

13 Nigeria, Ministry of Information, *Building the New Nigeria: Industry* (Lagos: Associated Press of Nigeria, 1971) pp. 15–16.

14 Walter Schwarz, *Nigeria* (London: Pall Mall Press, 1968) p. 292.

15 Damachi, *Nigerian Modernization*, pp. 89–90, for details.

16 Nigeria, Ministry of Economic Development, *Four Steps to National Stability* (Lagos: Government Printer, 1968) p. 6.

17 Nigeria, Ministry of Economic Development, *National Development Plan, 1970–1974* (Apapa: Nigerian National Press, 1970) pp. 3–4.

18 Ibid., p. 18.

19 Nigeria, Ministry of Labour, *Annual Report* (Lagos: Government Printer, 1965) p. 23.

20 The four organisations are: (1) the United Labour Congress (ULC); (2) the Nigeria Trade Union Congress (NTUC); (3) the Labour Unity Front (LUF); and (4) the Nigerian Workers' Council (NWC).

21 For details of these advantages, see Damachi, *Role of Trade Unions*.

22 *Nigeria Handbook*, op. cit., p. 77.

23 Ibid., pp. 77–8.

24 For details, see A. Y. Eke, *Eradication of Illiteracy* (Lagos: Academy Press, 1972.

25 Nigeria is a country which is trying to forge national unity out of tribal diversity. For details on the tribal differences, see Damachi, *Nigerian Modernization*, ch. 2.

26 These figures must be viewed with caution because of the dubious nature of the results of the 1963 census.

27 On the basis of the findings of the survey the unemployment figure for 1970 was estimated at 2 million, that is, about 7.8% of the estimated labour force.

28 Iwuji, *Employment Promotion Problems . . . of Nigeria*, p. 14.

29 *National Development Plan 1970–1974*, op. cit., p. 311.

30 For details, see Harbison, *Human Resources as the Wealth of Nations*; Ukandi G. Damachi and H. Dieter Seibel (eds), *Social Change and Economic Development in Nigeria* (New York: Praeger, 1973) ch. 5; International Labour Organisation, *Toward Full Employment in Colombia* (Geneva: ILO Publication, 1970).

31 S. O. Falae, 'Unemployment in Nigeria', *Nigerian Journal of Economic and Social Studies*, vol. 13, no. 1 (Mar 1971) 62–8.

32 Nigeria, Ministry of Economic Development, *Six-year Development Plan, 1962–68* (Lagos: Government Printer, 1962) p. 23.

33 Falae, 'Unemployment in Nigeria', p. 68.

34 Ibid.

35 *National Development Plan*, op. cit. *1970–1974*, p. 311.

36 Falae, 'Unemployment in Nigeria', pp. 69–70.

37 For a perceptive discussion of these shibboleths, see Mark Blaug, *Education and the Employment Problem in Developing Countries* (Geneva: ILO Publication, 1973). Also, see Falae, 'Unemployment in Nigeria', pp. 70–5.

38 R. O. Ekundare, 'Salary and Wages since 1946', *Quarterly Journal of Administration*, vol. 5, no. 2 (Jan 1972) 161.

39 Nigeria, Ministry of Information, *Report of the Commission on the Review of Wages, Salary and Conditions of Service of the Junior Employees of the Government of the Federation and in Private Establishments, 1963–64* (Lagos: Government Printer, 1964).

40 Nigeria, Ministry of Information, *First Report of the Wages and Salaries Review Commission, 1970, and Second and Final Report of the Wages and Salaries Review Commission, 1970–71* (Lagos: Government Printer, 1972).

41 Ghana, Ministry of Information, *Report of the Commission on the Civil Services of British West Africa, 1945–46* (Accra: Government Printer, 1957).

42 Ekundare, 'Salary and Wages', pp. 162–3.

43 *Report . . . on the Civil Services of British West Africa*, op. cit., p. 10.

44 Nigeria, Ministry of Information, *Conclusions of the Government of the Federation in the Report on the Commission on the Public Services of the Governments in the Federation of Nigeria, 1954–1955* (Lagos: Government Printer, 1956).

45 *Second and Final Report of the Wages and Salaries Review Commission*, op. cit., p. 23.

46 Ibid., p. 7.

47 It is called 'prismatic' because if a ray of light is projected through a prism on to a screen, the seven colours of the spectrum will appear on it. Similarly, indigenous planners by virtue of their expertise and being indigenous tend to have a clearer picture of the socio-economic problems. As a result, they document them easily and set bogus targets in the hope of solving them.

48 For the details of this strike, see Damachi, *Nigerian Modernization*, pp. 104–6.

49 James O'Connell, 'Political Constraints on Planning: Nigeria as a Case Study in the Developing World', *Nigerian Journal of Economic and Social Studies*, vol. 13, no. 1 (Mar 1971) 42.

50 Ibid., p. 42, for a detailed analysis of this conclusion.

51 Nigeria, Ministry of Information, *Trade, Not Charity* (Lagos: Government Printer, 1971).

CHAPTER EIGHT

1 D. H. Perkins, et al., *Agricultural Development in China 1368–1968* (Edinburgh: Edinburgh University Press, 1969).

2 In terms of cultivated acreage per male farmer the following comparisons are of interest (around 1950): China, 10 acres; Indian sub-continent, 8 acres; Africa, 6 acres; USSR, 81 acres; USA, 208 acres. Colin Clark, *The Conditions of Economic Progress* (London: Macmillan, 1960), quoted by N. R. Chen and W. Galenson, *The Chinese Economy under Communism* (Chicago: Aldine, 1969).

3 Textiles alone, produced by 859 factories, account for 42·4% of total industrial production in 1933. On Pa Sin, *China's National Income in 1933* (Shanghai, 1947).

4 Chen and Galenson, *Chinese Economy*.

5 During 1953–8 light industry received only 11·2 per cent of total investment.

6 In his programme entitled 'On the Question of Agricultural Co-operation' in which he encouraged the speedier progress of the co-operative movement and criticised the 'spontaneous forms of capitalism . . . and rich peasants springing up everywhere in the countryside'.

7 See page 20 for some statistics on the share of investible funds retained on the farms.

8 Because many were so big as to be unwieldy, the number was subsequently increased to its present (1974) level of some 70,000.

9 During the twelve months up to September 1958 the amount of stone and earth removed in land melioration works (58,000 million cubic metres) was the equivalent of digging 300 Panama Canals! E. C. Wheelwright and Bruce

McFarlane, *The Chinese Road to Socialism* (New York, 1970).

10 The peasants had lost the right to their private plots at the beginning of the Great Leap Forward, and received part of their income in the form of standard food rations in public mess-halls. Neither of these measures was popular or calculated to raise productivity.

11 This implied a departure from the received view in the Soviet Union about the stages of and prerequisites for the transition from socialism to Communism. It therefore lay at the roots of the ideological controversy between the two great socialist states. It was also the first open challenge to the Soviet position as arbiter of orthodoxy since Yugoslavia's defection and independent experimentation in the early 1950s.

12 In a famous speech in 1931 Stalin had insisted on the need for the Soviet Union to overcome a time-lag of fifty years' backwardness in the short span of ten years in order to survive the threat of attack from imperialist encirclement.

13 Teng Hsiao-Ping lost his post during the Cultural Revolution, but was reinstated after the Tenth Party Congress in 1973, both to the Politburo and to the post of Deputy Prime Minister.

14 The composition of these revolutionary committees, particularly the representation of the armed forces, has changed over time.

15 For a summary account on which the present description draws see Jacques Attali in *Le Monde*, 15 May 1973.

16 This is how Chinese spokesmen refer to their country's rung on the development ladder at the United Nations and in such international forums as UNCTAD.

17 The need for perseverance and faith in the attempt to master nature is brought out in the Chinese fable related by Mao Tse-tung of 'the foolish old man who removed the mountains'.

18 One of the most common Maoist slogans is 'learn to serve the masses better'.

References

Aboyade, C., 'Some Implications of Nigerian Imports Structure', *Nigerian Journal of Economic and Social Studies* (Mar 1962).

Adedeji, A., *Foundation for Sound Development: an Address at the Press Conference on the Second Development Plan 1970–1974* (Lagos: Academy Press, 1973).

Aguda, O., 'The Sudan Civil Service, 1964–1971', *Quarterly Journal of Administration*, vol. VI (Apr 1972).

——'The State and the Economy in the Sudan: from a Political Scientist's Point of View', *Journal of Developing Areas*, vol. 7, no. 3 (Apr 1973).

Ali Taha, A. E., *The Sudanese Labour Movement: Study of Labour Unionism in a Developing Society*, unpublished Ph.D. thesis, University of California, Los Angeles (1970).

Ambannvar, J. P., 'Changes in the Employment Pattern of the Indian Working Force: 1911–1961', *Developing Economies*, vol. XIII, no. 1 (Mar 1970).

Anderson, J. E., *The Struggle for School* (London: Longman, 1970).

Apter, David E., *The Gold Coast in Transition* (Princeton, N. J.: Princeton University Press, 1955).

Arkadie, B. V. and Frank, C. R., Jr, *Economic Accounting and Development Planning* (Nairobi: Oxford University Press, 1966).

Arrighi, G. and Saul, J. (eds), *Essays on the Political Economy of Africa* (New York: Monthly Review Press, 1973).

Austin, Dennis, *Politics in Ghana: 1946–1960* (London: Oxford University Press, 1964).

Attali, Jacques, *Le Monde*, 15 May 1973.

Baldwin, R. E., *Economic Development and Export Growth: a Study of Northern Rhodesia, 1920–1960* (Los Angeles: University of California Press, 1966).

Bates, Robert, *Unions, Parties and Political Development: a Study of*

Mineworkers in Zambia (New Haven: Yale University Press, 1971).

Berry, L. *et al.*, *District Plans? A Review of Aims and Attainments in Tanzania*, mimeo (Dar es Salaam, Dec 1970).

Birmingham, W. *et al.* (eds), *A Study of Contemporary Ghana*, vol. I, *The Economy of Ghana* (London: Allen and Unwin, 1966).

Blaug, Mark, *Education and the Employment Problem in Developing Countries* (Geneva: ILO, 1973).

Bostock, M. and Harvey, C. (eds), *Economic Independence and Zambian Copper* (New York: Praeger, 1972).

Busia, K. A., *The Way to Industrial Peace* (Accra: Ghana Publishing Corporation, 1969).

Cable, V., *Whither Kenyan Emigrants*, Young Fabian Pamphlet (1969).

Carey Jones, N. S., *The Anatomy of Uhuru* (Manchester: Manchester University Press, 1966).

Chen, K. I. and Uppal, J. S., *Comparative Development of India and China* (New York: Free Press, 1971).

Chen, N. R. and Galenson, W., *The Chinese Economy under Communism* (Chicago: Aldine, 1969).

Chen, P. C., 'The Political Economics of Population Growth: the Case of China', *World Politics*, 23, 2 (Jan 1971) 245–72.

Chesworth, D., 'Statutory Minimum Wage Fixing in Tanganyika', *International Labour Review* (July 1967).

Clark, Colin, *The Conditions of Economic Progress* (London: Macmillan, 1960).

Cownie, J. and Pearson, S. R. (eds), *Commodity Exports and African Economic Development* (Boston: D. C. Heath, Lexington Books, 1974).

Damachi, Ukandi G., *Nigerian Modernization: the Colonial Legacy* (New York: Third Press, 1972).

——*The Role of Trade Unions in the Development Process: With A Case Study of Ghana* (New York: Praeger, 1974).

Damachi, Ukandi G. and Seibel, Hans Dieter (eds), *Social Change and Economic Development in Nigeria* (New York: Praeger, 1973).

Dasgupta, B., 'Calcutta's "Informal Sector"', *Bulletin of Institute of Development Studies*, vol. 5, nos. 2/3 (Oct 1973).

Davidson, Basil, *The Growth of African Civilisation, East and Central Africa to the Late Nineteenth Century* (London: Longman,

1967).

Davies, Ioan, *African Trade Unions* (Baltimore: Penguin, 1966).

Deane, P., *Colonial Social Accounting* (Cambridge: Cambridge University Press, 1953).

Dutta Roy, D. K. and Nabey, S. J., *Household Budget Survey in Ghana*, Technical Publication Series no. 2 (Legon: University of Ghana, 1968).

Eke, A. Y., *Eradication of Illiteracy* (Lagos: Academy Press, 1972).

Ekundare, R. O., 'Salary and Wages since 1946', *Quarterly Journal of Administration,* vol. 5, no. 2 (Jan 1972).

Elkan, Walter, *Development Economics* (Harmondsworth: Penguin, 1973).

Falae, S. O., 'Unemployment in Nigeria', *Nigerian Journal of Economic and Social Studies,* vol. 13, no. 1 (Mar 1971).

Frank, A. G., *Capitalism and Underdevelopment in Latin America* (New York: Modern Reader Paperbacks, 1967).

Friedland, William H., *Vuta Kamba: the Development of Trade Unions in Tanganyika* (Standford: Hoover Institution Press, 1969).

Gaitskell, Arthur, *Gezira: a Story of Development in the Sudan* (London: Faber, 1959).

Ghai, D. P., 'Incomes Policy in Kenya: Need, Criteria and Machinery', *East African Economic Review,* vol. 4 (June 1968).

Ghana, Ministry of Economic Development, *Seven-Year Development Plan, 1964–70* (Accra: Government Printer, 1965).

Ghana, Ministry of Economic Development, *One-Year Development Plan, July 1970 to June 1971* (Accra: Government Printer, 1970).

Ghana, Ministry of Economic Development, *High Level and Skilled Manpower Survey in Ghana, 1968* (Accra: Government Printer, 1971).

Ghana, Ministry of Finance and Economic Affairs, *Guideline for a Five-Year Rolling Plan* (Accra: Government Printer, Sep. 1969).

Ghana, Ministry of Information, *Report of the Commission of the Civil Services of British West Africa, 1945–46* (Accra: Government Printer, 1957).

Ghana, Ministry of Labour, *National Employment*, Employment Report (1971).

Ghana, Ministry of Labour, *Employment Market Report* (Accra: Government Printer, 1959).

Ghana News, vol. 4, no. 3 (Mar 1966).

Günter, Hans, 'Social Policy and the Post-Industrial Society', *International Institute for Labour Studies*, Bulletin no. 10 (1972).

Hahn, F. H. and Matthews, R. C. O., *Surveys of Economic Theory*, vol. II, *Growth and Development* (London: Macmillan; New York: St Martin's Press, 1965).

Hall, Richard, *The High Price of Principles: Kaunda and the White South* (London: Hodder and Stoughton, 1969).

Harbison, F. H., *Human Resources as the Wealth of Nations* (New York: Oxford University Press, 1973).

Harris, J. and Todaro, M. P., 'Wages, Industrial Employment and Labour Productivity in a Developing Economy: the Kenyan Experience', *East African Economic Review*, vol. 1 (1969).

Hart, Keith, 'Informal Income Opportunities and Urban Employment in Ghana', *Journal of Modern African Studies*, vol. II, no. 1 (Mar 1973).

Harvey, C., 'The Control of Inflation in a Very Open Economy: Zambia 1964–1969', *East African Economic Review* (June 1971).

Hazlewood, A., 'Inter-State Trade in East African Manufactures', *Economic and Statistical Review* (Sep 1971).

Hobson, J. A., *Imperialism* (London: Allen and Unwin, 1902).

Holt, P. M., *A Modern History of the Sudan* (London: Oxford University Press, 1962).

Huang, Y. C., *Birth Control in Communist China* (Hong Kong, Union Research Institute, 1967).

International Labour Office, *African Labour Survey* (Geneva: ILO, 1958).

International Labour Office, *Employment, Incomes and Equality, a Strategy for Increasing Productive Employment in Kenya* (Geneva: ILO, 1972).

International Labour Organisation, *Labour Force Projections: 1965–1985*, pt II, *Africa* (Geneva: ILO, 1971).

International Labour Office, *Matching Employment Opportunities and Expectations: a Programme of Action for Ceylon* (Geneva: ILO, 1971).

International Labour Office, *Report to the Government of the Sudan on the Development and Implementation of a National Employment Policy* (Geneva: ILO, 1973).

International Labour Office, *Towards Full Employment. A Programme for Colombia* (Geneva: ILO, 1970).

International Labour Office, *Year Book of Labour Statistics, 1968* (Geneva: ILO, 1969).

Ishikawa, S., *A Hypothetical Projection of the Chinese Economy, 1966–81* (Tokyo: Hitotsubashi University Press, 1970).

Iwuji, Eleazar C., *Development Promotion Problems in the Economic and Social Development of Ghana* (Geneva: International Institute for Labour Studies, 1972).

Iwuji, Eleazar C., *Employment Promotion Problems in the Economic and Social Development of Nigeria* (Geneva: International Institute for Labour Studies, 1972).

Johnson, G. E., 'Chinese Urbanization and Economic Development', *Pacific Affairs*, 44, 4 (winter 1971–2) 580–4.

Jolly, R. (ed), *Education in Africa: Research and Action* (Nairobi: East African Publishing House, 1969).

Kaplan, Irving, *et al., Area Handbook for Ghana* (Washington, D.C.: US Government Printing Office, 1971).

Kessel, N. and Elliott, C. M. (eds), *Constraints on the Economic Development of Zambia* (Nairobi: Oxford University Press, 1971).

Kitching, G. N., 'The Concept of Class and the Study of Africa', *African Review*, vol. 2, no. 3 (1972).

Kuo, L. T. C., *The Technical Transformation of Agriculture in Communist China* (New York: Praeger, 1972).

Legum, Colin and Drysdale, John, *Africa Contemporary Record, Annual Survey and Documents, 1969–1970* (Exeter: Africa Research Ltd, 1970).

Lenin, V. I., *Imperialism* (Moscow: Foreign Languages Publishing House, 1951).

Leys, Colin, 'Politics in Kenya: the Development of Peasant Society', *British Journal of Political Science* (July 1971).

Leys, Colin and Marris, Peter, 'Planning and Development', in Dudley Seers and Leonard Joy, *Development in a Divided World* (Harmondsworth: Penguin, 1971).

McLoughlin, P. F. M., 'Income Distribution and Direct Taxation, an Administrative Problem in Low-Output African

Nations: a Case Study of the Sudan', *Economia Internazionale* (Aug 1963).

McWilliam, M. N., 'Economic Viability and the Race Factor in Kenya', *Economic Development and Cultural Change*, vol. XII, no. 1 (1963).

McWilliam, M. N., 'Notes on "The Economic Development of Kenya"', *East African Economics Review*, vol. 10, no. 1 (June 1963).

Marris, P. and Somerset, A., *African Businessmen: a Study of Entrepreneurship and Development* (London: Routledge, 1971).

Mboya, T., *Freedom and After* (London: Deutsch, 1963).

Morse, David A., 'The World Employment Programme', *International Labour Review*, vol. 97, no. 6 (June 1968).

Mukooyama, H., *A Study of Labour Law in China* (Tokyo, 1968).

Mustafa, M. E. M., *Manpower and Employment Problems in the Sudan, IEME 3052* (Geneva: International Institute for Labour Studies, 1972).

Myint, H., *The Economics of Developing Countries*, 3rd ed. (London: Hutchinson, 1967).

Myrdal, Gunnar, *Asian Drama: an Inquiry into the Poverty of Nations* (New York: Pantheon Books, 1968).

Nath, S. K., 'Balanced Growth', in I. Livingstone, *Economic Policy for Development* (Harmondsworth: Penguin, 1971).

Nigeria, Ministry of Economic Development, *Six-Year Development Plan, 1962–68* (Lagos: Government Printer, 1962).

Nigeria, Ministry of Economic Development, *Four Steps to National Stability* (Lagos: Government Printer, 1968).

Nigeria, Ministry of Economic Development, *National Development Plan, 1970–1974* (Apapa: Nigerian National Press, 1970).

Nigeria, Ministry of Information, *Conclusions of the Government of the Federation in the Report on the Commission on the Public Services of the Governments in the Federation of Nigeria, 1954–1955* (Lagos: Government Printer, 1956).

Nigeria, Ministry of Information, *Report of the Commission on the Review of Wages, Salary and Conditions of Service of the Junior Employees of the Government of the Federation and in Private Establishments, 1963–1964* (Lagos: Government Printer, 1964).

Nigeria, Ministry of Information, *Building the New Nigeria: In-*

dustry (Lagos: Associated Press of Nigeria, 1971).

Nigeria, Ministry of Information, *Trade, Not Charity* (Lagos: Government Printer, 1971).

Nigeria, Ministry of Information, *Economic and Statistical Review 1970* (Lagos: Government Printer, 1972).

Nigeria, Ministry of Information, *First Report of the Wages and Salaries Review Commission, 1970, and Second and Final Report of the Wages and Salaries Review Commission, 1970–71* (Lagos: Government Printer, 1972).

Nigeria, Ministry of Information, *Nigeria Handbook 1973* (Lagos: Academy Press, 1973).

Nigeria, Ministry of Labour, *Annual Report* (Lagos: Government Printer, 1965).

Nyerere, Julius K., *Freedom and Socialism (Uhuru na Ujamaa)* (Oxford: Oxford University Press, 1968).

O'Connell, James, 'Political Constraints on Planning: Nigeria as a Case Study in the Developing World', *Nigerian Journal of Economic and Social Studies,* vol. 13, no. 1 (Mar 1971).

Onyemelukwe, C. C., *Problems of Industrial Planning in Nigeria* (London: Longman, 1966).

Pack H., 'Employment and Productivity in Kenyan Manufacturing', *Eastern Africa Economic Review,* vol. 4, no. 2 (Dec 1972).

Pearson, Lester, *Partners in Development: Report of the Commission on International Development* (London: Pall Mall Press, 1969).

Pearson, Scott R., *Petroleum and the Nigeria Economy* (Stanford: Stanford University Press, 1970).

Proctor, J. H. (ed), *Building Ujamaa Villages in Tanzania* (Dar es Salaam: Tanzania Publishing House, 1971).

Prybyla, J. S., *The Political Economy of Communist China* (Scranton, Pa.: International Textbook Co., 1970).

Rempel, H., *Labour Migration into Urban Centers and Urban Unemployment in Kenya,* unpulbished Ph.D. thesis, University of Wisconsin (1970).

Richman, B., 'Economic Development in China and India: Some Conditioning Factors', *Pacific Affairs,* 45, 1 (spring 1972).

Rimmer, Douglas, 'The New Industrial Relations in Ghana', *Industrial and Labor Relations Review,* vol. 14, no. 2 (Jan

1961).

Robson, P. and Lury, D. A., *The Economies of Africa* (London: Allen and Unwin, 1969).

Rodney, W., *How Europe Underdeveloped Africa* (Dar es Salaam: Tanzania Publishing House, 1972).

Rosberg, C. and Nottingham, J., *The Myth of Mau Mau: Nationalism in Kenya* (New York: Praeger, 1966).

Rothchild, D., 'Citizenship and National Integration: the Non-African Crisis in Kenya', *Studies in Race and Nations*, vol. 1, no. 3 (1969–70).

Schwarz, Walter, *Nigeria* (London: Pall Mall Press, 1968).

Shabad, T., *China's Changing Map: National and Regional Development, 1949–71*, rev. ed. (London: Methuen, 1972).

Sigurdson, J., 'Report from China: Rural Industry, a Traveller's View', *China Quarterly*, 50 (Apr-June 1972) 315–32.

Simmonds, J., 'Mass Modernization Aspects of the Chinese Experience', *Asia Quarterly*, 1 (1972) 3–78.

Stern, N. H., 'Experience with the Use of the Little-Mirrless Method for an Appraisal of Small-holder Tea in Kenya', *Bulletin of Oxford University Institute of Economics and Statistics*, vol. 34, no. 1 (Feb 1972).

Sudan, Establishment of Central Ministries, *Republican Decree Number Four* (Khartoum: Government Printer, May 1973).

Sudan, Ministry of Education, *Self-Help in the Field of Education* (Khartoum: Government Printer, 1973) in Arabic.

Sudan, Ministry of Finance and Economics, *The Ten-Year Plan for Economic and Social Development, 1961/62–1971/72* (Khartoum: Government Printer, 1962).

Sudan, Ministry of Finance and Economics, *Five Years Plan of Economic and Social Development, 1970/71–1974/75*, (Khartoum: Government Printer, 1970).

Sudan, Ministry of Planning, *The National Income Accounts and Supporting Tables, 1969* (Khartoum: Government Printer, 1972).

Turnham, D. and Jaeger, I., *The Employment Problem in Less Developed Countries: a Review of Evidence* (OECD, 1971).

Tanzania, Ministry of Information, *Report on Methods of Determining Wages in Tanganyika* (the Jack Report)(Dar es Salaam: Government Printer, 1959).

Tanzania, Ministry of Information, *Report of the Presidential Com-*

mission on the National Union of Tanganyika Workers (Dar es Salaam: Government Printer, 1967).

United Republic of Tanzania, *Background to the Budget, 1968–69* (Dar es Salaam: Government Printer, 1968).

United Republic of Tanzania, *Tanzania Second Five-Year Plan for Economic and Social Development, 1st July 1969–30th June 1974* (Dar es Salaam: Government Printer, 1969).

United Republic of Tanzania, *The Annual Plan for 1972/73* (Dar es Salaam: Government Printer, 1972).

United Nations, *Demographic Yearbook, 1971* (New York: UN Publications, 1971).

United Nations, Department of Economics and Social Affairs, *Population Growth and Manpower in the Sudan* (New York: UN Publications, 1964).

Were, Gideon S., 'The Western Bantu Peoples from A.D. 1300 to 1800', in B. A. Ogot and J. A. Kieran, *Zamani: a Survey of East African History* (Dar es Salaam: East African Publishing House, 1968).

Zambia, *Second National Development Plan* (Lusaka: Government Printer, 1971).

Index

249